THE COMPLETE GUIDE™

# Writing Fantasy

## VOLUME TWO
## The Opus Magus

EDITED BY

## TEE MORRIS

&

## VALERIE GRISWOLD-FORD

Dragon
Moon

WWW.DRAGONMOONPRESS.COM

The Complete Guide™ to Writing Fantasy: Volume Two: The Opus Magus
(formerly The Fantasy Writer's Companion)

Copyright © 2004 Contributing Authors
Interior Illustrations © 2004 Anne Moya
Copyright © 2004 Dragon Moon Press

All rights reserved. Reproduction or utilization of this work in any form, by
any means now known or hereinafter invented, including, but not limited
to, xerography, photocopying and recording, and in any known storage and
retrieval system, is forbidden without permission from the copyright holder.

ISBN 1-896944-15-9

CIP Data on file with the National Library of Canada

Dragon Moon Press is an Imprint of Hades Publications Inc.
P.O. Box 1714, Calgary, Alberta, T2P 2L7, Canada

Dragon Moon Press and Hades Publications, Inc. acknowledges the ongoing
support of the Canada Council for the Arts and the Alberta Foundation for
the Arts for our publishing programme.

The Alberta Foundation for the Arts
COMMITTED TO THE DEVELOPMENT OF CULTURE AND THE ARTS

Alberta COMMUNITY DEVELOPMENT

Canada Council for the Arts

Conseil des Arts du Canada

Printed and bound in Canada
www.dragonmoonpress.com

# Save a Tree Program

At Dragon Moon Press, our carbon footprint is significantly
higher than average and we plan to do something about it.
For every tree Dragon Moon uses in printing our books, we
are helping to plant new trees to reduce our carbon footprint
so that the next generation can breathe clean air, keeping our
planet and its inhabitants healthy.

# Dedication

The editors dedicate

VOLUME TWO
## The Opus Magus

to

Glenn J. and Trudi Griswold

and

E. Wayne and Nancy Morris

who taught us the most important lessons in life:

Never underestimate the air-speed velocity
of marshmallows shot from crossbows

Nothing comes close to "Lagoon View"
and afternoons at Camden Yards

— and —

With determination, will, and faith, dreams happen

# Foreword

## BY HOLLY LISLE

We hold our dreams sacred, and the dream of becoming a writer is the most common dream people share; 80% of the population in the United States alone confess to wanting to write a book someday.

These dreamers and hopefuls spread out across the world, full of hunger and hope and in many cases naïveté, yearning to see their words on pages and between the covers of books and sitting on shelves in bookstores, but they're unsure of how to get them there.

And sharp-eyed schemers are only too ready to sell lies for money—to tell you how to find an agent in thirty-six hours, write a book in fourteen days, and how to write a guaranteed bestseller. Never mind that in the world of publishing, there are no guarantees.

The thing these schemers and liars have in common is that they have not done what they are teaching you to do. They are not selling their work to publishers or cracking the professional markets. They have instead picked up a few basics about writing, knocked together a handful of acronyms for basics in the trade that they call "technologies," and for a fee they will try to tell you that they and they alone have secrets that will make you rich and famous without years of work, without paying any dues, without you having to learn how to write well or to tell a complete story on your own.

Remember that, in writing as in everything else, if it sounds too good to be true, *it is.*

The folks whose advice you'll read in this book are all writers. They already are where you want to be, doing what you want to do, and all of them became writers the hard way—by learning how to write, by learning how to tell a story, and by being persistent enough in every phase of writing to get past the multitude of obstacles that stood in their way.

There is no *easy* way to get where you want to go. But there are ways, and if you want this dream of yours badly enough, you can have it. You have to be persistent above all else—you have be willing to look a hundred or more rejection slips in the eye and keep on writing, keep on submitting, keep on learning how to be better. You have to believe in yourself when no one else will. And you have to be careful about who you listen to. Avoid the tricksters who will tell you what you want to hear for money. Listen to the folks who have already found their way to the dream we all share.

Believe, above all. Your dream is worthwhile, it is a wonderful thing, and you have what it takes within you to make it happen.

# Table of Contents

# Please, Sir, I Want Some More:
## WELCOME TO *THE OPUS MAGUS*
## (FORMERLY,
## *THE FANTASY WRITER'S COMPANION*)

### BY TEE MORRIS

Welcome to the sequel to *The Complete Guide to Writing Fantasy*.

Yeah, I know what you're thinking: the *sequel* to *The Complete Guide to Writing Fantasy*?!

Believe me, I find it a little surreal myself when I tell people "Yeah, I'm editing a sequel to *The Complete Guide to Writing Fantasy*." I mean, if Dragon Moon's *Guide* really was *complete*, you wouldn't be reading this sentence. Or this one. Heck, you wouldn't even be holding this book in your hands right now!

Okay, is it just me, or does anyone else's brain hurt?

So, how did this happen? This unexpected sequel? And why? If there is a *Complete Guide*, what does this volume have to add?

Let's step into my Time Machine of Memory and travel back to an Age of Innocence. This Age takes place in a realm that is kept warm even in the throes of winter by the people who inhabit it. We join two intrepid heroes traversing from Point A to Point B in a car that's got gas in the tank, tunes on the radio and several boxes of books in the backseat...

I was somewhere in New Hampshire. Or maybe it was Massachusetts. I'm not sure. I always missed the crossing over state lines, but I was the guest of *Complete Guide*'s Valerie Griswold-Ford and I didn't want to complain that no one was letting me know that we were changing states. (Granted, I was silently theorizing that this was all some kind of conspiracy. New Hampshire didn't *want* you to know you were leaving the state for whatever reasons. The truth is out there...) You see, Val had presented to all the authors of *The Complete Guide* an innocent little invitation to join her for "group signings" in the New England area. Only one responded with a "yes"—me. At this point, the Micro-Tour was winding down. That's what Val and I were calling this little weekend of ours: a *Micro*-Tour. We were hitting a café, three bookstores and a library. No big deal, until you find out that we were doing these events in three different states: New Hampshire, Massachusetts and New York.

Wow!

So, we were coming back from one of our events and the topic of *The Complete Guide to Writing Fantasy* came up. We chatted about how good it felt being part of such a successful title, but we also mentioned the frustration over some people who took sadistic joy in telling us *"Well, is this really a complete guide, 'cause I'm lookin' at the Table of Contents, and I think there's a lot missing."* What do you say to something like that? *"Well, we say it's complete, but it's not completely complete."* That won't work. Maybe *"I just wrote for it. The title wasn't my idea."* Nah, that just makes me sound like a government employee. Perhaps *"Look, just buy the damn book, you pinhead!"* *While* I seriously consider replies like that to the more abrasive fans of Science Fiction and Fantasy from time to time, I always manage to exercise self-control.

But as we're chatting, the conversation took a dangerous turn...

"What we need," Val stated (and stated quite confidently, now that I think about it), "is a sequel."

"A sequel?" I asked. "A sequel to *The* Complete *Guide?"* (Hmmm, déjà vu!)

And while it was at night when we were having this conversation, I could see in the glow of the dashboard a certain glimmer in Val's eyes.

In retrospect, I knew what it was—an agenda.

"Why not?" she asked back, her glimmer now being fanned into a raging bonfire. *"The Complete Guide* is complete in its own way. It covers the basics of writing. What we need is a sequel that goes beyond the basics with very specific and particular topics for the writer who has finished *The Complete Guide* and wants more."

"Uh-huh," I said, going quiet for a moment.

It was clear that Val had spent some time thinking this out, and as she had nicknamed me "Quad-Boy" during the weekend (following a blurry night involving me and a quadruple-shot espresso), I was tempted to dub her "Agenda Girl." I also had to wonder if this agenda was completely her own. This wasn't the first time I heard the word "sequel" dropped into conversations centered around *The Guide.* Dragon Moon Press was using the "s-word" as sales for the title were exceeding all expectations. As publishing is a business at its core, it was only logical to begin planning how to make lightening strike twice.

But sequels are tricky. Look at *The Matrix: Reloaded* and *Revolutions* or *The Chronicles of Riddick,* for instance. On second thought, don't. Look at *The Matrix* and *Pitch Black.* With many offerings, the originals are always sharp, intelligent and incredible. You can go back to the theatre and catch something new each time, and still not burn out on them when they come out on DVD. But when sequels come around, something's usually missing. It would be nice to think that every sequel will be *Spider-Man 2,* but many follow-ups grant a few "cool moments" here and there with its ending regarded a blessed relief that the ordeal is done.

The Golden Rule of Writing Sequels: There is no reason to go back to the well if that puppy's dry.

And that wasn't even my biggest issue. "So, what do we call this new guide?" I asked.

Val and I spent a good amount of miles kicking around ideas, and here were some of the possible titles we came up with...

*The More-Than-Complete Guide to Writing Fantasy*
*No, Really, THIS Is The Complete Guide*
    *to Writing Fantasy*
*Just Buy The Damn Book, You Pinhead!*
    (A personal favorite of mine)
*Son of The Complete Guide to Writing Fantasy*
*Bride of The Complete Guide to Writing Fantasy*
*Revenge of The Complete Guide to Writing Fantasy*
*The Increasingly Misnamed Complete Guide*
    *to Writing Fantasy*
    (Val's favorite, but our publisher and our lawyers
    mentioned something about Douglas Adams'
    estate being able to sue, so we dropped it.)

After we calmed down a bit (and joked about finding the closest Starbuck's to gas ourselves up on quad-espressos), Val chimed in with "We need a title that lets people know it's an addendum. You know, a companion to the guide."

Well, that took care of the title. Still, I had a feeling that Val was going somewhere with this little brainstorm session of ours.

"So," I continued on my Devil's Advocate line of questioning, "who's going to edit this *Fantasy Writer's Companion*?"

Agenda Girl didn't say anything for a moment. She just drove, and smiled. A smile that still haunts me in my darkest dreams.

After I agreed to co-edit *The Fantasy Writer's Companion* with Val, we started to brainstorm on various topics it would cover. That was easy. Now came the hard part: getting writers.

Well, okay, maybe asking a writers' group "Hey, you want to get your work published?" wouldn't be considered "hard" but Val and I agreed we needed to take the title's participant list to a whole new level. *But, I thought, this isn't going to be a "get-rich-quick" title. And it's non-fiction...will the authors I've got in mind be interested?* And there were a score of other questions, anxieties, and worries that were popping into my head as I approached award-winning author Wen Spencer.

"Hey, Wen...I, um..." Yeah, already the words were getting caught in my throat. "I'm going to be editing a writer's guide. It's a sequel to *The Complete Guide to Writing Fantasy*..."

"A *sequel* to *The* Complete *Guide*?" she asked me.

By this time, I was really hating that title. "Ummm...yeah...and well, I wanted to know if you would like to write a chapter for it. About writing across genres."

Wen hesitated. "How many words would you want?"

Oh crap! Word count! That was something Val and I hadn't discussed! "No more than eight thousand. Five thousand, minimum," I stated confidently, while I thought *Okay, what part of my butt did that come from?!*

"And when will you need it by?" Wen asked.

*Let's see, it's December right now, so how about...* "May," I said.

"Oh sure, no problem!" she smiled. "Sounds like fun! Just e-mail me the details when you get home, okay? See you later."

When I left Philcon 2003, I had recruited an award-winning fantasy author, an award-nominated horror author and one of the top authors from Wizards of the Coast for our project.

Cool!

While there are some returning names from *The Complete Guide* featured in this title, the new authors appearing in *The Fantasy Writer's Companion* are all accomplished in the subjects they are writing on. Kim Headlee has received many distinctions for her Arthurian legend *Dawnflight*, Tony Ruggiero has raised many a goose-bump with his anthology *Aliens and Satanic Creatures Wanted* and his vampire novel *Team of Darkness*, and Michael R. Mennenga continues to indulge children's imaginations with his fantasy *Dragon's Fire, Wizard's Flame*. Even the non-published authors making their debut here are authorities in their own right. Evo Terra, the *Companion*'s writer for "Herbalism in Fantasy," is a licensed herbalist; and Lai Zhao, the author behind

"Worldbuilding in Asian Cultures," lives in Hong Kong, China. (Can't get more authoritative than that!)

So what do these talented authors have to offer that *The Complete Guide* does not? While *The Complete Guide* teaches you how to walk in your writing skills, *The Fantasy Writer's Companion* teaches you how to run. The basics of grammar, characters and the nuts and bolts of writing have already been covered. Now it is time to give your work that extra edge, to focus on what you want for your story, your characters and your universe. With their experiences from past publications or current works in progress, *The Companion's* contributors intend to be just that: companions in your epic adventure as a writer. Here, authors from across the country and around the world come together to share the good, the bad, and the ugly (*whistle…wah-wah-waoooowww…*) of what goes into great storytelling. If you have a question about creating a certain mood, are in need of inspiration, seek validation for a "gut decision" you've just made in your writing or just want an inside peek at the creative mind of a writer, then you're at the right place.

Prop your feet up, keep the notebook handy and take satisfaction that you are in a good company of writers who truly love what they do and want to share with you in this exciting voyage you are about to undertake.

Enjoy the ride.

NeverLand
CREATIVE LICENSE

NUMBER 8675309703425          EXPIRES 10-28-2010

VLADMIL, LAMSON
9218 SOUTH DRU        N.
SOMWARE              82

Bill Shakespeare

COMMISSIONER   Oscar Wilde

ORGAN DONOR
Y

REVOKED

# Revoking Your Creative License:
## MYTH BUSTING

### BY TINA MORGAN

There are many myths and misconceptions about what determines "good" content. Unfortunately, that is very subjective and no how-to book can teach you how to create the next bestseller or a great literary masterpiece. What I can help you do as a fan of the genre, a teacher of online creative writing workshops, and as a book critic and columnist, is avoid the mistakes that will undermine your confidence and mark you as an amateur.

## Myth #1: It's possible to write
### a perfect first draft.

No, it's not.

While there are major authors who have and do claim to write each sentence only once, they are only human and they do make mistakes. It defies the laws of nature for anyone to write a perfect first draft and even if it were possible, consider the time it would take to produce one perfect sentence after another. If it takes 3 hours to write each sentence, by the time you finished a story, you could have written and rewritten it at least twice. Agonizing over each word can make writing a tedious chore instead of an enjoyable pastime or occupation.

First drafts are often the place to explore our characters and settings more thoroughly. They allow us to go off on tangents that can take over the plot and become a more compelling story than we might have had outlined at the start of the process. Putting too much pressure on yourself to create that "perfect" copy the first time around can stifle the creative process for a lot of writers. Allow your first draft to be rough and imperfect. I know how hard this can be. I have a tendency to want to avoid rewrites myself. However, allowing your writing to flow the first time through just might reveal a diamond shining beneath the surface that wasn't obvious when you started the story.

While rewriting is often a time-consuming and tedious process, it helps to think about the difference you're making in your story. Bringing out the best parts of the plot and characters until your work shines is a gratifying experience.

## Myth #2: Spelling and Grammar checks
### will catch all of my mistakes.

No. Spelling only works if you misspelled the word, but if you used the wrong word the spell checker isn't going to pick up on that.

For example, you could type *"Eye understand that there going to the see, can I tap along?"* but actually mean to type *"I understand that they're going to the sea. Can I tag along?"* In both examples, Spell Check will approve what is there.

Many times, our eyes will see what we know should be there rather than what is really on the paper. Some of the mistakes in that sample are obvious but what about:

> Harriet wanted to go to the party. He hoped to meat up with her friends.

Leaving the "s" off the word "she" is an easy enough typo to make and it's a mistake that will slip past all spelling and grammar checkers. It's also a mistake that is easy to miss as you read through your work.

*Homophones* are those words that are pronounced the same but differ in meaning, derivation or spelling. Common examples that your spell checker isn't going to catch and a grammar checker will probably miss are:

> Meet - meat
> Pair - pear - pare
> Two - to - too
> They're - their - there
> It's - its

(The term *homonym* is often used to describe these types of words but a quick look in the dictionary will show that homophone is the correct label.)

There's no replacement for a good human editor. If you have a problem with grammar, typing or spelling, consider finding another writer who's willing to trade critiques. Another alternative is to pay a student (who performs well in the language you're writing in) to go over your novel. I've done this on more than one occasion and found it to be a more cost-effective alternative than paying for editing services.

## MYTH #3: HEROES SHOULD BE HANDSOME, CLEVER AND MUSCLE-BOUND, RIGHT?

If your hero or heroine is "too" perfect, you run the risk that they'll be labeled "comic-book" characters. However, take a closer look at some of those comic book characters and you'll realize many of them have more depth than previously imagined.

Superman is probably the most "perfect" of all comic book heroes. His only weaknesses are kryptonite and Lois Lane. He's almost too perfect to be believed—though he didn't do too badly at the box-office. A little closer examination of the character, however, reveals a tendency to be naive and innocent. These characteristics lead him to underestimate his opponents, which makes him more approachable.

Take a walk on the darker side and you'll find several characters that make readers (and movie audiences) come back for more. Wolverine's claws, strength and healing abilities make him seem invincible but his distrust and almost animal fear of human relationships lead him to use violence when he should be using his brain. Batman isn't really a "superhero"—he lacks physical super abilities but makes up for it with technology and brainpower. However, even Batman makes the wrong choices at times. Cynicism isn't always the dark-hero's best friend, though it's a common trait.

If these characters didn't make incorrect assumptions and decisions, their comic books and movies would lack conflict. They all need that "fatal" flaw that allows the villain the opportunity to succeed or there's no real danger and no suspense to keep the reader engaged in the story.

A trip through any bookstore's fantasy shelves will lead to the discovery of a lot of "less than perfect" heroes and heroines.

Lois McMaster Bujold's *Curse of Chalion* features an older hero who must rely on his brains rather than his strength. He has no money, no job and very little hope of returning to his former position in society. His journey through betrayal and deceit is even more enticing because the reader is cheering for this obvious underdog to triumph over evil.

Ian Irvine's Tiaan from his *Geomancer* and *Tetrarch* novels is the opposite of a regular heroine. The red-headed weakling and town joke, Llian, from the *View from the Mirror* series has no magic and no strength, yet manages to foil the greatest "mage" in the worlds. His friend, Karan, is also an anti-heroine for similar reasons. She has imperfect magic only. They all succeed without the huge muscles and perfectly controlled magic and their struggles are all the more engaging for having to overcome their flaws.

Beware of stereotypes. Just because a hero is strong doesn't mean he/she lacks in brainpower. Beauty does not equal perfection and intelligence is not automatically equivalent to common sense.

## MYTH #4: HORSES

Many fantasy writers use a medieval setting for their stories yet they forget to research the major form of transportation in that era: the horse.

The most common misconception: *You can ride at a gallop for 11 hours a day, right?* Only if you have thighs and buns of cast iron and the hide of a rhino. Not to mention a horse with beyond mythical abilities. In *The Complete Guide to Writing Fantasy* I included a section on horses so I won't rehash it all here, but I will include a few highlights:

- 20-30 miles per day is average for a horse and rider in good shape. Pulling a wagon? Expect that rate to drop to 10-12 miles per day. Given the terrain, a human on foot can out distance a horse & wagon.
- Horses do NOT lap water
- A horse's stomach is designed to consume large portions of roughage per day. Without it, the horse may become colic. Colic can be fatal. This means your horse cannot run for 20 hours and be expected to sleep and eat in 4.
- Horses cannot regurgitate.
- Carrying double is very hard on a horse and cannot be done for an extended period unless one or both of the riders is a very small child.
- Horses cannot change their own sex. A gelding is a surgically castrated male. In more than one critique group, I've encountered stories where a horse starts out a mare but the writer forgets and it becomes a gelding. Or it's a stallion at the start of the chapter yet is referred to as a gelding midway through and then a stallion again at the end. The terms are not interchangeable.
- Some horses are truly hateful and dislike being ridden. Just as dogs have a wide variety of temperaments, so do horses. Giving the horse your hero is riding a "personality" can add depth and sometimes comic relief to your story.
- Swords should never be sheathed in a girth unless you're trying to kill the horse or cut the saddle off. Girths must be pulled far tighter than you would ever wear a belt on

your own body. Regardless of length, a sword being held in place along a horse's side is going to restrict movement and if not sheathed in some sort of casing, the sword will cut the horse's side. Sliding a leather or metal sheath under a very snug girth is going to be difficult.

- Metal armor is incredibly heavy. The horses used by medieval knights were much larger and heavier boned than the average riding horse of today.

## MYTH #5: THE MORE WEAPONS YOUR CHARACTER CARRIES, THE TOUGHER HE/SHE WILL BE.

Not true.

Actually, a character carrying a large amount of weapons will be easier to catch on foot because the weight will slow them down. The same problem exists with armor. Chain mail is heavy and it pulls hairs and pinches. Only a character that enjoys pain would wear chain mail directly against his/her skin. The weight of metal armor will restrict the warrior's movement and tire him quicker. There are times for full armor, but sneaking up on an enemy encampment in the middle of the night is not one of them. There's no way to keep the armor quiet.

There comes a point in many action movies where one of the characters begins pulling weapon after weapon in an impressive display of firepower. Many writers remember these powerful scenes and want to invoke the same feeling in their own work so they will create the "Walking Arsenal" character. While their weapons may vary from yet-to-be invented laser guns to simple knives and daggers, they have one common trait: a multitude of weapons.

As writers, we need to keep in mind the difference between script writing and prose. What makes an impressive scene on the big screen can fall very flat in the pages of a book. Movies give the viewer the opportunity to watch the subtle body language of the actor/actress and to form an opinion of their character before they start drawing weapons. In prose, the character must be established in other ways before resorting to the obvious visuals of multiple weapons to make an impact.

Consider the following example of a captain being arrested:

*The guard approached Danaar and waited for him to remove his weapons. Without a word he unbelted his sword and laid it on Cridan's desk along with the dagger from his waistband and the two from his boots. Then he removed a matching pair of daggers from his forearm sheaths. Reaching behind his back, he drew a stiletto from its scabbard between his shoulder blades and placed it on the desk.*

Not a very exciting passage really. It's merely a listing of weapons the soldier is carrying and does nothing to expand on the relationship between characters. But what if I add Danaar's feelings and thoughts about what he's doing?

*Danaar knew Cridan expected him to struggle with the guard and he smiled bitterly as his lordship stepped to the far side of the room. The guard approached his captain with trepidation.*

*The captain regarded Lord Cridan for a long moment, hatred shining bright in his intense eyes. Without a word, he unbelted his sword and laid it on Cridan's desk along with the dagger from his waistband and the two from his boots. Then he removed a matching pair of daggers from their forearm sheaths. Reaching behind his back, he drew a stiletto from its scabbard between his shoulder blades. He slowly placed it on the desk, resisting the urge to plant it firmly in Cridan's eye socket. Cridan and the guard breathed a sigh of relief when Danaar turned and stalked from the room, his back rigid with suppressed anger.*

By including Cridan's audible sigh of relief, Danaar's rigid stance and his desire to throw his knife at his former master, the tension is raised to a level that can't exist with just a description of the number of weapons he's carrying. Visuals that would have been automatically seen in a movie must be expressed in the writing for your reader to feel the full impact of your scene.

### WHERE WAS THAT SWORD?

Another common problem with "Walking Arsenal" characters is how they carry their numerous weapons. Many time writers forget to take into consideration the size of their character and the length of the weapons he/she is wielding.

In my example, I have my captain removing daggers from sheathes on his wrists and boots. Previously in the story I have established the captain as a large man. He would be able to carry longer daggers on his wrists than a smaller man; however, because of the need to flex and move the arm in combat, the weapons are going to be limited in size and therefore limited in use to close fighting or throwing. The stiletto in the back sheath isn't going to be easy to remove during an intense fight and I would not have him use it in that manner.

One thing I did not realize about this descriptive passage, until my editor pointed it out, was that the use of a stiletto might create confusion. For the purpose of this example, I could have changed the weapon to a larger sword but there was a reason for the captain to choose this particular type of knife. Since it is a smaller weapon, it can be hidden from view. As back sheaths are not common in his world, he is rarely ever totally disarmed even when forced to leave his visible weapons at the entrance to another noble's home or city.

Before you include a lot of weapons in your story, do a little research and make certain you understand how the function, length, and weight of a bladed weapon will affect your character's strength and fighting ability. Attending renaissance festivals and actually handling the weapons on display can help give you a clearer idea of how your character would carry and use his/her weapons. Most of the swords, daggers and axes for sale at renaissance festivals are for decoration only. Reproductions of early weapons are made from more modern metals and have dull edges, yet they can give you an idea of how it would feel to swing a broadsword and the amount of shoulder and arm strength required for a prolonged battle. But before you go swinging a weapon around, ask permission of the store keep or Faire merchant first! Last thing you want to do is pull a "William Wallace" on someone Christmas shopping for that unique gift.

Research is also not limited to the able-bodied. If fighting with knives is beyond your abilities then consider observing a martial arts competition. Many tournaments will include weapons sparing and forms. Contact re-enactment or SCA (Society for Creative Anachronisms) groups in your area. Talk to the participants about their weapons, their physical reactions to using the weapon and how they would have been used in battle.

Whether you chose a medieval setting or just about any time in the history of man, you can find re-enactment groups and museums that are familiar with the weapons your story requires. Consider a trip to Williamsburg, NC if you're using a Civil War setting. If you're using modern weapons, locate a gun and/or archery range in your area. Ask for a demonstration on how to load the guns you plan to use in your story and observe the wrist strength needed to fire different size handguns. At this point, I would highly recommend that you find a copy of *The Complete Guide to Writing Fantasy* and read the section of "Arms and Armour" on weapons safety (pp. 267-268). You must remember that when handling weapons, especially firearms, you are handling weapons. Safety first. Make sure you are working with a specialist.

Always remember, *weapons of any type are not toys.* They were made for one purpose only: to kill, whether for food, defense or aggression. Guns are not to be handled casually and you should *NEVER* assume a gun is unloaded, even if you just removed the bullets yourself. If you treat every gun as a loaded and lethal weapon, then the possibility of an accidental shooting is greatly reduced.

Guns come in all shapes and sizes and despite the many TV shows and movies that would lead us to believe that even a small caliber pistol can do vast amounts of damage to the human body, this simply isn't true. A .22 caliber derringer is not going to create the same amount of destruction as a .45 caliber handgun. Nor do guns come with endless supplies of ammunition. Many movies portray the characters shooting continuous streams of bullets for prolonged periods of time when in real life, the gun would have been emptied in a matter of seconds. The old black and white westerns were notorious for their "twelve" shot six-shooters. These guns were called "six-shooters" because that was the number of bullets they carried. After the sixth shot, the gun had to be reloaded, yet many silver screen cowboys continued shooting for eleven, twelve times or more before inserting more bullets. Take care that if you use guns in your story, you know exactly how many bullets the magazine holds and don't expect your readers to believe the gun shoots endlessly without reloading.

Creating new weapons is another option but one that must be used with care. If the weapon doesn't make sense within the world you've created then it can jolt your reader out of the story. Imaginary weapons need to conform to the physical confines of your world. They need to have a consistent pattern of use and a measure of predictability.

For inspiration or possibly an idea of what not to do, consider some of the following movies and television shows: James Bond, *Equilibrium, Van Helsing* or *Xena.* Each of these shows featured unusual and creative weapons. Everything from gas-powered crossbows to laser shooting watches. Some of the weapons defy logic, others fit up sleeves that were too narrow to conceal much more than a knife. Still others flew through the air in totally impossible manners and injured multiple people when they should have stopped after the first kill. The advantage each of these shows has is the visual impact of these amazing weapons. Your world is in written form and lacks the benefit of cool special effects.

While it can be fun to include a character bristling with weapons who can decimate an entire army single-handed, it's not very realistic nor in the best interest of your plot. Your characters need a challenge to overcome and difficulties in achieving their goals or the story becomes as interesting as a grocery list.

Weapons use and research are popular hobbies for many readers. Don't try to fake your way through your descriptions.

### Amazing Arrows

Stereotypical races are trite and overdone, so avoiding the clichéd "all elves are excellent archers" is a good idea.

Weapons are a source of many faux pas in fantasy fiction. Crossbows do amazing things and rawhide bowstrings shoot even when soaking wet.

I expect this last misconception to be further augmented by the elves at Helm's Deep in the *The Lord of the Rings: The Two Towers*. The elves stood, drenched in rain with their bows strung, yet when the time came to shoot, they were exceptionally accurate and their bows preformed admirably. Now, it could be argued that Tolkien's elves were magic and weren't using "catgut" bowstrings, but their human counterparts had no problem with their equipment either. The movie *Braveheart* comes much closer to portraying the actual ability and flaws of ancient archery. While there are those who would say, *"But I'm writing fantasy, not historical fiction!"* this chapter is about *myth busting* and the true attributes of bows and arrows do not match what we typically see on the screen or read in many fantasy stories.

- Most medieval bowstrings were made from the cured intestines of animals used for food. This *catgut* stretches. That's an inescapable fact. Wet bowstrings would stretch too far and not snap back in order to propel the arrow accurately or with any degree of strength. Every time one of these strings was pulled taut, they began to stretch. Each pull of the bow lessened their power and they had to be replaced quite often.

- The bow would break and/or lose power if left strung. Strings were always removed and bows were never carried strung.

- *Crossbows* are short-range weapons and are not designed for accuracy or power over long distances. This is because the weight ratio vs. the short limbs. Also, many crossbows, especially the larger, more powerful ones, required more than one person to cock them, due to the stiffness of the limbs.

- *Self-bows* (the most common type of bow used for centuries) were only about 4 feet long and made from one growth ring of a tree. This wood took 7 years to dry before it was usable. If a greener piece of wood were used, the bow would break after only a few shots and was only capable of 20-30 lbs. draw-weight, which severely shorted the flight and power. Such a low quality bow could be made and used, but it would have to be replaced very quickly, requiring a large amount of wood to stock even a small fighting force.

- *Long* and *recurve bow* are approximately 1 1/2 to 2 meters (4 1/2 - 6 feet) long unstrung. Your character is not going to carry that type of bow through dense thickets, short caves or up into trees without having to compensate for the length and limited mobility. Stringing a bow requires: room, strength and knowledge. If a bow is twisted when strung, it can cause the wood to splinter and/or shatter when pulled back. An exploding bow can maim, seriously injure or even kill your character.

When a bow is drawn, the archer must hold the full pressure until the string is released. This is not true of modern compound bows. These bows have a *cam* or aluminum pulley that allows the archer to pull past the point of *let off*. This happens because the limbs of the bow do not flex. The power of the bow comes from the cables and pulley set-up. When the hunter pulls the bow to the point that the cam rolls over, he/she is holding a much smaller percentage of the draw-weight. For example, a 65lb bow with 80% let off means the archer will be holding 13lbs of pressure. While holding even 13lbs can be tiring, it's much better than the average long bow's 50-70lbs of draw-weight. This needs to be kept in mind when writing your action scenes. An archer isn't going to hold his bow nocked and drawn for more than a few minutes. To do so would decrease the archer's accuracy and with the older bows, it would have a detrimental effect on its performance.

### SWORDS

Metal weapons need the same consideration as bows. Stainless steel was not invented until 1911-1913 (who actually invented it is in dispute, but the earliest patent was filed in 1919). Weapons made prior to this time would have rusted when exposed to moisture. These softer metals would have dulled quicker as well. No self-respecting swordsman would have plunged his sword into the ground to clean it. Metal was too difficult to make and acquire to abuse it in such a manner. If it were available, a thin coating of protective oil would have been applied.

While I enjoyed the movie adaptation of Michael Crichton's *Timeline*, I can only imagine the scene where Marek takes the sword from Chris and thrusts it into the ground must have made both author and many audience members cringe. In the book, the character is an expert on medieval weapons and fighting techniques. He even spends time learning to joust with wooden lances. He would not have thrust his sword into the dirt.

## MYTH #6: SETTINGS MUST BE EUROPEAN IN BASIS

I'm not sure when it became so popular. Maybe it's the sheer volume of "Arthur" stories on the fantasy shelves but fantasy heroines do NOT have to be green-eyed, redheads with Celtic names. While many fantasy authors grew up with stories of Druids, magicians and Knights of the Round Table, there is no rule that your world has to spring from or be inspired by these myths.

Many editors are looking for "something new"—stories that are set in the Far East or on the Russian Steppes. Stories inspired by Mayan or Ashanti culture. Our world possesses such wide and diverse cultures and societies that we do not need to confine ourselves to Roman, Anglo-Saxon, Druid or Celtic legends.

One of the things I see quite often in my critique groups are authors who are creating new worlds yet still using the feudal style governments that are almost always European in inspiration and basis. Even if your characters aren't part of the government in the world you're creating, they are often affected by it. Subtle changes in the make-up of your world can make a richer and more unique reading experience. If you resist the urge to fall back on the things you've read in so many other fantasy novels or learned in primary school, you just might find an alternative to the "knight" and "lord" arrangement.

This can be a difficult challenge for a writer who's grown up in the US, where most of our formal education over governmental forms has been the US's relationship with the British monarchy and our own growth into a democratic state. When you add to that the inundation of fairytale films and cartoons based in European countries, it can be difficult but not impossible to think "outside the box." With the proliferation of the Internet and satellite television, the opportunities to study other cultures are far more available than they were just ten years ago. If you haven't read it already, check out Lai Zhao's chapter, "Culture Shock," which explores Asian world-building alternatives.

While you're exploring new worlds, remember that there is no reason to restrict your characters to Celtic or unpronounceable names. While naming your medieval knight Tyler or Bob probably wouldn't elicit the feel you're attempting to establish, you can choose a name with at least one or two consonants. Keeping the names of your characters in similar tone to the setting that you've chosen is important but using names your readers can pronounce is a good thing. (This means readers can talk to their friends about your book and refer to the characters by name and hopefully word of mouth will sell a few more books for you.)

## MYTH #7: THE SAME AGE

If your protagonist is twelve then you must be writing a "Young Adult" (YA) novel, right? Wrong. This misconception often comes up in critique groups and it always amazes me. The age of the protagonist is not synonymous with the age of the target audience. While Orson Scott Card's *Ender's Game* is science fiction, it is still an excellent example. Ender is a child when the story starts and throughout the bulk of the story is under twelve years old. The novel has currently been marketed for the YA audience but it was not written with that intent. The subject matter (genocide and war) is not aimed at a young audience, despite the protagonist's age.

Lynn Flewelling uses a young protagonist in her novel *The Bone Doll's Twin*, yet it is a dark fantasy novel that is not aimed at the pre-teen audience. Jacqueline Carey's Phedre starts out as a four-year-old child in her erotic fantasy novel, *Kushiel's Dart*. Carey's protagonist matures within the first few chapters while Flewelling's doesn't reach puberty until the sequel, *The Hidden Warrior*.

Another myth that can be a problem for readers and writers alike is that the age at which a person is considered an "adult" is the same regardless of era, culture or life expectancy. In a society with poor health care and limited resources, a person may be considered mature at fourteen, as opposed to our current legal age of eighteen to twenty-one. Prior to the 1950's, many women married before the age of eighteen and had their first child or more before they would be considered old enough to make their own decisions regarding sex and birth control in our society.

## Summary

There are a lot of misconceptions about what you can and cannot include in a fantasy story. Do your research on the things that you can investigate and remember that only you can tell the story that's in your head.

Your imagination knows no limits to where it can take you and your readers; but if your mode of transportation is an animal of some kind, the beast will have limits of its own. Your horses can run for days on end IF you make it clear to your readers that they're not reading about normal earth-based horses.

Knowing how and why technology included or created for your story works will make your novel more believable. If you want to include a gun that shoots 1,000 rounds per second for over an hour before running out of bullets, then do it, but give your readers a brief explanation how/why this works. Machine guns can fit on the front of shopping carts; *Minerva Awakes* by Holly Lisle proves that.

Every fantasy world should be true to itself. If you establish in the first chapter that you're writing about a medieval European world, then don't be surprised if readers protest when the technology doesn't match. However, if you want to use computers and stun guns in a society that still uses horses in some portions of their world, consider reading *Cordelia's Honor* or *Borders of Infinity* by Lois McMaster Bujold to see how she reconciles these seemingly incompatible elements. One of the beauties and thrills of writing fantasy and/or science fiction is the endless realms your imagination can travel.

"Almost anything is possible in fantasy,
even houses made of cheese."
—*Castle Roogna*, Piers Anthony

# It's Like a Novel, Only Shorter:
## WRITING SHORT STORIES AND NOVELLAS

### BY BOB NAILOR

A pound of truth can be found within the title of this chapter. Yes, short stories are the same as novels, only different.

So, what is a novel? Mr. Merriam-Webster.com says: *an invented prose narrative that is usually long and complex and deals especially with human experience through a usually connected sequence of events.*

A novella is nothing more than a condensed novel, hence the nomenclature, novella, or as Mr. Merriam-Webster.com says: *a work of fiction intermediate in length and complexity between a short story and novel.*

A short story, on the other hand, is just a condensed novella or an even more compressed novel, as Mr. Merriam-Webster.com would tell us: *an invented prose narrative shorter than a novel usually dealing with a few characters and aiming at unity of effect and often concentrating on the creation of mood rather than plot.*

Dictionary definitions are a good thing but at times tend to complicate the specifics. There are just a few items that one should remember, the most important being that a short story is not a novella and a novella is not a novel. The operative word that I used above is *condensed*, which doesn't entail just removing words. It means making each word count by deleting extraneous material and plot lines. Let me give you an analogy: a novel is equivalent to an ocean liner, a novella measures up to a yacht and, of course, a short story will be the rowboat. You can put a rowboat on a yacht and a yacht on an ocean liner, but you can't put an ocean liner on a yacht or rowboat. Sailing vessels and stories, all three types have the same basics and dynamics with size and details separating them.

By analyzing the basic structure of the three, we can learn the differences and similarities between a novel, novella and short story.

All of them (novel, novella and short story) have the same basic construction in their individual creations. Where they differ is in their construction. Only a brash person would assume that writing a short story is easier than writing a novel. The exact same methods are used for both, although the approach is slightly different and the time involved in typing the words is longer.

When I write a short story, novella or novel, I like to think of myself sailing the Seven Seas, or in this case, the *Seven C's.* Just like the seas of the world, they are connected, but each has its own quirks. The Seven Seas have changed during the history of mankind. In the days of Ulysses, Caesar and Sinbad, the Seven Seas were the Red Sea, Mediterranean Sea, Persian Gulf, Black Sea, Adriatic Sea, Caspian Sea and the Indian Ocean. Today, they are the North Atlantic, South Atlantic, North Pacific, South Pacific, Indian, Arctic and Antarctic Oceans. In writing terms, what I call the Seven C's haven't changed over the years, even as far back as Aesop. The Seven C's are *Concept, Capture, Character, Conflict, Climax, Conclusion* and *Collection.*

Join me in this nautical-narrative adventure through the Seven C's of writing, taking you into the creative process behind my short story, "Sea of Regret" recently published in the May 2004 issue of "The Emporium Gazette," online at www.emporiumgazette.com. This chapter provides you a chance to take a ride in the writer's mind and experience the thought process, planning, and plotting that goes into a short story. I will also point out possibilities that could have been added to make this into a novella or novel.

## CONCEPT

This is the idea that starts the whole process. It is the smallest and calmest sea that you will sail in your journey to write a story. There is a spark of imagination and suddenly a story comes into existence within your mind. Placing the idea for your story on paper will help you discover the size and scope of the project. It can be a simple sentence that says *"Create goddess legend with tigress using India as model for locale."* That was the *concept* for my short story, "The God Makers" which was also published at The Emporium Gazette. For "Sea of Regret" my concept was a simple sentence: *A young man, shipwrecked, afloat at sea, ponders regrets.* With my concept clear and concise, the vision was there. Now I had to take the journey.

The more I considered the concept, the more I knew this was to be a short story. It is a fine art of knowing whether or not the idea can be expanded to create a novella or even larger to novel size. As you expand your concept, you will glean a few aspects of your project and soon realize what could be the possible word count or which category your work will fall under. That "fine art" mentioned earlier includes realizing that throwing more characters into the story to stretch it for the sake of stretching, is, in fact, stretching. Every word in your manuscript should move the story forward, not be there just to up the ante of the tally. Your plot will also assist in this decision. A concept like *"Relic hunter searches for the Ark of the Covenant"* could be the foundation for a short story. After the first sentence of your concept is down on paper, you should then detail an outline of what will happen, listing characters and key descriptions that will be used. To expound on the detailing aspect using the earlier reference, you could add items like *"during Nazi reign, use Egyptian excavations for* clues, love interest for conflict, submarine challenge, desolate island for disaster." Depending on your details, the short story could easily grow into a novella or an epic adventure which, in this case, would be Indiana Jones' *Raiders of the Lost Ark*.

Word count, although not extremely important in this stage, will assist you to establish which category your story will be. A short story can go as high as possibly fifteen to twenty thousand words, while a novella will run from approximately twenty-two to forty thousand words. When you reach the fifty thousand word limit, it is normally considered a novel. There is some degree of wiggle on the word count; the final decision being made by the editor. This means knowing the guidelines of where you submit.

No matter what, getting your ideas on paper is the first step in your voyage. This is similar to charting your course on the waves. Some sailors like to set sail and follow the current but a good sailor charts. The same is true with writers. Some just start typing and let the story flow to the length that it will be. Others create a structure for the story which helps them define the direction and length. It is with this plan that the writer will know when the story is done. Sailing the unknown can lead to many dangers, one of them being that you are not on course. Still, that can be good, too, sometimes. Obviously, rules are not carved in stone; they should be liquid like the sea and flow but stay within the guidelines.

While I figured out what regrets my character would have, the plot developed. When the ending came into focus, of course, the regrets compounded.

## CAPTURE

Concept is only the beginning; the true start of the story is *capture*. This is the hook that catches the reader's attention. This is the hardest sea to journey out onto and although seemingly calm, be extremely wary; it is very deep and treacherous.

Whether it is a rowboat, yacht or ocean liner, each has an anchor, a *hook* so to speak, which is usually attached at the bow (front) of the boat. An anchor holds the boat stationary; the hook holds the reader. It can take you a great amount of searching to find your treasure, that one line that will capture your audience, in the depths of this sea.

You may begin to develop your story, be it novel, novella, or short story, only to find that your starting point doesn't hold—or hook—the reader. Now you have to wonder if you should have launched your adventure from a different port. This is a critical decision for you and your story. If you don't grab the reader's full attention in the first sentence or paragraph, you won't have an audience. Only a handful of readers will continue to read something found to be boring in hopes that it will get better. An empty ship seldom sails.

This is your bounty and treasure. You don't need to have this hook to start your story but you will need it by the time you finish. Some writers find that grand opening segment after they've completed their story and this may hold true for you. Just remember, you have to sail all seven C's which means if you skip this one early, you will have to come back to it. The hook to the reader in "Sea of Regret" was the first two sentences.

> Of all the things he remembered, there was only one he regretted: He would never see Shara Ki again. Afloat on the waves, the sole survivor of a shipwreck, he stared at the monotonous view.

You are caught in the web of mystery of what the main character is regretting; who or what is Shara Ki? At the same time, your imagination has been piqued with the idea of being shipwrecked. What exotic island will he find himself on? The reader's attention has been captured.

With the hook, or capture, a short story, a novella and a novel decidedly agree in the most compact manner, yet differ slightly. (Confused? Well...) A short story must capture in the first few sentences. A novella can use the first paragraph or two, while a novel has the luxury of almost a page. Each is in comparison to the length but there is no reason that a novel can't capture the reader in the first sentence.

There is no second chance on this sea, so don't wander about; a direct course is the best plan of action.

## CHARACTER

Once you have capture in control you need to evaluate your characters and that will be the third sea to chart: *character*. As stated earlier, in a short story you will have a limited number of characters. In a novel and novella, this number will increase dramatically. This sea has varying degrees of depth, color and action. Just like the waves of the ocean, the characters must come alive; they must rock, roll, crest and dip inside the reader's mind. If you have what I call an assembly line character (ALC), you have nothing. An ALC is just a cardboard silhouette with no motivation or depth, the stereotypical person. Like the alkaline residue when saltwater dries on metal, if touched, it will dissipate in the wind, leaving nothing. If your character is scrutinized, you don't want him or her to crumble like powder. To explain, what do you think of when you read the word "barbarian" or "sailor" in a story or novel? For the word "barbarian," it would probably be a very rough, heavily muscled brute with black, mussed hair and likely wearing a suitable amount of fur and with at least one knife and/or sword. Your first mental image of the word "sailor" is probably that of a young male wearing a white or blue bell-bottomed uniform with a white cap. He swaggers, drinks, smokes and has at least one young maiden in arm. Your character "can" be what everyone thinks is stereotypical but you must take care and make at least some attempt to discern him or her from the rest of the crowd. This can be done by using emotions, unique characteristics or the situation. In "Sea of Regret" I have a sailor but I have taken him out of his normal surroundings. He is now a victim of his own occupation and is not in control of any seagoing vehicle; instead he is adrift, lost:

> Seaman Second Class Hanson straddled his floating island of debris. The ship had exploded, that much he remembered.

I give more and more details about the character as the story unfolds, rather than droning on about physical features and boring descriptions of clothes. Many times the readers' imagination will fill in details or place themselves into the story.

> Shara Ki was the girl he'd loved and left behind. He wanted to marry her but just like other young men of his village, he had no money. Shara Ki's father had accumulated a tidy dowry for her and the manor lord's young son was quickly wedded to her. Hanson left the village the morning of Shara Ki's marriage; he couldn't stand to watch his beloved in the arms of another.
> The seaport of Tileth had beckoned to him and he answered the call. Four years later he had proven himself worthy and been promoted many times.

In just a few short sentences you have learned that the lead character is about twenty-five years of age and a village-raised lad of poverty. Lovelorn, he departs for a seaport, becomes a sailor and seems to be a very responsible and capable person. More and more details about Hanson are revealed as the story progresses.

In a novel, details would be much more vivid, embracing the reader's mind to see exactly what the writer has envisioned.

In this case, Hanson would have had many more characteristics embellished, perhaps to such a degree that you could have selected him from a group of strangers on the street. In a short story, that skill is not necessarily needed. Also, in a novel or novella, more time would have been expended on developing the detail of his love interest and possibly his adventures in Tileth and at sea. Friends, neighbors and other characters in Hanson's life would have come into existence and been carried along in detail to expand the story and give a better understanding of our lead character.

## CONFLICT

Sailing the fourth sea is fun. This is where you can mix characters with personalities to provide conflict and add excitement to the story. The waves are the ride and this is where all the action happens. Just like the sea, this one is filled with currents that move you from one point to another. Some seas have more than one current while others only have the single main current. This is true of writing. A novel has many plots, a novella has a few and usually there is just one plot in a short story. The main ocean current involves the plot and what it is all about. This is not just some insurmountable task to be accomplished but can be an inward change that happens to your lead character. Physical conflict is good but mental conflict adds a new dimension to your character and depth to your writing skills. This is where you can change the course of your voyage and have fun. Red herrings are great if sprinkled about with the proper amount of caution. Twists and turns keep the reader awake. There are many conflicts in "Sea of Regret" beginning with the accident at sea. Hanson finds himself alone, trying to stay alive. There is a lack of supplies. I saw no reason to have my character be allowed all the food he wanted.

*He'd discovered that he was alone. Hanson had shouted for any companions but been met with silence. He had gathered a wooden bench, three chairs and a lanyard pole with a small amount of rigging rope. He used the rope to hold his bounty together. He'd also found a floating wooden galley crate partially filled with fruit. The salty water didn't aid in preservation and it was quickly rotting and shriveling in the hot, tropical sun.*

So often in a stereotypical tale, an island is always in sight and paradise is there to accept the shipwrecked sailor to a haven of safety and leisurely pleasures. I made sure there was no land in sight and that can definitely sully even the happiest person's day.

*The ride was continuous, wave after wave, always rolling down into the trough and its myriad shades of blue and green, only to glide back up to the top where it was crested in white. The crest, where in the distance it was always the sea touching the sky. Land had been but a dream for the last five days as he floated under the scorching sun.*

Of course, when a mermaid introducing herself as "Ayala" appears, her presence might make one think they were going crazy. A mermaid may also add a sensual interest that could allude to other plots if the story was expanded to novella or novel length. Lest I forget, regret is one of the prime players of conflict in this tale; not marrying Shara Ki is only the first regret. Of course, the conflict of seeing Shara Ki's eyes in Ayala's face enhances this regret. We suddenly feel an empathy with our character and understand some of his newfound loneliness.

*They were the same ice-blue as Shara Ki's which caused tears to well in his eyes.*

This is the largest sea of the seven we will navigate and you have the ability to decide what weather will occur during the reader's voyage. A clear sailing day is beautiful but little happens during that time. Just like distant thunderstorms or wailing rains pelting you. Conflict adds excitement. A good storm (a.k.a. conflict) is necessary in captivating your reader. You can have a few squalls, if you want, even that distant chance of a storm, but there must be something that causes your character to have a problem or some form of consternation of his or her situation.

In a novel, entire chapters can be written on a single conflict, digressing with details that will keep the reader intrigued. At the same time, there are many other conflicts happening that will possibly influence the main conflict. Having a volcanic explosion in your story that will have no other impact other than a disaster in the distance is a waste of the reader's time, neither enhancing the story nor moving the story along. This is what I call a dead red herring because it does nothing except smell...

...and trust me, readers can smell a bad story quickly and easily.

Yet, that same volcanic explosion, with one lava flow heading toward a hospital where your spouse works and another flow toward your home and children, will keep the readers on the edge of their seats.

Whether it is a novel, novella or a short story, a sole conflict can be the vortex that sweeps your reader to the next sea.

## CLIMAX

In a story that works, the plot comes to a peak and is revealed with the resolution made apparent. Normally, all the conflict threads are resolved and finalized, but there are times when they are not, especially when the concept and conflict is leading to a different port—sequels.

This is the fifth sea, a small sea, a very small sea. It is where all the water from the prior sea is squeezed and channeled to literally squirt the reader to the finale of the story. In a novel, this will range from the last chapter or two to possibly the last few pages. In a short story, the climax usually occurs in the last one or two paragraphs.

In "Sea of Regret" our lead character, Hanson, after making friends with the mermaid Ayala, goes below the surface of the ocean, into her world. He cannot breathe, his lungs need oxygen.

> Deeper and deeper they plummeted. His lungs burned and he regretted not taking a deeper breath. Would he survive to surface again?

Hanson sees the other merpeople coming to greet him.

> In the distance he could see others swimming toward them. The sea was full of merpeople. They were coming to greet him.

It is at this moment he realizes what is happening.

> *Ayala turned to look at him and through the haze he could*
> *see that her eyes were dark, nearly black. They were no longer*
> *anything like Shara Ki's. In fact, Ayala's soft smile now twisted*
> *into a grin, an evil grin. The sharp teeth glistened from behind*
> *the curling snarl of her lips.*

Our short story has reached a *climax*, the wind has billowed the sails, the reader is speeding through the water. Our vessel is on course.

The only thing that can surpass a grand climax is a fabulous finale. The voyage is almost over. Don't let your reader down.

## CONCLUSION

This is a very, very important sea. It is the finale where the lead character discovers or reveals whether or not anything was learned or changed from the conflict. For the short story, this is the smallest surface to navigate in our Seven C's.

> *Seaman Second Class Hason regretted at that moment not*
> *paying closer attention to what Ayala had said. They ate*
> *whatever they caught.*

This is the final regret. Our character has matured and learned, unfortunately too late, one of the hardest lessons of the sea where everyone is involved in fishing, one way or another.

This is a vital section that leaves the reader with a lasting impression of your story. It must have impact. Many authors have left impressions on their readers such as Damon Knight in his short story "To Serve Man" with the immortal words: It's a cookbook. The novel *Make Room! Make Room!* by Harry Harrison was the basis for the movie *Soylent Green* and the words: It's (Soylent Green is) people.

It's not critical that it be spoken words that leave the impression; just a great ending that catches the reader, such as the ending Rod Serling wrote for the film based on Pierre Boulle's *Planet of the Apes*. Still considered one of the most chilling images in film, it is not the last lines of the film that make an impact, but the striking image of The Statue of Liberty and Taylor's discovery that this topsy-turvy world he has crash-landed on is Earth.

## COLLECT

You have now sailed the first six seas; this is the last sea. The final C. This particular sea will have more storms and calms than any of the others. Your true nautical skills will be tested to make sure that you are indeed a writer. This one will be the hardest and possibly the longest voyage you will have of the Seven C's discussed. If you don't submit your work, it definitely won't be published and you definitely won't *collect* any money.

This particular C hasn't changed over the years. Think of it. A storyteller sharing his inner wealth then later stretching out his open hand for some small token, in hopes to make a meager earning. If he didn't stretch out his hand, the money wouldn't come of its own volition.

Depending on whether you are trying to sell a short story, a novella, or a novel, the length of time to receive a reply can vary. Short stories usually have the quickest turn around of either days or weeks depending upon mailing methods. Today, many markets accept electronic submissions and a writer could have a reply in just a few scant hours or less. Fifteen minutes was the shortest reject—er, response—that I have received. Novellas and novels can take up to months, but anything over six months should be considered time to nudge the editor with a reminder, unless the guidelines state that it could take longer.

A good philosophy is to analyze the market for your story then select five places to mail it. Just to make sure we are all in the same boat, always start with the better paying markets first. Send out your story, making sure you've met the guidelines and have a one page cover letter. Two of the quickest ways to sink your boat, after navigating the first six C's, is to (1) not adhere to the guidelines of where you are submitting and (2) not being professional in your one page cover letter. Fancy typefaces (or *fonts*), colored ink(s), and cute stationary are for family and friends—not your manuscript.

A *cover letter* should be one page (have I emphasized that clearly?) and either be in a font that is recommended in the guidelines or else use 12 point Courier on plain white bond. Make sure there is a minimum of one (1) inch margins the top, bottom and right side. A one and one half margin on the left is nice.

What do you put "in" the letter? Make sure you include your name, address, phone number, date, name of manuscript and a short description of it. If you have any publishing credits, list the better ones. Make sure you have the name of the editor and publication to which you are submitting this manuscript *spelled correctly.*

If a paycheck comes back—great. Otherwise, you probably got a rejection letter that should be quickly reviewed. If you agree, make the appropriate adjustments in your story. Then, get out the list of five markets you chose earlier, check off the first one and mail your manuscript to the next one on the list. This mailing should be done no more than twenty-four hours after receipt.

If you have just received a rejection of your story back from the fourth place on your list, send it out to the last listed name. Now, sit down and review all the notes from the four earlier markets. There are a multitude of hints and suggestions in those rejects. Even "does not fit our needs at the current time" informs you that somewhere you missed a submission point, a similar story was just printed, not the publication's normal story type or possibly too short or too long. Now, re-evaluate your story and make changes. Look at the markets again and find five more places to mail your story.

Non-paying markets should not be relegated to the unusable category. It would be better to have your story published for no money than not printing the story at all. Your name on a story in the file cabinet does not help to make it a household word on the lips of raving fans. Evaluate the non-paying markets and decide which would sound the most impressive listed as a publishing credit. (Yes, even non-paying markets are publishing credits.) Also, non-paying markets are usually willing to work with unknown authors and help preen your writing skills.

That concludes the voyage across the Seven C's of writing and the basics in creating a solid story, be it a short story, a novella, or even a novel. As explained, there are differences and similarities between the three styles. Find the one that fits your niche and enjoy.

## ASKING THE BIG QUESTIONS

Of course, not only is there the "how" of writing a short story, novella or novel, but also the "why" which needs to be answered, too.

WHY WOULD YOU WRITE A SHORT STORY? Simple. A rough short story can be fleshed out in a few scant hours and polished in a day or two, ready for the editor and a paycheck. What is the down side to this? You are now in the slush pile; that enigmatic stack of papers clustered on the editor's desk, waiting. A short story has to carry punch. In order to do that, the writer must make each word zing to its fullest potential. Once you have caught the editor's eye and been published, then when your name passes his or her desk again, you may have a better chance of being elevated in that pile. No promises.

Just remember, a short story must have one very basic plot line, a couple of characters and not be mussed with superfluous characters and sub-plots. Short stories should be quick reads and eye candy for the brain. (Okay, okay...*mind* candy.) It should be quick-moving and make your reader feel satisfied when they are finished.

A published short story is your introduction as a writer to the world. You've caught the eye of an editor; now you hope to catch the eyes of readers and they will look forward to more stories with your byline. The single most positive aspect of getting a short story published is that publishing credit. If and when you decide to write a novel, it adds credence to your ability and skill as a writer; something the editor will acknowledge.

Magazines and anthologies are wonderful proving grounds for short stories because the editor can take a chance on a new writer without too much damage or loss of income. This chance is what makes a writer known to the reader and thus starts what the writer likes: fans. Writing short stories can get your name out into the public eye much faster and easier.

A final reason why: *quick money*. A full-time writer could type out two or three short stories a week and therefore, could see some respectable money. Short stories don't pay an immense amount of cash, but pennies do add up.

WHY WOULD YOU WRITE A NOVELLA? Sometimes the story can't be told in 6000 words or less. A good story needs to take the number of words necessary to give the reader a complete ride. Skimping in details will detract from your story; it could also cost you a publication. This is a good time to broaden your short story's scope and turn it into a novella.

A novella can take the short story and enhance it with more than one plot line and have a couple of sub-plots. More characters and depth of character can be fleshed out. Writing novellas is a great exercise for the writer to flex his or her skills. This is also a good medium for those who are afraid of the commitment to the number of words required by a novel, yet feel that short stories are too constrictive or restrictive. In addition, a novella can be composed and ready for mailing in a week or two.

Many magazines frown on novellas since they take a large amount of space in either one issue or extended over multiple issues. This is a conundrum since these same magazines will evaluate and occasionally print a novella to keep their readership hooked into buying the next issue in order to finish reading the next installment or conclusion.

Publishers, big and small, that print anthologies are the best markets for novellas. The same rules discussed in the earlier section on short stories apply regarding the publisher's issues.

Novellas usually pay more than a short story, hence the editor's need to evaluate a novella for publication.

**WHY WOULD YOU WRITE A NOVEL?** You can't put the history of the world on a 3x5 card or two, and there are those stories that just need more than three hundred pages of print. A novel can be written in anywhere from four weeks (Yes, a novel in a month! It is done every November at www.nanowrimo.org during National Novel Writing Month.) to any extensive length of time. Some authors have been working on a novel for over twenty years while some of their other published novels took only a few months. Each novel will take the number of words necessary to tell the tale but it should be in the range of 60,000 to 80,000 words, although the length of 100,000 is not totally out of range.

Novels, especially trilogies or series, are multi-threaded with plots and sub-plots and deep character development. A short story cannot allow that depth of writing. Yet, to the writer, a multi-threaded novel or trilogy can be a dangerous maze to tread. In a standard novel, the author must keep track of the main story line or plot, plus all the subplots. In a multi-threaded novel, there are multiple story lines with multiple sub-plots. This can be a daunting enterprise for even the best authors, let alone the novice.

One sure way to be able to track and make sure all the story lines work is to write a novella around one main plot. You should now have a modest 30,000 word project. Then write another novella revolving the other main plot that plays on the first novella but can totally stand on its own merits without the first. You should now have two novellas of approximately 30,000-40,000 words each. If you had more than two main threads or plots, a third novella could be written; more than three will make the next step very difficult or almost impossible.

Now, rewrite the novellas into one novel, chopping the sections and gluing it all back together. The final product should range somewhere in the 70,000-85,000 words and all the plots, sub-plots and characters have closure. Your reader is satisfied, and hopefully wanting to see more of your work.

Another aspect of writing a novel that happens is discovering characters that come to life and ideas that get born during the project. Yes, that happens and it adds bulk to your original idea which in turn adds more words. Be careful not to get caught in the premise of being too clever with your material. If you attempt to construct too complex of a story structure, you could lose control of what is happening and an editor will realize that faster than you, the author.

What do you do when a character comes to life? Go with it! This could be the added touch needed to turn the short story or novella into a novel. In addition, it makes writing much simpler. When you get ready for the final edits, this character may get scratched, but he or she has added to the quality of your story, whether he or she be in it. How is this? A character can add depth to your novel's realizations and be eliminated from the final version; yet he or she has enhanced the other characters with more depth, a depth that still exists in this character's absence.

Novels are the highest paid writing. When dealing with novels, it is best to have an agent that will assist you and make sure that your interests are being preserved.

**WHICH AUTHORS WRITE SHORT STORIES? NOVELLAS? NOVELS?** Andy Duncan wrote "The Pottawatomie Giant" and won the 2001 World Fantasy Award for Best Short Fiction. His novella, *The Chief Designer,* won the 2002 Theodore Sturgeon Memorial Award.[1] He basically writes short stories and has had the fortunate luck to have a book published which is a collection of his stories. For him, writing short stories has been successful.

Robert Jordan, well known for his novel series, *The Wheel of Time*, wrote a short story entitled "The Strike at Shayol Ghul" in 1996. It can be found on the internet at: http://www.tor.com/shayol.html[2] Jordan normally writes novels and this was definitely breaking new ground for him. *The Wheel of Time* series has currently [in 2004] consumed a total of ten books, which he promised would be the total number. The *New York Times* has called Jordan the American heir to Tolkien.[3] Before writing Tor's fantasy juggernaut, he used the *pseudonyms* of Reagan O'Neal and Jackson O'Reilly[4] to write other novels.

Pseudonyms are aliases (sometimes referred to as *pen names*) some authors tend to use in place of their real names or when they are established in another genre, are a very common practice in the writing world.[5] There are many reason why this happens, one could be the well-known author doesn't want the public to know it is him or her. Another could be as simple as the library is allowed to only have so many books by author X, so by using an alias, the same writer can have more books in the library. Also, the author could be known for novels and then writes short stories under an assumed nom de plume. Finally, the author just wants to hide his or her real name.

Roger Zelazny has written under the guise of Harrison Denmark. He has been writing stories since the 1950s ["And the Darkness is Harsh" (*Eucuyo, Euclid Ohio High School Literary Annual* (1954))][6] and also written many novels.

Even one of my favorites, Robert Heinlein, has used an alias or two or three or more: Anson McDonald, Lyle Monroe, John Riverside, Caleb Saunders and Simon York. Most of his pseudonym writing had been for anthologies that consisted of short stories and novellas. Robert Heinlein succeeded in novel, novella and short story writing.

Perhaps you've read *The Running Man* by Richard Bachman, or should I say Stephen King? While he is more famous for horror novels like *The Shining* and *Salem's Lot*, King (under the name Bachman) wrote the basis for the SF-action film starring Arnold Schwarzenegger. Remember, if you happen to read a story by John Swithen...well, you're still reading Stephen King.

Most readers associate Stephen King with novels but he has written novellas and short stories also. He wrote a novella, *Riding The Bullet*, that he made available for electronic download to the masses. It is still available at a modest price from Amazon.com.[7]

Lynn Abbey, another writer, has written many stories which are in the *Thieves' World* series. They range in length from short story to novella.[8] She has taken the short story and novella skills acquired and created a full-length novel of this world entitled *Sanctuary*.[9] Rest assured that Lynn Abbey has many other novels and short stories that range the fantasy gamut.[10]

Tara K. Harper primarily writes novels. Her *Wolfwalker* series currently has six novels, but she has many more already started, almost forty-eight[11]. She works on each as the notion strikes her. She also has three novels published in the *Cat Scratch* series.

Can a person write a first novel and be published immediately? Ask Christopher Paolini, author of *Eragon,* and the soon-to-be released sequel *Eldest.* At the ripe age of fifteen, Christopher graduated from high school in 2000 and started working on his novel. He is now nineteen and his first novel, *Eragon* was released in 2003.[12]

Jane Welch launched her first book in 1995. *The Runes of War* became the basis for her trilogy which followed with *The Lost Runes* in 1996 and finally *The Runes of Sorcery* in 1997. Had she been published prior? No. Jane Welch has gone on to write another triology, *The Book of Önd,* and has another set already in the works.[13]

Not all authors remain writers; some work their way through the process and become editors.[14] Kristine Kathryn Rusch began her career as a prolific writer of short stories, then novels, while still composing short stories. She is the wife of another well-known writer, Dean Wesley Smith, with whom she has co-written many novels. She has been writing since 1987.[15] She was editor of *The Magazine of Fantasy and Science Fiction* for six years before stepping aside in 1998 and giving the reins of the magazine to another author, Gordon Van Gelder. Even while serving as editor of *MFSF*, she wrote short stories and novels, still keeping her hand in the business of writing.

This small list of authors only proves that it doesn't matter whether you write a short story, a novella, or novel; all three or any one of them can lead you to publication and success.

WHERE CAN YOU SUBMIT? Short stories and novellas can be submitted to any number of places. The best place to begin your market research would be to purchase or check your local library for a current copy of *Writer's Digest Novel and Short Story Writer's Market*. This is a handy reference of guidelines each possible magazine or publisher wants and the going rate of pay. A really nice feature of this title is listing websites if one exists for that market.

Another current method of keeping up with the changing market would be to subscribe to WritersMarket.com.[16] This online subscription service is updated daily and keeps writers informed on submission guidelines for publishers and magazines, agents, who is in business and who is not, and other news in the writing world and its various markets.

Another favorite place of mine for fantasy and science fiction markets is Ralan's Place[17], an online resource that is consistently kept up to date with paying and non-paying markets for short stories, novellas and novels.

Finally, if you use Google or Dogpile for searching the internet, I would suggest using the following words enclosed in quotation marks: "writers guidelines," "fantasy guidelines," "magazine guidelines" and "fantasy magazines. CAUTION: you may find much more than what you were looking for, especially when you use the word "fantasy."

WHY SHOULD YOU WRITE A SHORT STORY, NOVELLA, OR NOVEL? There are many reasons and here is a simple, short list of why:

- *Recognition? Not really.*
- *Money? You have to be kidding.*
- *Awards? They're nice.*
- *Because it is inside you?* We have a winner!

You write a short story, novella or novel because you have it inside you. It is the burning desire to tell a story, be it very short or very long or somewhere in between. You are a writer — nothing else really matters.

## ENDNOTES

1. http://www.angelfire.com/al/andyduncan/#bibliography
2. http://www.tor.com/shayol.html
3. http://www.tor.com/jordan/media.html
4.http://www.highbeam.com/library/doc0.asp?docid = 1G1:58633 344&refid = ink_d2&skeyword = fantasy + writing&teaser = ROBERT +

JORDAN + WRITING + AS + JACKSON + OREILLY. + Forge + 23.95 + (24 0p) + ISBN + 0-312-86486-8 + Long + before + Jordan + (The + Path + o f + Daggers) + became + a + bestselling + fantasy + novelist + be + wro te + swashbucklers + and + westerns + under + the + pseudonyms...

5. http://www.myunicorn.com/pseudos.html

6. http://zelazny.corrupt.net/stories.html#old

7.http://www.amazon.com/exec/obidos/ASIN/B00005BB4A/ qid = 1087168058/sr = 2-1/ref = sr_2_1/103-2555718-9703036

8. http://millennium.fortunecity.com/kibble/275/1983.html

9. http://millennium.fortunecity.com/kibble/275/thievesworld4. html

10. http://www.lynnabbey.com/Bibliography/bibliography.htm

11. http://www.tarakharper.com/faq_wrt.htm#time_write

12. http://www.randomhouse.com/teens/eragon/ christopherpaolini.htm

13. http://www.sfsite.com/05a/jw80.htm

14.http://www.sfsite.com/06b/kkr83.htm

15.http://isfdb.tamu.edu/cgi-bin/ea.cgi?Kristine_Kathryn_Rusch

16.http://www.writersmarket.com

17.http://www.ralan.com

# Culture Shock:
## WORLDBUILDING IN ASIAN CULTURES

### BY LAI ZHAO

#### ONCE UPON A TIME IN CHINA

I am browsing in an English language bookshop. Lofty ceilings, soft but bright lighting, Feng Shui comfortable atmosphere and setting. A forest of full, shiny mahogany bookshelves greeting me the moment I step through the square-arched doorway. From the adjacent café, coffee aromas and chocolate gateau scents wash over me, but it is the dry, wood smell of new books that calls, intoxicating. Interspersed amongst the shelves are tables showcasing the newest arrivals. People stroll through the aisles, looking for their preferred texts, their perfumes and colognes floating past.

I head for the Science Fiction/Fantasy section.

The first book I pick up: Celtic settings, names, peoples, gossamer-winged faeries, philosophies and viewpoints. It goes back on the shelf. A little further down, I select a second book. More Celtic- and Gaelic-based tales with crosses, winged dragons, knights in restrictive metal plates and unicorns. Hmm. Next row. European milieus, Finnish-based names. Well, you get the picture. I walk towards the Chinese section because I've given up with the English selection. One step...two...three. Stop. Backpedal one, two, stop. Blink. Blink. Surely this isn't real?! Surely...but no, *there it is*. Amongst hundreds of Western fantasy novels, a book cover with a distinctively Oriental character in armor reminiscent of which Far East nation? A little bit of all with a dash of imagination. I pick it up and start reading the first page.

Moments later I blink at the watery vision of someone shaking me, asking me in Chinese if I'm okay. What happened? Me, who never faints, has fainted. How embarrassing! What a way to lose face—in a bookshop where the staff recognizes me, and among Saturday afternoon shoppers. Mortification sets in!

But why did I pass out? (Note to self: must not make this a habit!)

While the use of Earth cultures in fantasy worldbuilding is not new, there has long been a tradition among Western authors to only use Western cultures. What's wrong with the Western cultures? Nothing. But why stop there?

## Beyond European Borders:
### Advantages of Alternative Cultures

Using alternative cultures provides you, the author, with a greater range of choice when worldbuilding. Clearly, you construct as much of your world as you need to in order to make it seem real to your reader. You could do this with the Western cultures, but why not try something that makes your work stand out from others?

Alternative, in this case, means non-Western. Middle Eastern, perhaps. Russian maybe. How about Australasian or Eurasian? Or, Asian? But if Asian, to which part of the continent do you refer?

The countries and cultures most often thought of when "Asia" or 'Asian' is mentioned are China and Japan, usually in that order. And yet the vast size of the Asian Continent gives lie to this "mis-association." Asia includes every country from Eurasia (e.g., Turkey) to the Middle

East (e.g., Tajikistan) to the Far East (e.g., Mongolia). Still, why only China and Japan? They are fascinating countries with rich histories that extend thousands of years into the past.

Just as the East craves things Western, so the West craves things Eastern. You only need to look at the popularity of Feng Shui, martial arts, Hong Kong cinema, anime (Japanese animation), manga (Japanese or Chinese comics) and any number of "authentic" oriental product imports to see the craze. But what else can such countries offer, especially in terms of worldbuilding for the writer?

Going beyond the modern façade, you can find ancient traditions still firmly entrenched. For instance, the tea ceremony (originated in China, adapted for Japanese needs), the celebration of the New Year (in China, the date is approximately February; in Japan, around January), ancestor worship, seasonal festivals and lion and dragon dances. Even here, the similarities between these nations are apparent. Aspects of these practices bring rich and unique cultural touches to your work's world. Other advantages include a more "exotic" feel to your world's written language (Chinese ideographic and Japanese onomatopoeic), fashion styles (the Chinese *cheongsam* or *keipo* and the Japanese *kimono*) and music (Chinese *yiu-wu* and Japanese *kokyou*).

Alternative cultures can also offer a sense of childlike wonderment because it may be seen as something "new," different and more interesting. "Fresh" would be an appropriate term. As a friend told me when I asked what he thought, stories that are set in a culture with which you are too familiar contain themes that are ignored; however, set the same story in another culture and the theme becomes interesting and can be further emphasized. For instance, girl meets boy in a version of Ancient China by traveling through a book (*Fushigi Yuugi*, by Yuu Watase) or girl meets half-demon boy in Ancient Japan by falling down a well (*Inu-Yasha*, by Rumiko Takahashi), seems to be far more intriguing than girl gets together with boy from Hell in a skyscraper American city. All three stories contain the theme about selfless sacrifice to save what you believe in and love.

Such ancient cultures, like China and Japan, can provide the setting for much amusement and potential conflict for your characters. For example, in *Morevi*, (by Lisa Lee and Tee Morris), Earth Captain Rafe Rafton encounters Askana Moldarin, First Queen of Morevi. Unfortunately for Rafe, he commits a few taboos. Morevian culture is based on the Chinese and Japanese worlds. In Oriental cultures, even those who can seemingly travel wherever they wish in the Imperial palace would still have had to acquire the Emperor's permission and seal first. Rafe, on the other hand, just goes where he wants without seeking approval—a trait of (over) confident British Pirates (Rafe calls himself a Privateer, but we shan't go there!). This causes Askana to lose face. A bull in a china shop? Perhaps, but not as clumsy and a good deal more intelligent!

*Keep a sharp eye for fortune cookies throughout my chapter. These are exercises in worldbuilding inside Chinese, Japanese and other Asian cultures. You might just find some good advice or food for thought in these sweet treats for writers.*

## SECTION 1: SOCIETY & ATTITUDES

### OVERVIEW

China and Japan have long histories. Their ancient worlds are a far cry from their Western counterparts. Each nation is steeped in tradition and beliefs in harmony and beauty. Ancient China and Japan are very similar, both in attitudes, formation and gender roles. For instance, before the rise of the feudal era in Japan, women had prominent roles in society. And they were also as capable as the men.

### WAR & FATALISM

Both Ancient China and Japan were formed by warring states and regions being united under a single ruler. In China, the feudal system was male-dominated, while in Japan, male-dominated rule came during the Feudal Era. However, it's interesting to note that "might is right" was the prevailing attitude in Ancient Japan.

Both nations could also be seen as "fatalistic," as in *"if it happens, it happens."* This is not to say that neither is proactive; they merely believe in conserving their energy for things they can change and/or control.

The illustrated version of *Hua Mulan* (Xu Deyuan and Jiang Wei) shows this attitude quite clearly. In this version of the legend, Mulan thinks to herself "Why don't I disguise myself as a man and join the army for father? So long as I am not discovered, I can come back to look after parents in one or two years' time once the war is over." (p.16)

*When building your world, slipping in snippets of Chinese or Japanese war strategy and hinting at warring states would serve you better than obvious mentions.*

## EMOTIONAL DISPLAYS

Both nations very much emphasized using instincts and feelings to help make decisions and judgments; however, both also stressed the importance of neutral displays of emotion. For instance, expressing anger or upset at any incident, except funerals or vengeance, etc., was a frowned-upon weakness. Such displays were interpreted as the goading party drawing out your "worst" side.

You were expected to keep your emotions within, whether you were in the presence of your family or otherwise. "Inappropriate" emotional displays, e.g., failure to bow respectfully to a government official you detested or appearing aggressive or arrogant when you were merely confident, could land you with a death sentence. Behind closed doors was another matter.

Such was the society in which both nations lived that putting on a false face became second nature; it was a way of survival.

*Whether or not your story is a comedy, in the ancient Far Eastern societies, consider how embarrassing a character would find it to show his affection for, or verbally describe it to, his girlfriend. The opposite is also true.*

## HUMOR

Both nations love to laugh. Yet humor can be so blatant it comes across as crude. It can also be so subtle that unless you are highly educated, you won't understand the joke.

Because the Ancient Japanese society was so serious, the people had to find ways to relieve stress. One of those methods was laughter. Their humor can be seen in the myriad depictions of their life, from comedic acting to stories.

In Ancient China, humor was socially regarded on a more serious level. Joking within your own intimate group was generally more open than when in a group with those you considered acquaintances.

### CORRECT HUMOUR

Correct etiquette in both societies also meant correctness even in humor. While you could be loud and rowdy with your best friends, you were expected to behave better around your employers (if they deigned to invite you or join your entertainment time) and anyone of higher status than you as seen in *Four Scholars* (http://tvcity.tvb.com/drama/four_men/main.htm). *Four Scholars* is a period costume series that tells the story of four talented scholars who are employed by the Emperor to help administer matters of state. The tale follows the scholars' exploits and their lives. The series is filled with humor, wry comments and numerous references to China's ancient society.

*Generally, make sure humor is subtle and tasteful. It does not need to be laugh aloud funny, but it should be harmless and should not cause a friend to lose face. Of course, if your characters are spiteful, feel free to be vicious. Humor can be biting.*

*Note though that much humor is expressed not through jokes and punch lines, but through puns, subtle references and vocabulary. (Numerous Chinese and Japanese words have multiple meanings while pronunciation (and tone) does not change.)*

### FORM & TRADITION

From an observer's viewpoint, both ancient nations are polite, rather formal and terribly tradition- and customs-oriented. They are also strict about hierarchy, correct forms of address and appropriate behavior.

However, if you become an insider, you'll find that behind closed doors, quite a few people will buck the trends and traditions when there is good reason to do so! (It's not a good idea to do this whimsically; you could end up being executed if discovered.) Terry Pratchett exaggerates the use of formal language in *Interesting Times*, but this title is a good illustration of the type of vocabulary you had to cultivate within societies that adhered so strictly to correct form.

## Mentality/ Beliefs/Values

It's important to understand that Ancient China and Ancient Japan value "face"—honor, decency and self-sacrifice for the good of all. These aspects of both nations are deeply ingrained and can be seen not only in their histories (e.g., *Hua Mulan* and Samurai Era), but also even now in their modern states (e.g., Chinese Olympic Gold medallists and Japanese business discussions).

While both nations would like you to believe that they have always been so imbued with such sense of worth, the reality is far different.

### Losing Face

One of the most notable aspects of Asian societies overall is the concept of "face." In Ancient China and Japan losing face is unacceptable.

Both nations go to great lengths to avoid actions or words that would cause a person to lose face in front of anyone. For example, if your friend has said or done something that affronts the one to whom you're speaking, you could say, "he is still young and does not fully understand the situation, please forgive him;" however, you should not say, "he's twenty-plus years old, he should know better" then turn to him and demand he apologize. You could get away with the latter in Western societies, but in Far Eastern ones, you could easily land yourself in a vendetta. You have caused him to lose face and, in this case, the only way to redeem himself is to declare vengeance. That usually meant the offending party would have to kill you, and that's a bad way to end an evening between friends.

On the other hand, if the subject causes herself to lose face (through words or action), a variety of methods exist for redemption, from the profuse apology to suicide. It's worth noting that suicide for women in Japan was a cut across the throat; men were expected to perform *seppuku* (Japanese ritual suicide by slicing open the belly). In China, women's suicides tended to be hanging, the "rope" usually made from a scarf or other long garment that could be slung around a roof beam or sturdy branch. Men usually fell on their swords or a sharp instrument of their trade.

### Shame

In both ancient societies, closely related to *losing face* was *shame*. This is especially true and apparent in Ancient Japan (and is still firmly evident in today's Japanese society). The Ancient Japanese would go to great lengths to avoid it. Phrases, words, actions, appearances—all were designed to project humility and prevent you from shaming yourself or another.

In China, you also went out of your way to avoid causing shame to yourself and others. One such way to shame yourself was to be caught in a compromising situation with the opposite sex.

### SEX & NUDITY

Many examples of sex and nudity can be found in Japanese scrolls from Ancient epochs; they are also prevalent in modern times, particularly in manga and anime.

In Ancient China, it was considered insulting or wanton to show more than the wrist; the entire body was covered—unless you were bathing (privately).

In both societies, men and women were generally respectful of each other. And while prostitution was legal, those who were born into self-respecting families (regardless of rank) were not "wanton" (i.e., they were modest, humble and respectful of self, family, relatives, friends and country).

In Ancient China, particularly, if you were female and pregnant out of wedlock, you were blamed for the pregnancy and punished. In Ancient China, if discovered, a pregnant, unmarried woman would be beaten with a bamboo cane while witnesses looked on. Such scenarios illustrate the mentality of the times: women were seen as seducers of men, using their wiles to exploit them; women were also blamed for causing men to feel lustful. This is one reason behind the written word *yiu* (妖 meaning in one sense "demon") containing the word for "woman" or "female."

### HONOR

And on the flip side of the *shame* coin is *honor*.

This idea was deeply ingrained in both nations. You were expected to work hard, study hard (if you had the opportunity) and contribute to society and family. At all times, you needed to protect the family's honor; women's reputations were particularly closely guarded (Ancient China), while men were expected to be discreet (Ancient Japan).

### HARMONY

Both nations seek harmony in everyday life. This stems from Buddhist teachings. However, while in China full Buddhism and Confucianism were the religions, in Japan, there were three: native Shintoism, the

Zen path of Buddhism and adapted Confucianism. (Later, Japanese religion also included Bushiddo.)

Two non-fiction titles that illustrate this harmony with the world around them are *The Tao of Pooh* and *Zen in The Martial Arts*. In *The Tao of Pooh*, written by Benjamin Hoff, the harmony sought after in life is explained through the adventures of Pooh, Piglet, and the many colorful characters of Hundred Acre Wood. *Zen in The Martial Arts*, written by Joe Hyams, explores the balance of power and peace as well as the philosophy of many martial arts. (The book also documents several intimate conversations between its author and The Dragon himself, Bruce Lee.)

Even the architecture and décor depicted harmony. Much of Ancient Japan's buildings and formal gardens were imported from China during early history, from the red-tiled roofs and the layout of the gardens incorporating bridges, large ponds filled with lilies and goldfish or *koi*, to the monasteries and temples dedicated to (Zen) Buddhism.

Illustrations of Japanese pagodas, Chinese Winter and Summer Palaces, formal Chinese and Japanese gardens, and so on, will demonstrate the similarities as well as highlight the differences between the two cultures.

## FORMS OF ADDRESS

When it comes to forms of address, both Ancient China and Japan get complicated.

Depending on which "status" you hold within the family, you would address your elders in one way while addressing, say, your younger cousins in another. Additionally, the station you hold in life also determines how you address a stranger, a citizen of higher "rank," someone below your level and also how you would refer to yourself.

### FAMILY & RELATIVES

Both societies stress the importance of family. Children are the most treasured. Their well-being, their future, is a priority. However, both societies stress manners at all times.

In Ancient Japan you would hear "honorable mother" or "honorable father;" you would also encounter "Honorable Elder Sister." Other terms would be "your honorable mother" or "honorable paternal grandfather." In Ancient China, you would encounter the same type of forms of address, but wouldn't necessarily hear the "honorable" prefix.

### THE IMPERIAL FAMILY & COURT MINISTERS

As a Court Minister, you would address the Emperor as "Honorable Imperial Majesty," or "Honorable Emperor." Even if you know his name, you would never use it. The Empress would be addressed in much the same way, too. You would also refer to the Crown Prince or a Princess as "Your Imperial Highness." You might get away with using their names plus the suffix "Imperial Prince" or "Imperial Princess" if either allowed such.

If you had to greet or refer to the Queen Mother, you would likely go with "Honorable Emperor's Mother" or "Honorable Predecessor's Empress."

Referring to other Court Ministers would go along the lines of "Honorable [Surname][Name] Brother Minster" or "[Surname] Brother Minister." You would use the term "Elder Brother" in this case.

Talking about yourself was done in the third person. You might have used "this unworthy person," "this humble servant" or "this uneducated (or uncouth) person."

Indeed, at Court and with other Court Ministers, you had to stay polite and calm. Showing anger, particularly in Ancient China, was the worst way to lose face and credibility amongst your peers. Before the Emperor, it could be disastrous to your reputation as another Minister might use the "losing face" moment against you.

Consider *Interesting Times*. When Rincewind visits the Counterweight Continent with Twoflower, he ends up attending a banquet with the Emperor and the Vizier. Pratchett creates a comic affect by exaggerating the type of vocabulary used, but he comes close enough to the reality.

If you were going for a comical effect, vocabulary you might use could include anything from "delicate flower of the moon" and "light of the world's eyes" to "most precious jade jewel of the crystal ocean."

However, for something that's not so frivolous, take a longer look at *Morevi*. The language used to address the Queen is not so flowery, but it is still polite. If you look at period costume series that involve Ancient Chinese Emperors and the court, like *Duke of Mount Deer* (Louis Cha), you would encounter polite, mildly-voiced phrases. Another example would be *Quest for Qin* (author's translation) by Wongyi.

## DON'T TAKE MY WORD FOR IT:

### TITLES THAT LOOK BACK TO ANCIENT CHINA

Whether you find them in modern settings or in medieval ones, the beliefs and traditions of both nations are dramatized in many anime titles. *GTO* (*Great Teacher Onizuka*, by Tohru Fujisawa) is the story of a 22-year old biker gang leader called Onizuka. He has major anger management issues and is lecherous. Nevertheless, he becomes a teacher. For his students, he will do anything to help them understand life—from saving one from suicide to setting up a joyride with apparent death as the climatic end, and everything in between. For his students, he will lose face, forego dignity and be a clown. He will do anything as long as it doesn't compromise his decency and honor.

This story is just one of many examples of how the values of decency, honor and self-sacrifice pervade the Japanese culture, from ancient eras to modern epochs. Further examples include Kenshin (*Rurouni Kenshin*, by Watsuki Nobuhiro), Taro (*Ranma ½*, by Rumiko Takahashi), Yu Yu Hakusho (*Yu Yu Hakusho*, by Yoshiro Togashi) and even Sesshou-Maru (*Inu-Yasha*, by Rumiko Takahashi).

In Chinese culture, the same is represented, particularly in the legends and stories of *Hua Mulan*, *Feng Shen Yan Yi* (Japanese manga adaptation is called *The Houshin Project* by Xu Zhonglin and Fyu Fujisaki respectively)) and *New Heaven Sword and Dragon Sabre* (by Louis Cha). You can also see how these values are taught to and learned by Suen Ng Hung (Cantonese), a.k.a. the Monkey King in *Journey to the West* (Chinese version, a TVB broadcast description can be found at www.tvb.com/singhe/b5/drama/journeytothewestii/) and again in the story of Nezha, the boy with spinning fire wheels (who makes an appearance in *Feng Shen Yan Yi*). Nezha is the oldest son of General Li, one of Heaven's top generals.

### THE HOUSHIN PROJECT VS. FENG SHEN YAN YI

*The Houshin Project* (manga) differs quite a bit from the original novel. The manga contains twenty-three volumes, while *Feng Shen Yan Yi* has a hundred chapters. A translation of the novel is available as *Canonization of the Deities* (translated by Gu Zhizhong). Both stories tell of a boy (who is human but was raised in Heaven) sent on a quest to "seal the deities" that were wreaking havoc and disharmony in the world. And there the similarities end. Both stories are worth the read, with each showing what idealized life was like in ancient societies and their beliefs.

### MANGA VS. NOVEL

It may be obvious that manga are comics and novels are, well, novels. However, their writing styles may not be so clear. Manga, more specifically Japanese manga and to a lesser extent Chinese manga, are tales told using film storyboards. You could conceivably take a manga and use it as a storyboard for a feature length animation. Manga are very visual. Novels, on the other hand, require much adaptation and faithful ones are very hard to do.

### MY *MULAN* VERSUS *THE MOUSE'S MULAN*

While Disney's version of *Hua Mulan* brought this ancient tale of Chinese folklore into modern mainstream America, it is a far cry from the actual legend. For a summarized but detailed narrative of the legend, peruse *Hua Mulan, China's Sweetest Magnolia* (Asiapac Books PTE Ltd) and *Mulan Joined the Army* 木兰从军(Canfonian PTE Ltd).

The main differences between the historical records, Chinese legends and Disney's animated feature involve two points. Mulan was not discovered to be female until after she had returned home from the war; nor did she invite to dinner the general who came calling. These elements were part of Mulan's "Westernization" to make the story more appealing to the family audience.

*Hua Mulan* embodies the Chinese civilization's two traditional concepts of value—filial piety to your parents and the spirit of patriotism. However, the legend also performs a greater service. It highlights the fact that women were as able as men when it came to protecting their countries and families. This is especially significant and commendable since China's feudal society was male-centered.

## SECTION 2: THE LANGUAGE

## EDUCATION

In Ancient China, it was considered unseemly and unsuitable for young ladies to be educated in the same way as young men. (The Chinese legend *The Butterfly Lovers* shows how Zhu Yingtai disguised herself as a man because her desire to study poetry, writing, etc. was so strong—http://www.wku.edu/~yuanh/China/love.html.)

In contrast, in Ancient Japan before the rise of the feudal era, women had very prominent roles. They were educators, proprietors, teachers, empresses with power and so on.

In both nations, the learning was done by rote. Students repeatedly copied the written language and recited ballads and poems. Any student not performing to his best ability was punished. How this punishment took form depended on the teacher.

### SENSEI VS. SHIFU

In Ancient Japanese, the word for teacher was *sensei*; in Ancient Chinese, it was *laoshi*. A Martial Arts master was also *sensei* or *shifu* respectively. (The words haven't changed, either.)

## FACE READING/CHAIR READING/PALMISTRY

One practice the Ancient Chinese and Japanese put much faith in was reading people—mainly through facial features, expressions, and actions. You could tell much from a person's facial features. Large lips meant you had a talent for singing, while crooked or loosely-spaced teeth meant you had a tendency to lie.

Seating also gave clues as to status within a company. Take the example of the Emperor and the Court at a banquet. Those sitting closest to the Imperial Throne possessed high ranks; those furthest away were of the lowest Court echelon.

As in the West, palmistry looks at the lines on your palm, the thickness of the heel of your hand and the length of your fingers.

## WRITTEN LANGUAGE

Chinese is *ideographic* (a picture or symbol representing a thing or an idea) while Japanese is *onomatopoeic* (the naming of a thing or action by a vocal imitation of the sound associated with it). Ancient Japanese, however, borrowed heavily from Chinese; much of Japan's documents were written in Chinese.

Ancient Japanese documents were written in Chinese, the script of the educated. Hence, one reason that so many Chinese words are found in the Japanese language. Chinese was used for law documents, official records and most of the poetry and other written works. It wasn't until later that the Japanese developed their own system (largely owing to women taking a positive lead in developing the language and education).

## Spoken Language

There are many dialects for each nation. From region to region, the dialects could differ so much that it would sometimes be impossible for speakers to communicate.

In Chinese, only Cantonese has kept its full tonal system, yet all the dialects are filled with rising, level, falling and dipping then rising tones. Japanese, on the other hand, while regional dialects are also numerous, do not contain tones.

Historically, Chinese and Koreans settled what is now Japan, integrating with the native Ainu. As far as spoken language goes, Japanese was greatly influenced by Korean. If you study spoken Korean you'll find many similarities to spoken Japanese. Yet, you'll also discover, perhaps frustratingly, that Cantonese and Mandarin (or "Putonghua") pronunciations are often used.

### Cantonese vs. Mandarin

Cantonese is, in fact, far older than Mandarin, which originated from the north (around Manchuria.)

### North or South?

The legend goes that there was a vote as to where the Ancient Chinese capital should be located; which would the people prefer? According to the story, the Emperor liked both the northern and southern locations. Unfortunately, a southern lord offended the Emperor and he chose to base the capital in the north. The vote of the people conveniently disappeared. Hence, Putonghua became China's official language.

## Naming Conventions

*Zhongguo*—Middle Kingdom

At the time, the Ancient Chinese believed China was the centre of the world. But there is another interpretation you may find useful for worldbuilding. Both Ancient China and Japan subscribed to the myth of Three Kingdoms—Heaven, Earth and Hell. In this sense, *Zhongguo* could be taken as a reference to mean, literally, "the kingdom between Heaven and Hell," i.e., "the middle kingdom."

*Zhongyuan*—Originating Centre

*Nippon*—Day's Birth or Land of the Rising Sun

In one sense, *Nippon* means "the day's origins," or "the day's birth," hence a reason behind Japan's marketing tagline, "Land of the Rising Sun."

As legends tell it, centuries ago the Chinese had explored as far West as America, long before Columbus sailed into the country. The Ancient Chinese had also traveled as far east as they could go without hitting "West" again. The land considered to be furthest east, the direction from whence the sun flowed over the horizon, was *Nippon*, a.k.a. Japan.

*Names are given according to the description (e.g., Meiguo means "beautiful country" (scenery), i.e., America), the smell (e.g., Xianggong meaning "fragrant harbour," i.e., Hong Kong), the location (e.g., Hokkaido meaning "north sea passage," i.e., Hokkaido), etc.*

## AUSPICIOUS NAMES & (MIS)FORTUNATE SURNAMES

If you are born into a family with a "misfortunate" surname, like *Ng*, it was customary to give the child a name that would counteract the "misfortune." Ng could be taken to mean "no" or "misunderstood" or "lacking." To negate this less-than-positive connotation and give the child some good luck in life, you might choose a name like "Chun Chun," meaning "Always improving."

The flip side to this, is if you were born with a surname like "Huang," meaning "king" or "emperor." Because the surname was so strong, you had to be very careful with the child's name; it would have been prudent to choose something that would balance the "power" of the surname.

On the other hand, if you named a child "Long," or "Dragon," you had to be sure the child could carry this name and be the best. Dragons are seen as the greatest and wisest of creatures; they are also believed to be very successful and are natural leaders. If the child couldn't live up to the name of "Dragon," the name would become a burden and the child would suffer throughout life.

*Girls were not normally given the name "Dragon;" usually a boy would carry it.*

## Section 3: Food & Tea

### Overview

Both the Chinese and the Japanese love their food; taste is particularly important. The Japanese not only savor the taste of food, but also the aroma, visual appeal and texture. As an appreciation of art and beauty instilled itself in Japanese culture, preparing, cooking and serving food took on a new level.

Fish, shellfish, wild game and acorns formed the main diet of the Japanese until the end of the Neolithic period (about 300 BC). Early agriculture began around then, too. Chopsticks were imported from China during the Tang Dynasty (618-906 BC).

### Soup's On: Cuisine and Culinary Arts

In Ancient Japan and China, there was a hidden dialogue and even a respect shown for social status in the preparation and presentation of food. While there are many modern myths behind "traditional" Oriental/Far Eastern meals, selecting from communal dishes was hardly the norm. Enough food per individual was served. However, as time passed, China began serving communal dishes, provided it was a meal amongst friends. You wouldn't be sharing dishes with strangers. Along with table settings, there were other aspects of revels and repast that spoke a silent commentary on one's standing with the table's host.

#### Appearance

Depending on where you were and whom you were serving, the appearance of dishes could range from the uninspiring to works of art. If you were, say, serving family, whatever is easiest would work. But if you were serving the Emperor, appearance was one of the first things on which you would be judged. Displeasure could cost you more than your livelihood—it could end up costing you your head.

#### Textures

A primary concern for both nations. If the dish being served was supposed to be tough or leathery on the outside and the inside was meant to be soft but the dish you served was nothing like it, there would be trouble—particularly if your customer happened to be of high rank with an irascible temper.

Foods eaten mainly for textures include shark's fin (Chinese) and *junsai* or *water shield* (Japanese).

### FLAVOR

If it looks good, it should taste just as good, n'est-ce pas? The nice answer would be "yes," but that's not always the case.

If the dish is not palatable, depending on the customer's temperament and status in society, they may put up with it, return it, scold you, throw it on the floor (plate included) or merely beat you up.

Flavor is very important to both nations, not just in the sense of taste, but also aroma. Usually it's the smell of food that either whets your appetite or causes you to wrinkle your nose and get as far away as possible.

### WITH RICE, WITHOUT RICE

A Chinese meal does not necessarily require cooked rice to be called a meal. However, if a Japanese meal does not include a bowl of cooked rice, the meal is considered a "snack."

## DISHES

In both cultures, the variety of dishes is vast, particularly with regards to Cantonese cuisine.

### CANTONESE VS. MANDARIN CUISINE

In my experience, the difference between Cantonese and Mandarin cuisine is minimal. However over the centuries, the Cantonese have developed the ability to prepare and cook literally anything that's edible. Next time you're at a traditional Cantonese restaurant, ask if you can have a copy of the Chinese-only menu to take with you. When convenient, ask a Chinese friend to translate. You might find the Chinese-only menu includes dishes the bilingual menu doesn't.

The following dishes come from various eras. Because worldbuilding requires more variety than reality may provide, I've listed this selection of foods for review and reference; the variety is greater than presented.

| CHINESE | | JAPANESE | |
|---|---|---|---|
| **NAME** | **DESCRIPTION** | **NAME** | **DESCRIPTION** |

| CHINESE | | JAPANESE | |
|---|---|---|---|
| **BREAKFAST** | | **RICE DISHES** | |
| Baozi | Steamed buns<br>Various fillings | Gyu-don | Thinly-sliced cooked beef on rice |
| Congyoubing | Spring onion-flavoured chapatti<br>Fried in oil<br>Small | Hayashi-raisu | Meat & vegetables with rice |
| Doujiang | Sweet soy milk | Kare-raisu | Japanese-style curry |
| Shaobing | Sesame seed pancake | Katsu-don | Fried pork cutlet on rice |
| Youtiao<br>Xifan/zhou | Fried bread sticks dripping in oil<br>Resemble doughnuts<br>Savory | Ten-don | Battered shrimp on rice |
| Xifan/zhou | Congee (rice porridge) | **NOODLE DISHES** | |
| Zhu rousing | Dried string pork | Agedashi-dofu | Deep fried tofu in fish stock |
| **TYPICAL DISHES** | | Ginnan | Ginko nuts |
| Bai mifan | Steamed rice | Hatsu | Chicken heart |
| Chao fan | Fried rice | Hiyashi-chuka | Cold noodles |
| Chashaobao | Steamed barbecued pork rolls | Kake soba/<br>udon | Plain noodles in broth |
| Guotie | Fried dumplings | Kata-yaki-soba | Crunchy fried noodles |
| Huntun | Small meat dumplings<br>Served in soup<br>i.e., Wonton | Negima/<br>hasami | White chicken pieces alternating with long onions |
| Mantou | Plain steamed bun (a staple) | Tsukimi soba/<br>udon | Noodles with raw egg |
| **LUNCH** | | Shiro | Intestine |
| Beijing kaoya | Beijing duck | Sushi &<br>Sashimi | Assorted |
| Dongpo menrou<br>Gongbao jiding | Pork fillet<br>Marinated, boiled & steamed till pork is tofu-tender | Yaki-onigir | Grilled rice ball |

| | CHINESE | | JAPANESE | |
| NAME | DESCRIPTION | NAME | DESCRIPTION | |
| | LUNCH | | NOODLE DISHES | |
| Gongbao jiding | Sichuan dish Chicken stir fried with peanuts & chili | Zaru-soba | Cold noodles with seaweed strips Served on a bamboo tray | |
| Jiangbao jiding | Marinated chicken breast Stir fried in special sauce | | | |
| | | | WINTER FAMILY FOOD | |
| Jiaohua ji | "Beggar's Chicken" Marinated chicken wrapped in bamboo leaves Roasted | Chanko-nabe | Meat & vegetable stew Sumo wrestler's potage | |
| Muer rou | Pork stir fried with wood ears (mushroom) | Oden | Fish cake, bean curd, kelp rolls, konnyaku (gelatin-like ingredient) & vegetables in broth | |
| | | Yudofu | Bean curd in broth | |

*You might stress the dishes' colorful and artful presentation, the aroma's mouth-watering effects, the texture's smooth and crunchy sensations, and the way the flavor compels you to eat serving after serving. The last is also effective if you need to poison a character using food but need the character to eat the entire dish for the poison to be effective.*

## Chinese Soups

**Note:** The variety of soups is endless. They range from savory to sweet, from clearing the palate to clearing your digestive tracks, and from general good-health soups to medicinal broths. A few are listed below:

*Bean curd claypot soup*
*Dried scallop soup*
*Egg Flower soup*
*Egg-drop soup*
*Green pea soup*
*Lobster soup*
*Lotus Root soup*
*Sizzling rice soup*
*Hot & sour soup*
*Pickled vegetable soup*
*Whole Wax Gourd soup*

*While many soups use vegetable and meat ingredients, there are even more that use herbs and medicinal plants. The latter sometimes reek and are incredibly bitter, yet they help the body heal and clear ailments that conventional medicine does not always cure. On the flip side, if your character is allergic to various medicinal plants or mistakenly uses the wrong proportions of plants, the ingredients are better than manufactured poison—plants are natural as are allergic reactions.*

## Tea

Both nations during "ye olde days" are primarily tea-drinkers. This list is only a small representation of a great variety available.

| Chinese | Japanese |
|---------|----------|
| Camomile | Bancha |
| Chinese herbal | Chinese |
| Chinese | Fresh |
| Chrysanthemum | Green |
| Green | Gyokuro |
| Iron Buddha | Japanese green |
| Jasmine | Oolong |
| Longzheng | Powdered green |
| Oolong | Sencha |
| Pu'er | Tea |
| Shoumei | Tea powder |
| | Wheat |

*Allergic reactions to a tea like "Bitter Summer Grass" could include lack of blood clotting—fatal to those who are wounded. Other teas may cause headaches, while others may cause reactions similar to a caffeine overdose.*

## ALCOHOLIC DRINKS

The following are a selection of alcoholic drinks from Ancient China and Japan.

| CHINESE | JAPANESE |
|---------|----------|
| Beer | Beer |
| Chinese wine | Rice wine / sake |
| Mao Tai (Chinese) | Distilled spirits (various grains and potatoes) |
| Rice wine | |

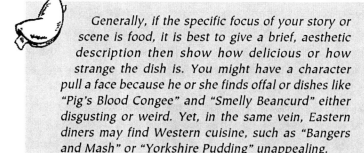

*Generally, if the specific focus of your story or scene is food, it is best to give a brief, aesthetic description then show how delicious or how strange the dish is. You might have a character pull a face because he or she finds offal or dishes like "Pig's Blood Congee" and "Smelly Beancurd" either disgusting or weird. Yet, in the same vein, Eastern diners may find Western cuisine, such as "Bangers and Mash" or "Yorkshire Pudding" unappealing.*

## SECTION 4: GAMES PEOPLE PLAY

### OVERVIEW

Many games in Ancient China and Japan were games of strategy, training the mind to think and overcome adversaries. Games taught children and adults about life and how to handle their emotions. For instance, if you were always emotionally involved in a game, you increased your chances of losing.

### Complete this Verse

In Ancient China, particularly at Court, advisors or noted scholars were asked to entertain the Emperor. Usually in the form of "complete this verse." Participants ("players" is usually taken to mean that the participants are voluntary, which wasn't always the case in the Ancient Chinese court) would be pitted against each other. Sometimes the Emperor would cite a verse and the participants would have to supply the second half of the verse. In this case, "verse" can be taken as a long stanza. If the verse was taken from literature, the participant who completed the second half correctly was the winner. If the verse was created, the participant who created a pleasing and intellectual second half won.

### Go

The two-player board game originated in China around three thousand years ago and was imported to Japan. In both nations, the rules and strategies are much the same since the game's creation; in fact, it's one of the oldest games to remain true to its origins.

Traditionally, it was played on a grid of 19 x 19. There are two sets of stones, black and white. Black usually goes first. The aim of the game is to obtain the highest number of points, which is earned by surrounding territory and opposing pieces. While *Go* sounds simple, the moves that can be made are many, thus complicating the game.

Go is a game that illustrates your thinking and how you see time. Your moves represent the way you consider the present and the future—are you a long-term strategist, or a present-moment tactician, or are you both?

For a very good look at how the game is played, the excitement and intensity that can surround the game, as well as Ancient Japanese fashion, have a gander at the manga *Hikaru no Go* by Hotta Yumi and Obata Takeshi. It tells the story of Hikaru, training to become an excellent Go player. His mentor is Sai, whose goal is to attain "the Hand of God;" Hikaru's rival is Touya Akira.

### Wrap, Cut, Hit

Interestingly this game, far from being exclusive to China and Japan, is prevalent throughout the world under the name *Rock, Paper, Scissors.* Traditionally, kids played it to determine who would be the leader of another game. The winner was the last one left.

### PICK-UP STONES

An ancient game played in both societies that predates the game "*jacks.*"

You sit cross-legged or kneel on the ground. Assembled before you are small, rounded stones. With only one hand, you pick up one up, throw it vertically into the air, snatch another from the pile and catch the first; you throw both into the air and swipe a third and catch the first two. The game goes on until you either fail to catch the stones thrown in to the air (in which case you lose), or you have picked up all the stones and caught them all (in which case you win).

### MAHJONG

There are many versions of it, from Shanghai to Taiwan, from Chiuzhou to Japan, but this game—now gaining popularity in the West—began in China. Mahjong is designed to keep the mind nimble and the fingers quick, and can be played with or without money.

Four players sit at East, South, West and North points. One hundred and forty-four tiles are arranged in four walls two tiles high that form a square with approximately four tiles sticking out beyond—like a square with each line extended beyond the corners.

Three players begin with a set of thirteen tiles; the "first" player has fourteen. When play commences, player one discards one of the fourteen. The aim is to assemble four sets of three tiles and a pair, and obtain points by collecting the right Flower and Wind.

The tiles are divided into:

*Characters* (the words translate as 10,000, 20,000, 30,000 and continue all the way to 90,000)

*Sticks* (pictures of bamboos from two to nine; one is a picture of a bird)

*Balls* (stylized pictures of *tongzi* (lit. trans. "Coins")—old Chinese currency. They were small, flat copper discs with a hole in the middle that allowed them to be strung together.)

*The Winds*—East, South, West and North—four of each.

*The Dragons*—White (a blank tile decorated with a frame); Green (the word is Chinese for "prosperity"); and Red (the word is Chinese for "center"). There are four tiles of each Dragon.

*Eight Flowers*—Four Blue Flowers and four Red Flowers. Both sets are numbered from one to four. Depending on when your turn is, you can pick up points for getting the correctly numbered flower.

Similar to Mahjong's Western equivalent Gin Rummy, players assemble sets: four sets, and a pair. Possible sets are normally a run of three and/or three of a kind. Sometimes, you can also assemble four of a kind—which gives you an extra turn, and extra points if you win. The scoring system is relatively simple, but to score high, you need to collect the appropriate tiles. If you need one more tile to win and someone throws out the one you need, you can claim it. However, if two of you are waiting to win, whoever is on the right of the player discarding the tile wins.

There is one combination of tiles called "*Su(p) sam yiu*" (Cantonese), that is, *The Thirteen Orphans*, that would provide you with, literally, full points. It's also the hardest combination to assemble. Each tile is either the first or the ninth of the first three sets (as listed above); the rest of the thirteen tiles need to contain one of each Wind and one of each Dragon; the last tile of this combination needs to form a pair with any one of the assembled thirteen.

The game isn't as complicated as it sounds; however, when played expertly, it is fast and filled with strategy. Four rounds complete a game.

## Do You Feel Lucky: Gambling

The street is crowded but the noise level is bearable. Shops, restaurants and brothels on both sides are filled with customers. As you stroll down the street, vague calls become louder and clearer. You pause before a wooden-fronted building, indistinguishable from its neighbors, except for the occasionally deafening cries. You glance at the sign above the door. How's your luck holding these days?

The room you enter is hot and sweltering, filled with body heat and tobacco smoke. Crowded, noisy, but you can still feel the excitement. Somewhere you hear the muted clink of money being won or lost. Shouts of dismay, of success. You push your way to the front of the crowd. Before you there's a table. On it is a large sheet of paper sporting the word "Big" on one side and "Small" on the other. The middle box is blank. Bets are called and placed. Rattling in a china bowl distracts you. Looking up, you see the banker standing on the other side of the table vigorously shaking a covered bowl. He slams it on to the table. People start chanting either "Big" or "Small" depending on the majority of bets. The banker reveals the bowl's contents. You peer inside. Dice. And there is a pair of single red ones and a three. Around you the gamblers yell their cheers or lament their losses. You have just taken part in a game of *Big/Small* (author's translation).

Accustomed to the din now, you weave your way through the gambling den's crowds to another table. This one is just as noisy as the first. Again you worm your way to the front. Another table with another large sheet of paper on it. This time, the paper is painted with a fish, a prawn and a crab. Other symbols include money, lose and a blank square. As before, bets are called and placed. The banker shakes what you assume are dice, in a covered china bowl. He slams the bowl on the table. The crowd leans in. He lifts the lid. And three dice lie in the center. You frown. They are not the usual dotted dice. Two show a crab each while the third shows a prawn. Around you, those who lose yell while those who win cheer. This is *Fish/Prawn/Crab* (author's translation), another popular game of chance.

## GUESS THE NUMBER

Finally, we have a drinking game. First, you all guess how many fingers there will appear. With great enthusiasm, you and friends each use your right hand and snap out as many fingers as you want, one to five; if you use a fist, it means no fingers, or zero. The loser(s) drinks a predetermined amount of whatever alcoholic beverage is making the rounds.

*Many games in Ancient China and Japan were addictive, not just because you could win obscene amounts of money, but also because of the mental workout. They also offer opportunities to show off your settings and character reactions. For instance, just as in Poker, in a Mahjong game, little movements will tell the other players what tiles you have. Take a look at Granny Weatherwax's reactions in "Cripple Mr. Onion" in Terry Pratchett's* Witches Abroad. *She pretends to be a novice player; you could use a similar technique for your Mahjong-addicted character. Or, study Ranma's reactions in* Ranma ½ *(Rumiko Takahashi) when he plays cards to try and win back everything Soun lost. (Also note the surroundings.)*

## SECTION 5: ARTS & ENTERTAINMENT

### OVERVIEW

Both societies found entertainment mainly in the form of street theatre, martial arts displays, tournaments, plays and music. Both also considered each form art. Because martial arts and their tournaments as well as traditional music are prominent even now, I'll focus on theater.

### CURTAIN GOING UP: THEATRE

### JAPAN

| THEATRE | DESCRIPTION |
| --- | --- |
| Bunraku | A musical puppet drama accompanied by a lute-like instrument with three strings |
| Kabuki | (Strictly speaking, this form of entertainment appeared around the 16th Century. However, for purposes of worldbuilding, it's been included here.) This is a musical drama in which both male and female roles are played by men<br>The front part of the stage is elevated<br>A revolving stage may also be used |
| Noh | Stylized movements, chanting and elaborate costumes and masks characterize this type of play<br>Dancing is part of the play<br>Music accompanies the play<br>There is a space for an orchestra<br>Comic interludes between acts are integrated into the overall performance<br>A chorus provides background and supporting vocals |
| Yose | Popular theatre<br>(Certainly doesn't sound as old as Bunraku or Noh, correct? Well, again, for worldbuilding purposes, the more information you have, the better the detail of your world.)<br>Yose includes historical story-telling, story-telling and singing, comic story-telling and comic dialogue |

## CHINA

The most famous theatre type is Opera. The costumes are colorful, the headdresses dazzling and the face painting regarded as artwork. While Opera didn't evolve until much later in China's history, it's worth noting here for research references. Opera traditionally permitted only men to perform in them. It was considered disgraceful for women to appear on stage.

Opera may tell the idealized or stylized stories of ancient heroes and heroines through a musical medium. Female character voices were high while male character voices were low. However, the "pinched" and nasal qualities of the voices so specific to Chinese Opera rendered the male voice higher than you would expect.

The most frequently seen forms of opera are Beijing Opera and Cantonese Opera.

*In some regions, you were expected to participate if performers, particularly dancers, dragged you "on stage." It was considered bad form to refuse. If you need a comical situation for your character or merely a breather, consider using dancing, theatre or Opera for the occasion. This circumstance is entertaining especially when your character does not know the lines and is given no chance to rehearse. (An example of such a situation can be seen in Final Fantasy VII, the role-playing game on the Sony PlayStation One — http://www.us.playstation.com/games.aspx?id = SCUS-94163.)*

### CHINESE OPERA ONLINE REFERENCES

http://chineseculture.about.com/sc/traditionalopera/
http://www.chinapage.com/opera/mask.html
http://www.chinavoc.com/arts/perform/opera/beijingopera.htm
http://www.chinavoc.com/arts/perform/opera/kungu.htm
http://ajet.kghs.kh.edu.tw/garden/theater/chinese.htm
http://www.paulnoll.com/China/Opera/China-opera-seet-1.html
http://www.princeton.edu/ ~ his325/week3/Opera/opera.html

## SECTION 6: DRESSING THE PART:
## FASHION OF ANCIENT CHINA & JAPAN

### OVERVIEW

Clothes, hairstyles, posture and language spoke volumes about an individual's societal status. Life was hard and your appearance dictated your station. For example, if you were poor, you wore homespun, simple garments; if you were rich, you would be seen in expensive silks. Hairstyles, particularly for women, broadcast status.

### HAIRSTYLE

Hairstyle in both nations could be used to distinguish between the more obvious ranks of peasant and nobility, and also between married or unmarried women.

For example, young, unmarried women wore their hair in complicated knots and braids, or tied back and left to hang down their backs. Hairpins and decorative combs were usually "cute" and "young." Older, married women, on the other hand, would gather their hair and tie it up, away from their face and necks. Hair adornments appeared more "mature" and "stately." Prostitutes' hairstyle would reflect that of maidens'. The head prostitute or owner of the establishment, usually an older woman addressed as "Mother," would wear her hair like a wife's.

### FASHION

Depending on your station in life, you could be wearing clothes made of coarse material and drab colors, or clothes made of silk and dyed in bright pastel shades.

In both societies, ordinary citizens wore work-convenient clothes that mainly consisted of tunic, loose-fitting trousers and boots. For those who were born into noble houses or attended respectable schools, clothes were usually patterned and may have been embroidered.

#### SLEEVES

Sleeves usually ended about mid-forearm where they met the cuffs. Typical white tunic's cuffs reached to the mid-forearm and were stiffer and embroidered using gold or silver thread; they could also be dyed a vibrant pastel color. The outer robe and the white tunic would be gathered at the waist with a "cummerbund/sash" belt of any color; again it would be one that matched or contrasted with the outer robe.

The white tunic/robe would fall to the man's feet, split at the sides for ease of walking. The outer robe would also be this long. Loose white trousers were tucked into calf-high, black leather boots. This was the stylized fashion for men of above-average status.

Women wore a variation of this style. They had the same white tunic (with decorated cuffs), loose-fitting trousers and boots, but their clothing was less severe. *Return of the Condor Heroes* and *The New Heaven Sword and Dragon Sabre* (both by Louis Cha) show women of above-average status wearing outer robes that were dyed vibrant pastel colors. The wide, flowing sleeves ended around mid-forearm or elbow length while the body of the robe was gathered at the waist, using a "cummerbund/sash-style" belt.

From the waist hung an "over skirt," usually of the same color and material as the outer robe. The skirt hung to the knees, but may have been shorter on one side. Hems may or may not have been embroidered, yet such robes and skirts would have sported patterns of some sort.

In these period-style pieces, if you were of average status or below (e.g., ordinary citizen or inn proprietor or employee as opposed to a scholar or martial artist of a renowned school, etc.), you would be invariably dressed in drab colors. The outer tunic would be belted at your waist and reach mid-thigh. Loose-fitting trousers would be tucked into calf-high boots.

However, compare the stories to the illustrations of reality. Depending on the era, you might find a stark contrast between fictional fashion and historical fashion. For instance, in Mulan's time, men and women were depicted wearing long robes with wide sleeves that fell to the ground. Robes were wrapped around the body and tied at the waist with a sash. Men wore white under-robes while women wore bodices, arched upwards in the center, under the outer robes.

*Rurouni Kenshin* (by Watsuki Nobuhiro) illustrates the type of clothes worn in Samurai-era Japan. While idealized, the fashion is accurate. Warriors usually wore the wide sleeved-robes and wide trousers tied at the waist. The trousers were gathered at the calf and ankle and feet were covered in white "socks." *Yukata*, wooden "slippers," were worn outside the house.

*Inu-Yasha* (by Rumiko Takahashi) shows the simple robes worn in Ancient Japan by both men and women, the main difference being that men mainly wore baggy trousers and women usually wore skirts. This type of simple clothing is very similar to Ancient Chinese styles. *Easy Way to Learn Chinese Idioms* presents sketches of Ancient Chinese fashion.

In *Ranma ½* (by Rumiko Takahashi) you can see the long robes that men and women wear during the New Year festival — they resemble a Geisha's clothing. These robes are about peace and harmony, hence the meaning of the name: harmonious garment.

Ancient Japanese fashion can be found in any number of manga, anime, historical texts and fictional works. The traditions are still very much entrenched in today's Japanese society.

*Up the stakes for your characters: Have them appear in something taboo or unacceptable in these ancient societies. If your characters are trying to be inconspicuous, but are scantily-clad, they will draw hostile, disapproving stares.*

## Armor

Armor and military uniforms of both Ancient China and Japan also did not much differ. The main visual differences are the weapons used (*Kozuka, Tanto, Wakizashi, Katana*) and design in the twelfth and thirteenth centuries, the Samurai wore the *O-yoroi* armor. Basically, small iron plates decorated with lacquer combined to make protective plates for the shoulders and upper arms, chest and back, and a "skirt." If the "skirt" hung long on the sides and short on the front, it usually meant that the Samurai was a mounted archer. The helmet itself contained "wings," a "veil" at the back, and horns. It was fastened beneath the chin.

A particularly clear visual representation can be seen Takahashi's *Ranma ½* when Soun and Saotome take on a challenge to fight. Both Soun and Saotome are, essentially, cowards. Soun is dressed in medieval Samurai armor, while Saotome shakily marches along in his Panda form.

You can also find such depictions of similar Chinese armor in the live action, costume period series (broadcast by TVB) *Quest for Qin* (by Wong Yi; English title is author's translation) which tells the time-travel story of Hong Siulung and his adventures in Ancient China, approximately a few years before the start of the Qin Dynasty (221 BC). The live action series can be considered a satirical look at life in Ancient China (http://tvcity.tvb.com/drama/steppast/story/index.html).

*Artwork by Lai Zhao*

1. Helm
2. "Scarf"
3. Shoulder-plates
4. Chest armor ("Hauberk")
5. "Belt"

Both countries' traditional armor were similar, but you could take the Chinese version to be simpler than the Japanese Samurai version. In most depictions of Ancient Chinese armor, the helmet (1) is made of metal while the "wings" and "rear veil" are either light chain mail or leather. At its top are red tassels. Both types of helmet are tied beneath the chin.

It was not uncommon to find a scarf-like shawl (2) knotted at the throat.

Shoulder-plates (3) hung over the upper arms. Chest (4) and back armor (the Western equivalent would be akin to the hauberk), were worn beneath a "belt" (5).

The contrast between the two styles isn't vast, but it is very noticeable.

*For the Japanese, since Ancient times, it is a sign of respect to remove your shoes or boots before entering another's dwelling. In China, removing your shoes upon entering is a more recent custom.*

## FASHION SHOWS

*Cooking Master Boy* (an anime directed by Nobuyoshi Ogawa) was broadcast again as a TVB period costume series in the nineties. Essentially, both version narrate the story of a young man who travels through Ancient China pitting his cooking skills against others who claim they are the best. He is dressed in a short tunic with long sleeves ending in decorative cuffs. It's tied at the waist with a cloth belt that resembles a combination of a sash and a cummerbund. Loose trousers are tucked into calf-high leather boots.

There are variations of this simple style presented in stories set in Ancient China. The examples that come immediately to mind are from Louis Cha's works. They are martial arts, historical fantasy epics set in an idealized Ancient China.

In *Adventures of Chor Lau Heung* (www.tvb.com/xinghe/b5/drama/ thenewadventuresofchorlauheung/index.html), the men are seen wearing a white tunic/robe under a light, colored outer robe. There were no restrictions on color and it would usually be made from a light, quality fabric; the robe may or may not have had embroidered hems. Invariably, it had wide sleeves.

Again, looking at *Morevi*, the described clothing style is reminiscent of the kimono but also includes elements of simple Chinese robes: aesthetically pleasing and comfortable to wear. Silk was the main material used in Ancient Chinese and Japanese fashions; unique properties include keeping you cool in the hot, humid summers, and maintaining warmth in the harsh, dry and bitter winters.

## BRAVE NEW WORLD

The cultures of Ancient China and Japan can be easily researched either in a library or online, and with resources such as *The Fantasy Writer's Companion*. This chapter presents Asian cultures' physical aspects that are important to worldbuilding that will provide your work-in-progress a different backdrop with greater depth. The intangible aspects of these cultures will be presented in a subsequent volume.

If your Cantonese or Japanese is limited, no need to worry. You don't need to understand the spoken or written form to appreciate or experience the cultures. The fantasy anime *Ninja Scroll* gives a view of Japan's Feudal Era as opposed to *Rurouni Kenshin* (Watsuki Nobuhiro). *Cooking Master Boy* (directed by Nobuyoshi Ogawa) provides detailed glimpses of cooking in Ancient China while *Judge* (directed by Hiroshi Negishi) and *Journey to the West* (www.tvb.com/singhe/b5/drama/ journeytothewestii/) offer visuals of the Lords of Hell, the Gods and the demons of both nations.

Perusing *Morevi* (Lisa Lee & Tee Morris) in detail shows how the rich background of the Orient can be used to deepen a fictional world while also providing an exotic atmosphere. A closer look at Askana and the Morevian culture reveals both Chinese and Japanese influences. Note the graceful movements of the Queen in combat; the descriptions resemble Chinese Kungfu and Japanese martial arts. Also, *Interesting Times* (Terry Pratchett) will make you laugh while giving you a taste of how language works in the Ancient Orient—exaggerated workings of the vocabulary, that is.

Alternative cultures not only broaden your personal knowledge but also open up a plethora of hitherto unexplored worlds. The imagination takes off and your thoughts pelt down a different path and scramble up steep mountains of information. Not because it's "new," but because it's exciting. Different possibilities, ideas, inspirations. Wow!

Even immersed in the Chinese culture, I ended up browsing and reading for hours because of interesting facts that led me down so many trails. Naturally, everything is interlinked, yet the information is vast and pinning down what you should use and should not means you still require more data to make such a decision.

Two cultures so similar yet, in some respects, worlds apart. This is a journey that continues far beyond this chapter. And, as the old adage goes, "The teacher can open the door, but only the student can walk through it."

The door is open. Enjoy the journey.

## TIPS FOR FURTHER RESEARCH

The quickest way to find information and sources is, obviously, the Net. Search strings you might use could include (as written):

> *"Ancient China" + Chinese culture*
> *"Ancient Japan" + Japanese culture*
> *"Chinese Opera"*
> *"Ancient Japan" + Shinto*
> *Buddhism + Zen + Confucianism*

You might also ask the local university's Asian Languages Department for help and information. I've discovered that experts, or those who want to be seen as such on a subject, love to talk shop. Even the Chinese or Japanese restaurant manager loves to talk about their country! Just do a little background research first and list your questions, then watch them give you all the information you could possibly want!

Other ways of research include visiting the appropriate museums and libraries, and obtaining tour guides and brochures from your local travel agencies. Talking of travel, one absolute must when researching such a vast topic are language phrasebooks. They not only provide useful phrases, they also help you out with the cultures, too!

If you're after very quick immersion into the Chinese and Japanese cultures without going on holiday to these two countries, you could immerse yourself in manga, anime, Hong Kong cinema, Mandarin music, Beijing Opera, and Noh and Kabuki. You could also visit your favorite restaurants in your local Chinatown and Japanese communities. Just order tea and snacks—keeps your costs down and also provides a place for you to soak up the atmosphere.

Start with summaries of the countries and eras you want to research. Once you have basic knowledge, you will find narrowing down the information you need much easier and faster.

St. Ignatious
1st Grade   P.S. 666

# The Art
## of Never Growing Up:
### WRITING FANTASY
### FOR THE YOUNGER READER

### BY MICHAEL R. MENNENGA

When you think of children's fantasy, several things may come to mind, but consider this—almost everything written, televised, or produced for kids is fantasy-related. From Santa Claus to the Easter Bunny—tales of children's horror, apprentice wizards, educational TV shows filled with fuzzy characters and even big foam purple dinosaurs—it all falls into the realm of fantasy. Today's children live in a rich world of fantasy media, so it only makes sense that a fantasy writer would want to target this vast group of readers.

Writing children's fantasy can be exciting, challenging and a highly rewarding experience—one that every fantasy author should try at some point in his or her writing career. The world of young adult fantasy has been blown wide open by the mega-successful young wizard books of late. You know, the kid with the glasses and that tell-tale scar across his forehead? Because of J.K. Rowling's fantasy phenomenon, even more attention has been given to the entire genre.

It used to be that books written for children were required to teach some sort of a lesson, and followed strict rules of reading levels. This is no longer the case. Children's books now focus more on being fun to read, and less consideration is given to life lessons taught. These books still require some attention to reading level and age groups who are best suited for the content, but this is no longer a *primary* requirement. This New Age of children's literature tackles all types of tough subjects, dark themes and even some very controversial topics. Movies, video games and TV shows have become more mature (and edgy) over the past several years. Shielding children from these themes is no longer as much of a concern. New publishers and new markets are searching for the next great Children/Young Adult Fantasy series. But more importantly, kids are reading, and these flocks of new fans are open to anything new that will ignite their highly active imaginations.

It is the readers that makes writing Children's/Young Adult fiction (or simply called YA Fiction) so exciting. Kids are natural lovers of fantasy because it sparks their dreams and fills their lives with wonder. Wizards, magic, mythical creatures and all the other wondrous things that live in flights of the imagination are still within the realm of a child's possibility. It is very rewarding to see the joy in a child's face as they talk about one of your characters. It is fulfilling to know a child has become a fan of your creation, and you can be assured that their children will be introduced to your work as well. Touch a child's imagination, and it will carry him or her through the rest of their lives.

Writing for younger readers is not that complicated anymore. However, there are many subtle techniques that must be incorporated and pitfalls that should be avoided. Whether you are writing for the very young, grade school age, or teens, YA Fantasy requires only a good imagination, attention to detail and a willingness to target your work for specific groups of readers.

So with that in mind, a good place to start would be to determine which target audience appeals to you the most.

## Getting to Know Your Audience: Who are these younger readers?

There are many categories of children's fiction, and before you start writing for a young audience, you need to know (in general) who comprises that audience. Are you interested in writing for pre-school or kindergarten? Or perhaps a story appealing to teens is more your style. You could also just write the story, and figure out where it falls into the list below when you are finished.

Regardless, it is best to have a basic idea of what age you are writing for before you begin, but every author has his or her own approach, so I leave you to use the information as it fits your style.

## Hardly Child's Play: The Breakdown of the Children's Book Genre[1]

There are many facets to the term "children's books." It spans everything from picture books to teen novellas, and each of these categories has its own specific guidelines.

### Picture books

There are a few variations on this general heading, and it spans a wide age range. As the title implies, these books tell stories mostly through images and illustrations, but the text involved is anything but simple. In many cases, this is the most difficult type of children's fiction to write. Because of word limitations and the very basic sentence structure required, telling a complete story becomes more difficult. Furthermore, you are trying to teach something (colors, numbers, shapes, etc) about the world around them. Obviously, the consumers of this type of book are parents, so it is best when developing an effective storyline to appeal to what a parent would want their child to learn.

Picture books break down into the following classifications:

INFANT OR BABY BOOKS (During the first year) A few of these types of books are devoid of text completely. Or they are books of rhyme or lullabies. Very little of the content requires extensive writing. These books occasionally hold some fantasy themes, but they are generally whimsical, involving animals or identifiable characters. They are mostly used to stimulate the child's recognition of simple shapes and faces. Because of this, the entire book normally only covers one basic idea. (What is a horse, what is the color blue, etc) A good example of this type of book would be *Moo, Baa, La La La!* by Sandra Boynton, or *Toes, Ears, and Nose!* by Marion Dane Bauer & Karen Katz.

**TODDLER BOOKS** (Ages 1-3) These are children's books that follow a theme, and are normally early-stage learning books that teach things like colors, animals or numbers. These books are less than 15 pages long, and have fewer than 500 words of text. They also contain novelties like pop-ups, hidden windows, or electronic sound effects, things designed to keep a child entertained while they are being read to. These clever gizmos are also intended to entice the child to "play" with the book at times when the parent or a reader is not present. Some fantasy themes exist in these books, but they are few and far between. At this stage, the books are still teaching basic ideas. Look at: *Buzz-Buzz, Busy Bees* by Dawn Bentley & Heather Cahoon (Illustrator), or *What Color Is Your Underwear?* by Sam Lloyd.

**STORY BOOKS** (Ages 4-8) These books begin telling simple one-dimensional stories, their writing normally contained to one or two sentences per page. Each page carries an image or illustration designed to reinforce the sentence. Books of this nature contain one thousand words at the most. All types of fantasy themes show up in these books (fairies, talking trees, witches, cartoon characters, etc) but again, they are very whimsical and simple. This is the beginning stage that books target the child's imagination for learning. Look at *Little Yau: A Fuzzhead Tale* by Janell Cannon, or *Ricky Ricotta's Mighty Robot Vs. The Jurassic Jackrabbits From Jupiter* by Dav Pilkey & Martin Ontiveros (Illustrator), or the classic *Elves and the Shoemaker*, by Jim Lamarche.

Easy-to-Read, or Easy Readers (Ages 6-8) These books have illustrations on each page, with one sentence *or paragraph* supporting the accompanying image; but unlike Story Books, Easy Readers increase in word count and pages. Typically around two thousand words, and up to fifty pages in length, these are books for children who are starting to read by themselves. Fantasy themes develop multi-layered qualities in these books, but storytelling still remains simple. There are no complex storylines, and only one character is focused on per book. Supporting characters are few, and the writing structure is limited to only one idea per page. Still, these books begin to get more exciting for authors, as they do actually tell a basic tale consisting of a real plot, something lacking in earlier books. Try *Frog and Toad Together: (I Can Read Book Series: Level 2),* by Arnold Lobel, or *Dinosaurs Before Dark (Magic Tree House Series #1),* by Mary Pope Osborne & Sal Murdocca (Illustrator)

## Illustrated Chapter Books

Targeted for ages 6-10, Chapter books (also called Bridge or Transitional Books) are still telling stories in an easy-to-read style, but are normally three to five thousand words in length. Here the books begin to take on a more traditional formatting. Themes begin to take shape, plots achieve some depth and illustrations are only used to reinforce the general subject matter overall. Paragraphs are still short and sentence structure is limited to single topics. These books begin to cover more complex ideas of fantasy: magic, mystical creatures and supernatural subjects. The characters are a bit more plausible and lose much of the whimsicalness seen in earlier fantasy works. Subjects like ghosts, monsters and the idea of "bad things" also gain a strong foothold with this reading material. Look for *Summer of the Sea Serpent (Magic Tree House Series #31),* by Mary Pope Osborne & Sal Murdocca (Illustrator), or *The Meanest Doll in the World* by Ann M. Martin, Laura Godwin and Brian Selznick (Illustrator).

## Middle Grade Books

Middle Grade Books (Ages 8-12) quickly gain in complexity and storyline. These books are a more standard size (in between a hardcover and typical paperback) and the page count jumps beyond

100 pages. Illustrations fall to the wayside as well, with only a handful of images being displayed on chapter headings, if at all. No longer limited to simple story structure, these books begin to develop rich characters and full plotlines that keep the reader wanting more. For this reason alone, fantasy authors should feel at home. This is also the stage where we begin to see a demand for *sequels*. The limitation in these books is in word usage and sentence structure. The author needs to be careful not to overwhelm this age group with complicated terms or words. Keep it simple, tell a good tale and have fun with any topic. This is the key to writing to Middle Grade Books. A great example is: *Captain Underpants and the Big, Bad Battle of the Bionic Booger Boy, Part 1: The Night of the Nasty Nostril Nuggets* by Dav Pilkey, or *The Amulet of Samarkand (The Bartimaeus Trilogy, Book 1)*, by Jonathan Stroud.

## Young Adult Books

By far, the most popular area of children's writing today! J.K. Rowling, Terry Pratchett and a multitude of others fill this category. Normally considered only for ages 12 and up (or ages 10-14, depending on which publisher you are looking at) these books are breaking out of their specified age groups and gaining popularity with both children and adults. The reason for this (besides the success of *Harry Potter*) is that these books are filled with fully developed storylines, fascinating and engaging characters, thrilling suspense, dark themes and all the wonderful things that are found in the adult fantasy market...*with one exception*. These stories are written in simple language, with easy to follow sentence structure and clear, decisive paragraphs. These are the books that are being used in adult classrooms to teach illiterate and non-English speaking adults how to read. They are used in high-school classrooms to get teenagers excited about reading again. And they have become a rich source material crossing the media lines. The only thing you need to watch when writing YA material is overly complicated words, sentence structure and "mature" themes. It is advisable to maintain a 4-6 grade reading level, (more on this in a minute) but that is not difficult to do, considering a 5-7 grade reading level is the typical e-mail. Just keep it simple, don't get carried away with the long descriptions and you are there.

## TEEN BOOKS

Books written for teens are slowly being merged into the Young Adult Category. Often you will see them incorrectly listed as young adult, or sometimes called "Juvenile Fiction" or "Junior Novellas." These books are—for the most part—just like traditional novels, only shorter. The big difference here, and what classifies them as teen, is raging emotion. Think of bad daytime soap opera or better yet, after school specials. These books are filled with emotional turmoil, betrayal, peer conflicts and budding sexuality. Most authors find this a difficult category to write because of the need to relate to such high running emotion, but there are many who do it well. Fantasy is surprisingly absent in this arena, primarily because these books tend to focus on social relationships relating to real-life situations. These books also cover some very heavy topics: drug use, homosexuality, terminal illness, etc. Nothing is out of bounds here. It is possible to bring fantasy effectively to this category, but it may have limited success, and will most likely be placed in a YA category by bookstores. Look at: *Stoner and Spaz* by Ron Koertge, or *Green Angel* by Alice Hoffman

Most anyone out there will recognize these groups, but the industry is always reinventing itself. New categories are splitting up the major groups, and trying to bridge some gaps; but mostly, it is just the publishers trying to generate even more excitement in a market that is already exploding.

## WHEN WORDS COLLIDE: READING LEVEL

Reading level and educational value is a very important distinction between writing for the young and all other types of writing. Any good story will be entertaining, but to give it weight as a learning tool will require an extra parameter not needed in the normal fantasy novel. Do a quick search on any online bookseller, and in the children's book section you will find—added to the book's information listing—something unique to literature: *reading level*. Teachers, parents, publishers, publicists and reviewers are going to want to know what age group your book is best suited for, so in that respect you must evaluate and classify for a reading level group. Grades K-3, Ages 7-9, RL4.5, etc. are all classifications given to YA books, and each has specific meaning to different people, but it all means the same thing: these books are targeted to specific age groups and reading levels.

It makes sense that the more information you can give a perspective reader, parent and/or publisher about what is contained within the covers of your book, the better.

Their are other resources available on the Internet covering how to evaluate a book's reading level and the educational value it holds. If you are interested in learning more (and you should be), a simple search on "reading levels" will return several very good sites on the subject. I also recommend that anyone seriously considering writing for younger markets take some time and talk with teachers. Gathering information on how books are used in the classroom and how educators evaluate them is time well spent.

Is it possible to write young fiction without this input? Absolutely. Many of the books published for younger readers have received no educational consideration at all, and many YA authors have never considered classifying their work to a specific reading level or age group, but I personally feel that it gives your book a bit more of an edge in the marketplace, and this extra footwork and research is a important step in your creative process. The focus on books for younger readers is—and always will be—education.

## Teach Your Children Well: Educational Value

I agree with the statement that *all* books have some educational value. I am not suggesting that in order to write children's fiction authors must hold some sort of degree in education. As stated earlier, the simple fact is that books targeted for kids are going to be evaluated for their educational value, whether that evaluation comes from a parent considering your book for their child, or a teacher in a classroom looking for new curriculum that will keep their class interested through a lesson plan.

You can argue that reading level and educational value should not be important factors in writing fantasy or being an author, and you would be right. The new thinking in the children's book industry is that books should be fun to read first, and educational second. Nonetheless, these books are being read by kids, and do influence their lives, so there is some responsibility on the part of the author to temper the themes appropriately. (The term *age appropriate* applies here.)

What this means is that no matter what you write or how you write it, any book that is written for kids is going to be placed under special scrutiny by parents, professionals, reviewers, publishers and anyone that is concerned about what children are being exposed to in the media. How you approach this fact is completely up to you.

So what does all this have to do with the way you write fantasy? The short answer is, "Not much." Telling a story does not change. The basic elements remain the same no matter what age group you are writing for. And with the new thinking in the industry, no subject is considered taboo, as long as it is approached in a tasteful and age appropriate manner. However, there are a few tips that will help you capture this young reader and keep them engrossed in your story.

Think of younger readers as blank slates. They do not come into your story armed with preconceived notions, so they are willing to accept many storylines that would leave an older reader flat. This can be helpful, as well as difficult at times. The most important part of writing for kids is to make sure the reader can actually read it, understand it and identify with what is going on. Beyond that, the sky is the limit.

## Ready or Not, Here I Come: Some Tips to Start

Here are a few do's and don'ts in writing YA Fantasy. You should find these helpful no matter what kind of writing you do. The key part of writing is to consider whom you are writing for.

### Simply Read.

I know, this is so cliché, but it is absolutely true. No matter what genre you are trying to write in, it is important that you read in that genre to get a feel for what is being produced in your market. Getting the inside scoop on what other writers are producing will give you the best chance of finding that unique and exciting twist that will make your book the next heavy hitter in the checkout line. So before you sit down in front of the word processor, curl up with a good book and let your imagination run free.

### Implementation of Complicated and Disproportional Vocabulary (or, Working Within Reading Levels)

It astounds me how many times I see words that no young reader would ever be able to understand without a companion dictionary. Young Adult books are graded by reading level, which means that you should try to follow the rules of reading level and grade. It is sometimes difficult to keep your prose in check when writing, and there are certain words that you just can't get around. (Descriptive words, scientific words, places, etc.) So you can toss in the *occasional* college level word or two when necessary. But if you do throw in a word or two that may be over the reader's head (hydroelectric, for example) you should spend at least one sentence restating it for clarification. (i.e., the stream of water turned the generators to power the town.) That way, all readers will be able to keep up, and you don't have to dance around the word too much. On the other hand, there is also no reason that you have to fill your book with unnecessary, overly-complicated words just because it makes your book sound better. Remember—kids are your readers.

### Keep It Simple, Stupid...

Unless the kids you are writing for are astrophysicists, I would suggest that you keep your science fairly simple. But keep in mind, kids these days are much more in tune with math and science, because of the highly technical Internet subculture. So they can grasp some *deep* concepts—just not all of them. You can put in any kind of science that you like, just take it easy on how deep you get. If you are writing about a particle accelerator, all that is required is mentioning that it is a machine that makes atoms go really fast. (Okay, that is a bit over simplified, but you get my drift.) You don't need to include the latest research from MIT to get your point across. Don't be afraid to teach them something new, but temper the technical details, and be careful not to write so far above their heads that you lose them.

The most important part of your approach in writing for children is conveying your story in a simple and concise way. You do not need the big flowery words or long run-on sentences to get your point across. Kids like real-speak, so tell them your story in the same way that you would talk to them in any normal situation. Simply pretend that you are telling your story to a couple kids who are sitting on your couch. This way you will keep your writing light and informal. It is not important to wow them with your prose. It is important that you capture their attention, spark their imaginations, and keep them on the edge of their seats wanting to know what happens next.

### ...But Not Too Simple, Genius.

Children are not stupid. Don't treat your readers like morons, don't talk down to them and most definitely don't baby talk. They are kids, not idiots. Today's child is more in tune with the world than you might want to admit. They know about many things and are comfortable with tough issues. Many of them have grown up with two wars and a day of terrorism on U.S. soil none will forget, all of which was presented in real time on TV and throughout the news media. The TV shows that they watch and the movies they see all address hard-hitting issues, and treat them in a mature and intelligent manner. If your story's tone begins talking down to them, your book will get tossed aside in favor of another, more appealing pursuit.

### MOVE ALONG...NOTHING TO SEE HERE.

Kids get bored easily, so be careful how far you take a particular thought or concept. Overly long explanations of scenery and the weather will have your young reader drifting to the video console. I recently read a young adult book that spent four pages describing a mountain range. It had nothing to do with the story. The author just felt like giving detail to this particular mountain. I assure you that only a handful of younger readers actually read the entire four pages. All the kids I know either skipped to the end or gave up and tossed the book aside. So the extra pages of filler were ultimately pointless. As writers, we tend to get fascinated with all the little details of the world that we are building, but kids do that for you in their mind's eye. Give them enough information to start their imaginations, and then move on. Let them do the rest. It will be a richer experience for them in the end.

### ACTION, ACTION, ACTION

Don't forget the action. In a world filled with high quality video games, interactive Internet and all the electronic gizmos of our modern age, keeping the attention of a young reader is a challenge. Consider what you are presenting in your story, and find places to punch up your action. Don't make your fantasy one long fight sequence, but any place that you can add conflict, drama, suspense, or action will only help to keep the attention of your audience. This is where writing fantasy is also a plus. Fantasy builds worlds that the young reader cannot find anywhere else, and to that end, you have the advantage of giving them a unique experience.

### ANTICIPATION

In fantasy, this is the life-blood of the genre. It is important that you keep your reader wanting more. Make them want to keep going to find out what happens next. This may seem obvious, as it is an integral part of any good book for young or old, but anticipation is paramount in YA fiction. It is essential to build suspense in the first line of the book, and sustain it right to the last page. As one conflict is resolved, be sure to have the next drama well-established. Young readers are not as patient as older readers, so they tend to look ahead as they read. If they know something exciting is coming up, they will stick with the story while you set it up for them. Keeping the mystery alive for the younger reader will ensure that they remain with you to the very end.

### Don't Skimp on the Melodrama.

Your younger reader is an emotional creature. They have not earned enough life experience to draw on, so their worlds tend to be based on feelings and situations they create in their minds. Tension and conflict in your characters is the fastest way to draw a young reader into your story. Make them feel what your characters are feeling. Make parallels to things that readers may relate to. Humiliation, failure at learning lessons and punishments are all major issues in the young person's life. Although they may seem small to us as adults, it is important to remember what it was like to be a kid, and the impact that not getting ice cream at the park last week had on your world. You should also remember that the modern child deals with some very heavy life issues that children's literature is now willing to address. Divorce, death, abuse and drug use are all themes seen in modern children's fiction. Harry Potter lives with his abusive Uncle Vernon and Aunt Petunia during the months off from Hogwarts, Artemis Fowl's father comes home after five years in prison in *Artemis Fowl: The Eternity Code* by Eoin Colfer, and these are just two of many works to cite. Fantasy affords us the chance to work these types of themes into our writing. Using non-human characters and fantastic situations, younger readers can explore these ideas and issues. The main point here is to not be afraid to tackle the hard subjects. Nothing is out of bounds these days, as long as it is incorporated into your work in a responsible and tasteful way.

### Free Your Inner Child.

"Be a child." This is something that I tell new authors and many times I get blank stares. It is not as hard as it sounds. For many of us, that was a long time ago, but it can be done. The greatest advantage that we as fantasy authors have is our imagination (since most of us have never really grown up anyway).

Kids have incredible imaginations and just naturally visualize more than adults. They are much more apt to incorporate your story into their mind's eye than an older reader. Kids fully accept fantasy concepts of dragons, wizards and unique races. These are the things that stimulate the imagination. They take fantasy at face value, because they have not been beaten down with the reality of our world yet, so wonder and magic still have a place in their belief systems. For this reason alone, it is a great audience to write to, and it is important that you as the author are able to tap that resource. Free your mind. You need to become a child again and remember what it was like to not know that things don't live in the clouds, that nothing is lurking under the bed, or that elves and fairies don't exist.

## MISCONCEPTIONS AND OTHER TRAPS:
### "YOU WANT TO DO WHAT?"

I was going to avoid talking about this. Mostly because the second that you tell someone "it can't be done," someone comes along and does it. Still, there are a few things that are not the "preferred" way to go, and tend to make it more difficult to write effectively. I'll speak my peace, but by no means will I tell you "it can't be done." Take these cautions with a grain of salt. And if you throw said caution to the wind, be careful how you incorporate these things in your work.

### CUTE TALKING ANIMALS & FUZZY CREATURES

I know that I'm going to get called on this one, but I have to make the point. It is best to avoid the talking woodland creatures and cute fuzzy animals if at all possible. The main reason that I say this is that it gets old fast, and older kids quickly reject the "talking animal" idea. As I have said, kids are not stupid. They only have limited life experience, but they know enough that animals don't talk. I see attempts at this all the time in movies, books and games, and I'll admit to some extent it works. The concept, though, is overused, and not nearly as effective as people think.

However, let me quickly pull a complete 180 on you and say that as fantasy authors, you do get to pull a trump card on this. If it happens to be magic that makes them talk, or if it is some strange mythical creature that is blabbering on, then you have found the key to unlock this door. It is possible to make talking creatures work in fantasy, but it is not an avenue that I would suggest. I have personally done it before, and have encountered great difficulty. In *Dragon's Fire, Wizard's Flame*, I set a cast of animals on a journey with a fireless dragon and wrote myself into a corner. As the three animals began to encounter other creatures, it began to seem odd that they could all understand each other. I was able to work it out in the end, but it led to more difficulty for later books when I tried to introduce a human character into the mix. In the end, I have spent far too much time trying to work out the talking animal concept. Since then, I have talked with many authors that have had the same problems. Take a long time to consider before using this in your own work.

As for cute, fuzzy, animals—the girls may love it, but the boys will hate it, and why turn off half of your audience before they even open the book? The same can be said for snarling monsters, ultra-powerful wizards or battling ninjas—the boys will love it and the girls will be left flat. The only way this risk pays off is if you are intentionally marketing specifically to girls or boys. Now admittedly, you see this all the time in the industry. It can be very successful, and many have made it big with the "target specific market" approach, but this strategy must be carefully planned. Animorphs, Strawberry Shortcake, Bionical and many others have done very well, but if you decide to take this direction, it wouldn't hurt to have a large merchandising contract in place to make up for losing half of your reading audience.

### Too Many Characters

You have just added your twentieth Space Ninja to the Divine Order of Alpha Centarui's Sho-Lin, and you're only on Chapter Three. Guess what? Your young reader has not been taking notes and is hopelessly lost in a sea of characters. This is an issue all writers face whether writing for adults or kids, but in the case of young readers, many times they do not even pay attention to names. (Mostly because fantasy writers like to come up with all these weird monikers that even the adults can't pronounce) Kids know who's who in your story by what the character is (i.e. the Dragon, the Princess, the Woodsman). Names are an afterthought. So if you have thirteen ninjas that are exactly the same except for their names, you have a problem, and your young reader will get confused, then frustrated, and then they'll stop reading all together. If you must have a large number of characters, then write them as groups. You can pick out individuals to spotlight, but don't make them *individual characters* to the story. That may seem strange at first, but think about that for a second: "A group of bears walk out of the forest, a small brown bear in front stops for a drink, when a larger one, walking too close, knocks him into the water." They are a group, but you can pick out characters without naming them, or turning them into fully developed individuals. Tricky stuff, but possible. Look to *The Teenage Mutant Ninja Turtles* as an excellent example. The author has established names for each, but writes them as a group. It is not until late in the book that he begins to separate them and make them individuals. The main point here is not to overwhelm your young reader with a cast of thousands. Just deliver a story that will fire their imagination.

### CONTINUITY

Kids are mistake magnets. If it was night ten chapters ago, and you do a flashback to that moment of the book and it is suddenly day, they will let you know in a big way. They may not care about characters names, or what deeper meaning the main character holds, but they *do* care about the storyline. How far have they traveled? What color were the trees? How long are the swords? These are details that adults tend to give little thought to, but kids lock onto them and hang on for dear life. The reason for this is that we take our surroundings for granted, and when we see a reference to a sword or a pine tree, we have a perfect image of what that looks like in our heads. Kids often do not have that to draw on, so they use the little detail you give them to build images in their minds. If you change that image by mistake, you change the story for them and they have to stop and essentially start over. Sweat the details. They (the children *and* the details!) will come back to haunt you if you don't.

### AND THE MORAL IS...

Not to have a moral. Don't preach to kids. It is not necessary that every book be laced with a life lesson. This is the main idea behind the change in the industry's thinking, and the momentum behind making books fun for kids. Children are smart enough to know when someone is trying to teach them something. (They are in school learning stuff most of their lives at this point!) It isn't necessary to cram your personal opinions or values down a young reader's throat, or to be their parent. It is your job to tell them a story and entertain them. This does not mean that your story can't have a moral or depict values. If the story is told well, and makes them think, then they will draw their own conclusions. Bonus! There is just no need to blatantly point out to the reader a moral. Just a simple "good vs. evil" story relates a moral. However, it does *not* beat the reader over the head with it. Focus on telling your story and show both sides of the situation. That is all that should ever be required of an author. The reader will decide what they want to take away from your work.

## THE FIELD OF CHILDREN'S DREAMS:
### IF YOU WRITE IT, THEY WILL BELIEVE.

There is a responsibility issue that must be considered, one that has been put to the test with the juggernaut fantasy series about the boy wizard, Harry Potter. Although kids are the final consumers of these books, it is the parents that are the monitors. The final decision of whether or not a book falls into the hands of a young reader rests with the parental filter. Because of this, it may be advisable to temper your book's themes with this question: "Will a parent find your subject matter appropriate for their child to read?" or "Would I be okay with my kid reading this?" I am not suggesting that you should write books that appeal only to the Moral Majority. I am suggesting that is not possible to please everyone, but it can be argued that some topics are universally agreed upon not appropriate for younger readers. These are themes best left to adult audiences. It is possible to effectively write any theme into a young adult book, but it requires a lot more finesse than a regular novel.

I close with asking a question asked earlier: "Would I be okay with my kid reading this book?" As long as that answer for you is *yes*, then let the writing begin.

## BIBLIOGRAPHY

Some of the information here was found at the following websites, you should visit them:

www.write4kids.com
www.hoagiesgifted.org
www.donjohnston.com/catalog/stflexilelevelsd.htm

## FOOTNOTES

[1] List information source—www.write4kids.com

# How Do You Like Your Fantasy: Light, Medium, or Dark?
## Incorporating Horror in Fantasy

### BY TONY RUGGIERO

Is this chapter sounding like a recipe for a cookbook? Well, this topic could be thought of in that light. Have I confused you already by the second sentence? Bear with me for a little while and it will all become clear, I promise. Just give me your literary, as well as culinary, indulgence for a page or so and allow me to explain where I'm going with this analogy. *Trust me—we are going to have some fun here.*

When you write or read, don't you look for certain ingredients in a story? Perhaps it is the characters, the plot, or the setting that entices you to sit and nibble on the story to see if it is to your taste. As you read, your mind asks: Does this satisfy my hunger? Or does it leave my literary stomach rumbling? Does what you're reading have that special interest you seek, or does it leave you searching for excitement that can only be quelled by just the right morsel? If you answered *"yes"* to any of the above, then you are not alone. Many readers out there are starving as well, looking for something to satisfy their literary hunger.

Now ask yourself this: When you write, are you one of those writers that incorporates ingredients that you find tasteful, or are you one that serves a special recipe? You know what I'm talking about: that unique dish with those secret little spices you add to shake up your audience, so much that it always makes you a little nervous when using it. That hot and spicy number that gives you the reaction you want—perhaps the raise of an eyebrow or one of those special looks from a friend or loved one. That's what writing is all about, isn't it? Getting a reaction.

Okay, so what the heck am I talking about? I'm talking about spicing up your fantasy writing by adding a dash of something additional, something you think the reader might find interesting. How much you add will depend upon the reaction you are trying to obtain. Now as to exactly what spice I am referring to? Read on...

First, I promise...no more food association jokes on the subject. Let's get down to the meat... sorry...the heart of the topic: using horror in your fantasy.

*HOLD IT!* I can see it happening already. Some of you are getting ready to flip to the next chapter without even giving me a chance. What is that you say? You don't use horror in your fantasy, or there's no place for that in fantasy? Tsk-tsk-tsk. Stop lying to yourself, come out of the coffin and admit it: either you do use horror or you really want to. Sure, you might call it something else and you may not think it is horror—but it is. You're just going through a phase of horror-denial, because many of you don't like or *want* to admit it.

Poor horror. Abused as a child, it has been given the reputation associated with gory books and sensationalistic movies that usually contain nothing resembling a plot or characters. Sure, the men and women are usually dressed skimpy enough to arouse *some* interest, but beyond that...well, what can I say? What I am planning to do in this chapter is show you what I call the good side of horror and how to use it within fantasy. You're just going to have to trust me for a while and tag along as I ramble through what I think is the best use of horror in writing. Grab one of those frozen drinks from the refrigerator—oh, and grab me one while you're up.

*If it's nighttime where you are, you might want to turn on an extra light in the house as well. You never know who...or what...is also burning the midnight oil with you...*

To set your mind at ease a bit, why don't we sidestep a little? I'm not talking "The Time Warp" or anything, just something to ease you into this. There are varying degrees of horror we can use in writing fantasy. For those of you whose blood pressure jumps or can't breathe every time someone mentions the "H" word, we will call it something else: dark fantasy. In this chapter, we will refer to "dark fantasy" in its various states of light-medium-dark or just say "H" instead of saying "h-o-r-r-o-r" to avoid alienating those dark fantasy writers who remain in hor—sorry, "The-Genre-That-Must-Not-Be-Named" denial. I'll go along with it. Just remember, we may not call it *horror* but it's there...lurking in the pages of that first or next fantasy novel you are planning to write.

My goal in this chapter is to explain how I think you can use "H" effectively in your fantasy writing...and heck, even have fun with it. But first, we need to define what "H" is. We all have our own thoughts on the matter, but for the sake of brevity, let's see what our good and longtime friend Mr. Webster has to say:

> HORROR: 1. A strong feeling of fear, repugnance, terrified, alarm, etc. 2. A quality, experience, etc., that arouses such feeling. 3. Intense dislike; aversion. 4. *Informal* Something very unpleasant, ugly, etc.

Do you see something you like? There's a lot there to work with but I want to mainly focus on the word *feeling*. Did you notice it appears twice in the definition? This is what "H" is all about—conveying that *feeling* of something that is nasty or horrible to the reader, to make your audience *feel* the nastiness and horribleness of a particular person, place or (most of the time) *thing*. You do that and you're set, because we all fear something.

As Stephen King says in *Bag of Bones*: *"FEAR means F--k Everything And Run!"*

Our interpretation of that "something"—whatever it is—is what scares the crap out of us. So all you have to do is lay out the groundwork and let the reader's imagination do the rest. Let them try it on for size. One way or another, they'll find a way to make it fit their own personal fear. After all, it's just the human nature in all of us.

*Oh by the way, did you turn that extra light on? I would if I were you...*

Before I go any further, I think there is another point I need to make clear. When I'm discussing the big "H," I'm approaching this from my own personal preferences in this genre. Now hold on...don't start saying stuff like I'm stuck up or snooty, or I'm some literary hotshot because I have a master's degree in English, and so on and so on. I think perhaps you will agree with me on this one. And if you don't...hey, it's a free country and all that good stuff. Just don't blame me if that seven-foot-tall, slime-covered, multi-eyed creature standing behind you gets pissed.

Anyway, where was I? Oh yeah, I was saying the only true form of "H" that is worthwhile to pursue is what I call *realistic* horror, the only true form of "H" that is believable. It's probably easiest to begin by explaining what "H" is not. Believable "H" *is not—is not—is not—*the kind where you take a character, any character for that matter, from the bravest to the weakest, whether human or not—and have everyone tell him or her to *not go* in the basement under any circumstances. What do they do? They go into the basement, of course. But wait a minute...it gets worse! Not only do they disregard everyone and head down to the basement, but they go at night when there isn't anyone else around during the fiercest thunderstorm to ever hit that region. On account of this, the power is out and the phone doesn't work. And, of course, the flashlight's batteries go dead...just as they hear a mysterious sound coming from under the basement steps. Come on now! Who in their right mind would go investigate said sound? The answer is either an incredibly stupid person or an unbelievable one—take your pick. Either way, it doesn't work for me or for most people. In my humble and esteemed opinion, there is no credibility in that type of lame "H," unless of course you enjoy watching the hack and slash type of "H." If you are one of these types, then you can probably live with this type of situation...hey, *Carpe Noctis* (Seize the Night) and all that good stuff, whatever makes you happy. Have you finished that drink yet? I'm ready for another if you are.

*Oh and while you're up, check that light.*

I call it *realistic* "H" when you use a *realistic* setting under *realistic* conditions. Hmmm, I'm sure you noticed that I repeated the word *realistic* three times in one sentence. Not the best use grammatically but you know what, I really want to get your attention on this point so excuse my bad grammar. In order for "H" to work, it must be a situation where you ask yourself what would you do? Put yourself in the place of the character you are about to send down into the dark basement. Given the example above with our character, if that's me, I'm going to wait until daylight, have three close friends right there with me, be armed to the teeth and have my cell phone in hand (with fresh batteries) before I venture into the basement or anywhere else I have been told not to go. Disappointed? Don't be. Things can happen and still be scary. In fact, if you obey the rules of common sense and stuff happens, it works better because you have been true to the laws of common sense, you take precautions and yet you *still* got screwed!

Isn't that a closer resemblance to real life?

Let's look at some possibilities: you could have been smart and taken along some buddies with you into the basement and have your friends just go poof and disappear, or maybe evolve into some primordial type creatures from the Jerry Springer show. (Now that's scary!) And of course, there's the old faithful—the cellar door slamming shut and locking itself, but you can see it, you feel it and most importantly you can believe it. It's okay now because you had the character do the things any rational person like you or I would do. If they are consumed by some flesh-eating entity at this point, too bad for them; at least they did it under conditions that were plausible and not stacked against them before they even took the first step into the basement.

My personal favorite would be to have absolutely nothing happen in the basement, but have whatever creature, entity or hard luck little elf waiting in the kitchen, patiently having a cup of coffee and a cigarette. As your character emerges from the basement feeling that everybody was just full of it by saying to not go down there, then the fun can begin. Let your imagination do its worse and you'll feel good about it.

*What was that? You don't hear that scratching sound coming from your basement? What? You don't have one. Hmmm, it must have just been the wind. Don't worry about it.*

Let's talk briefly about the "H" classifications I mentioned earlier. As I said, I'm talking about degrees here, a way by which you can use horr—oh sorry, "The-Genre-That-Must-Not-Be-Named." Let's try this again. How about using some of the lesser-utilized elements of the human psyche to spice up your fantasy? Sound better? I thought so.

Let's define these three areas—light, medium and dark—give you some examples to consider and maybe provide you with new or favorite titles to read. I'm an example kind of guy; it just works better for me. That way I can even brag about some of my own stories.

Why not, I'm writing this chapter, after all?

*Okay, buckle in and let's hit the road...oh, wait a minute...do you feel that itching sensation...kind of like a spider or something crawling up your leg, huh?*

## PART I: THE LIGHTER SIDE OF "H"
### OR UP IS ALWAYS THE SAME DIRECTION,
### BUT NOBODY KNOWS HOW FAR...

By light, I am referring to using "H" elements in an amusing way. How can "H" be amusing, you ask? Where is the fear, the repugnance? Oh, it's still there, tucked away inside the bodice of a tavern wench somewhere, but we are going to have some fun with it. Let's think of some things that conjure up feelings of fear or repugnance, such as the traditional figures of "H" and discover how these mainstays of the genre can be depcited in a light, humorous way.

Let's begin by taking your standard "Grade A" blood-sucking type vampire and transforming him or her (must be politically correct about these things) into something else, or as I like to say, turning the tables on your audience. How about a vampire who has to give blood in order to survive, loves garlic and hates the darkness. Then place him in a personal relationship with a traditional female vampire and you get a kind of *When Harry Met Sally* kind of relationship—*I'll have what she's having.* This is the short story "Normalcy Sucks," featured in my anthology *Aliens and Satanic Creatures Wanted: Humans Need Not Apply.*

What I did was to give the audience a sense of attachment with the vampire. In fact, they actually feel sorry for the sucker (no pun intended). The story shows the problem of the male/female relationship, not from a human perspective, but from the vampire's. The audience walks away chuckling and I'm satisfied because I used something traditionally scary and made them laugh about it. *Score!*

Staying with this favorite icon, *Fat White Vampire Blues* by Andrew Fox is the story about a vampire in New Orleans. Living in the French Quarter, this once-dashing, once-alluring creature of the night has "swelled up on the sweet, rich blood of people who consume the fattiest diet in the world." Things have gotten so bad that "when he turns into a bat, he can't get his big ol' butt off the ground." Now, as he's trying to figure out how to make his victims more Atkins-friendly, a new leaner and younger vampire comes to town so the old guy decides to get tough and get back into shape so he goes on a diet. Again, here you have an "H" mainstay used in a light and humorous way. I'm chuckling. How about you?

I have to mention some of my television and movie favorites such as the old Abbot and Costello comedy movies I remember watching as I was growing up. If you remember them as well, I guess we are around the same age. If you haven't seen any of them, you should. They are the first attempts to successfully use mainstays of "H" and truly poke fun at them. In their zany adventures on the silver screen, Abbot and Costello meet Dracula, Frankenstein and even the Wolfman; and sometimes, all three would meet up with the comedy duo in one movie. No matter how these creatures try to convey the macho "H" image, Abbot and Costello kept making them appear funny and inept. It is truly an art to watch them perform and a good source for some inspiration.

Of course I cannot mention Count Dracula and pass George Hamilton's perpetually suntanned nosferatu in *Love at First Bite* (1979). Although the humor is slapstick with such quips from Dracula as, "Without me, Transylvania will be as exciting as Bucharest... on a Monday night," and "I never drink wine, and I do not smoke shit," the movie easily provides amusement at the expense of a traditional horror staple.

Frankenstein gets his due in the movie *Young Frankenstein* (1974). As in *Love at First Bite*, the humor is pure farce, yet reminiscent all at the same time. Gene Wilder (Dr. Frederick Frankenstein) and Marty Feldman (Igor) are constantly trading witty banter, poking fun at both classic characters:

> Dr. Frankenstein: *"I'm a rather brilliant surgeon. Perhaps I can help you with that hump."*
> Igor: *"What hump?"*

...and later in the film...

> Dr. Frankenstein: *"Igor, would you give me a hand with the bags?"*
> Igor: *(doing Groucho Marx) "Certainly, you take the blonde and I'll take the one in the turban."*

Even the recent movie *Van Helsing* (2004) takes quite a few shots on the classic "creature feature" icons by giving them wicked senses of humor, although dark as it may be, it still works well. Let's take a peek at some dialogue:

> Van Helsing *(played by Hugh Jackman): "Vampires, gargoyles, warlocks, they're all the same—best when cooked well."*

And:

> Count Vladislaus Dracula *(played by Richard Roxburgh): "Igor... Do unto others..."*
> Igor *(played by Kevin J. O'Connor): "Before they do it unto me!"*

And:

> Frankenstein's monster *(played by Shuler Hensley): "Let me go!"*
> Carl *(played by David Wenham): "Where are you going to go? I don't know if you've looked in the mirror lately, but you kind of stick out in a crowd."*

Okay, let's try another. How about the devil? Good old Lucifer, another "H" mainstay who's shown up in many works. Use his basic traits that we all know: liar, cheat, contract for the soul and all-around-conniving, good-for-nothing kind of being, and then...place him in modern day Los Angeles, on a crusade to save the world.

Outrageous, you think? Well, before he was Lex Luthor's dad in *Smallville*, actor John Glover gave the Devil a slightly humorous due in *Brimstone*. In this exceptional offering on television, former police detective Ezekiel Stone (played by Peter Horton) is released from Hell, sent on a mission from Satan to retrieve 113 escaped souls. In every episode, Glover's Satan appeared in a variety of guises. His appearances ranged from the unsettling ("Good Humor" man) to the timely (LAPD officer), and he would pay Ezekiel the occasional visit to "help" in the return of his fugitive souls. In the form of a college counselor, the Devil gives a shapely college co-ed the best advice he could:

> The Devil: *"Stacey, if I were you, I'd tell mom and dad to go to hell. You're not at home any more, you're at college, so why should you play by their rules? If you think the only way to pay for college would be stripping at bachelor parties, I say 'Go, girl!' (Sees Ezekiel outside his office.) Ah, my next appointment. Think about what I said. (to Ezekiel, after Stacey leaves.) Sweet kid...I'm trying to get her on the wrong path."*

As *Brimstone* showed week after week, the Devil's work is never done. And there is no better environment to see the God of Hellfire hard at work than at a place that suits him best. In the short story "Lucky Lucifer's Car Emporium" (by yours truly), the consummate con-artist of Hell runs a used car lot where he takes people's souls as trade-ins on cars. He's having a hard time making his sales quota and he's desperately looking for a signature on the standard 666 form. In walks the standard mark every salesman dreams of, a nice guy looking for a change. Lucky Lucifer attacks and thinks he has scored another soul but we later learn that the car buyer has friends in high places. In both of these offerings, the writers took the embodiment of all evil and "de-horned" and "de-hooved" him, creating a character the audience could laugh at...and even grow to like.

Wasn't that fun? And you said "H" couldn't be amusing. See, you learned something new today. Let's summarize by admitting that we can use "H" in a humorous way by changing the roles of traditionally horrific characters by either bestowing human characteristics upon them or by use of the comedic elements. In other words, we take the inverse of what has been typically portrayed and defeat them with something unusual or foolishly simplistic. Whichever method works for you will probably work for the reader as well. Maybe you can even come up with another way in which to use "H" on the lighter side.

But do me a favor, keep it to yourself at least until after my next book is published. A guy has to make a living right?

*Did you hear that? It sounded like it was coming from your refrigerator...that dripping sound...*

## PART II: THE MEDIUM SIDE OF "H"
### OR DON'T FORGET TO PICK UP MILK, BREAD,
### AND TWO POUNDS OF CONTROVERSY
### ON YOUR WAY HOME.

Now we will move onto the next category that I call medium "H." In medium, the key word that comes to my mind is "controversial." What you want is for the writer (that is yourself, in case you've forgotten) and the reader (that's the other person) to not really be sure where these characters reside in the grand scheme of things. Are they in the light or in the dark? How about in the middle? Perhaps they are the type that can swing either way, back to humorous, our light setting, or perhaps to the dark side of true "H" which we'll talk about later on.

"Medium" is the area that has the most potential for development. Many readers are becoming disillusioned today with the proverbial happy endings that many publishers insist on. Readers finish the last page of a book and say something like "It shouldn't have ended that way," or "That's not right, there is no way the good guy could have won." See my point here? I am one of those types of people that like a little controversy in their stories. It's like when you are sitting in a restaurant and have just ordered your entrée. The waitress asks you what side dish you would like. Numerous choices flow from her mouth as she recites them for the hundredth time, her demeanor overwhelmed by boredom. You are also overwhelmed...overwhelmed by the choices and you can't decide. That feeling is what you want to covey to the reader—you just aren't sure what you want and likewise, the character you are working with...well, you're just not sure if he is good or bad.

What I must emphasize here: in order to be successful, the key is to not give anything in the story away by making a stand either way. Just lay it out there and let the reader stumble upon it, look at it, fondle it a little (depending on the mood you're in) and let them come to a decision.

Still not sure where I'm going with this? To put it another way, for those of you who reside in dreamland beyond even the broadest terms of fantasy and insist upon believing there are only good (wearing white doublets) and bad (wearing black armor) characters, I would say you are a wee bit out of touch, or to put it more bluntly: you are dead wrong.

I know this comes across a bit strong. In defense of the idealists, it is called fantasy for a reason. Anyway my point (and yes, there is one here somewhere) is that there is another character you can work with in your story. This kind of character is more honest and who possesses both good and bad qualities, and resides in the middle of good (white) and bad (black), equaling (yep, you guessed it) *gray*.

Now here it comes: my point. Ready? This gray category is for all practical purposes identical to the medium I am describing. Like the medium "H" stories, the gray character can have good days and not so good days. It just all depends upon what you want to do with the story.

*By the way, is that dripping sound from the kitchen bothering you?*

When it comes to working "Medium," concepts usually considered bad are given redeeming values. Their end results, even bad, remain justifiable considering the options as seen in one of my favorites: Stephen King's *The Dead Zone*. If you haven't read the book, you really should. King makes the concept of assassination of a future President seem...well...very plausible and worse, he gets the reader agreeing to it as well. King is famous for this kind of manipulation. (God bless him!)

While we're here hailing the King, let's take a look at one of his other novels, *Misery*. How is this novel controversial? (Apart from a fan depiction that keeps all authors awake the night before a book signing?) King shows us the inner workings of a woman's mind, and *whoa boy*, it's enough to keep me away from anyone in the medical profession. He takes a nurse, the symbol of tender loving and supportive care that millions of people need and depend upon, and makes her a raving lunatic who decides who will live and who will die at hospitals. Need more disturbing news? This nurse comes to the rescue and saves an author's life, but not just any author...her *favorite* author. She brings him back from the brink only to keep him prisoner, promising to carry out her own personal death sentence on him unless he brings back her favorite character from the grave. Oh, and did I mention that she is this author's "number one fan?"

How many of you writers out there have read *Misery* and then looked for that quirkiness in fans at book signings? I'll admit it: *I'm one.*

The reverse is also a known variation. Dean Koontz is another master of this category. An example is his novel *Fear Nothing* in which he takes a young man, Christopher Snow, and his faithful companion, his beer-lapping dog Orson, both of who appear normal...well sort of. Chris has xeroderma pigmentosum (XP—a condition that forces him to avoid light), and his dog drinks beer. What's so wrong with that? (I like a cold one every once in a while, too.) Koontz creates a scenario where they find out that they are anything but normal, the stoic and lifelong image of all things that are good—a man and his dog—ends up...well, let's say in a controversial position. (I refuse to spoil the book for you.) Are they the result of genetic manipulation or the new order to come? You read and decide.

Let's look at another example of a classic open to a lot of interpretation: Bram Stoker's *Dracula*. The book gives us a terrifying vampire with no ulterior motive other then to kill and feed. We can easily decide that our *original* vampire is "dark," by all measures. (Something we will delve deeper into later.) Now let's look at Francis Ford Copolla's movie *Bram Stoker's Dracula*, perhaps one of the best ever made as they add an element not found in the original text. The count meets Mina Harker, a woman who looks very similar to the count's dead wife who took her own life centuries ago. So the count comes to England in search of Mina, his lost love. Can you see where I'm going? They have added an emotional element into this classic creature, evoking sympathy from the audience. Now, in this modern telling of Bram Stoker's hor—er, dark fantasy epic—Count Dracula is not such a bad guy. He's doing all this in the name of love. Is that so bad? No. Probably not. But now some of the audience is almost feeling sorry for the poor vampire because they can understand his motive of lost love. How's that for a little controversy?

Before Dracula was given a sympathetic angle on the silver screen, Mary Shelley left a lot in question with *Frankenstein*. I don't mean Dr. Frankenstein himself. (He's got a beach house deep in the dark regions of fantasy.) Frankenstein's creature, on the other hand, is well within the gray. Did the creature ask to be created, and then abandoned? No. Would you abandon your own child, or simply cast it out? Absolutely not. Does the creature that has been shunned by society make an unreasonable demand for a mate? All he asks for is companionship. In return, he promises to disappear. Once again, we have the embellishing of human characteristics we can all relate to on Frankenstein's monster; a monster, lonely and unloved, driven to murder those that his creator loves. It doesn't get much more controversial than this.

Since we are mentioning horror staples placed in controversial settings, I threw my own Navy commander's hat into this medium setting with the staple being vampires and the controversy consisiting of my audience being forced into a position of not being sure who is the protagonist and who is the antagonist. In *Team of Darkness*, Dimitri— the leader of this small brood of vampires—seeks only knowledge, peace and an understanding of his role in the life of the undead. He (and his fellow vampires) feed primarily on livestock, humans only when provoked by them. Okay, we have some redeeming qualities there for these vampires, right?

Well, our vampire Dimitri is captured by the US Navy SEALs and *they* (catch that emphasis...*they*...the *humans*) force him and the rest of his brood to kill members of South American drug cartels. Okay—you're probably saying how can you force a vampire to do anything they don't want to? Military engineers devise a method of control so that if the vampire doesn't do what it is suppose to do, the officer-in-charge presses a button. Poof, the vampire dies. (Sound a little like slavery, doesn't it?)

So, who is the bad guy here? The vampire is just trying to live his own isolated life until the military comes along and thrusts him into a life and death struggle *against his will*. And you said you didn't like a little controversy in your life? Believe me, we all have some in our lives and that is one of the reasons that these type of things work so well in stories. It's somehow comforting to us that not only are *we* inundated by choices or decisions made by others, but so are the *characters* in our fantasy stories and that equals association and developing a relationship with the characters. Life is good. See, a little "H" in your life is a good thing, even if it is controversial.

What we want to achieve in the medium category of "H" is to appeal to the controversial side—walk the line between good and evil because that is where reality is really roosting at these days. Take traditionally good and bad characters, and write from their true perspective, not being judgmental but allowing the reader to have a part in the decision of what they truly represent. To keep the association with the reader, keep the issues at a level that most can comprehend or have been through themselves. And please, please remember, it's okay to have good guys make mistakes or have un-pure thoughts; after all, they're human. Well maybe, most of the time...but you still get my point.

*Speaking of point, do you hear that sound? I thought it was dripping but now it sounds like a knife being sharpened. Do you own a knife sharpener?*

## PART III: THE DARK SIDE OF "H"
### OR THERE IS NO LIGHT AT THE END
### OF THIS TUNNEL...

Okay, we've gone through the light and the medium so we have arrived at the last category, which you may have guessed by now, is *the dark*. This is your expected final stop, provided you have been paying attention to me and not those strange noises coming from your kitchen. "Dark" leaves behind any doubt in regards to the storyline. Light may have its humor, medium may have its controversy, but dark is flat-out nasty. This type of "H" is pure scare and goose bump land and not for those of the faint of heart. If you are of weak constitution, turn back now...

You might be wondering what is so different about this form of "H?" Bad guys are evil. Vampires kill for pleasure. Werewolves maul their victims viciously. So what? Dark is all that, sure; but writing dark goes far deeper, taking traditionally good images we have of people, relationships and settings, and—you guessed it—twist them around into unrecognizable, unfamiliar and terrifying situations.

Maybe that's why people say I am a twisted sort of guy. But you know what? When I get that kind of reaction, I feel satisfied because that is the reaction I want. What readers usually mean by those comments is that I twisted *them* around when they read the story. Or in other words, they didn't get what they thought was going to happen. To that I say: *SUCCESS!* I've achieved my goal!

Another characteristic of working dark is the story's ending, usually the kind of ending that leaves you with whiplash and bags under your eyes because you're either looking over your shoulder or refusing to close your eyes and go to sleep. Working dark reaches its apex when you come up with that "one last line" you leave with your audience, to haunt them for the rest of their lives.

Don't believe me? Take a look at some of these unforgettable last lines:

> *"It's a cookbook."*—Damon Knight, "To Serve Man"
> *"Then...some idiot turned on the lights."*—Ray Bradbury, "The October Game"
> *"They'll see and they'll say, 'Why she wouldn't even harm a fly.'."*—Robert Bloch/Joseph Stephano, Psycho

And here is a favorite last line of mine: *"Why don't we just wait here. See what happens."* If you don't recognize the last name, maybe this will help you out: "Who Goes There?" written by Don Stuart. Still nothing? Well, Don Stuart was the pen name for John W. Campbell, and his short story "Who Goes There?" was re-released as "The Thing from Another World" that scriptwriter Bill Lancaster and director John Carpenter turned into the 1982 roller-coaster horror film, *The Thing*. (Yes, yes, yes, I know this is SciFi, not Fantasy...but we're talking the big "H" here, and I've got a hall pass from the editors, so...) In this film, a group of scientists in Antarctica rescue a sleigh dog being relentlessly hunted down by a group of Norwegian scientists. (A safe assumption those silly Norwegians were suffering form cabin fever.) A closer inspection reveals the Norwegians were hardly mad, just terrified of their snow dog...and soon, the Americans find out why as the dog reveals itself as a host of an alien lifeform. This movie plays less on the fear of aliens from another planet and more on the power of paranoia, drawing the audience into the dangerous guessing game the American scientists play with one another, right down to the ending line where two survivors remain and neither one knows for certain who is human and who is not.

This is the impact, not to mention the fun, in working dark: the human psyche, both the characters' and your audience's, is your playground!

In the earlier mentioned short story "The October Game," author Ray Bradbury takes the reader into a mind not on the brink of snapping, but well beyond that point. The story centers around Mich Wilder, a man consumed by guilt, vanity, selfishness and a loveless marriage. Doesn't really sound like a guy you would give a second thought too, huh? Ah, but Ray Bradbury is at the helm, and you can't help but feel a twinge of sympathy for him in not finding the blessings in his healthy daughter, Marion. So, Mich quickly becomes more of a tragic figure...

Did I happen to mention Ray Bradbury was at the helm?

"The October Game" continues to pull readers deep into the mind of a man determined to make his wife suffer as much as he suffered under her. The ending *"Then some idiot turned on the lights"* remains one of the most haunting in our genre's history as Bradbury effectively pulls the reader into a tortured mind, and then leaves us to paint the final scene with our imagination.

Another bonus in working dark is that everyone is fair game. The less suspecting the reader is of whom the bad person is, all the better. There is no rule that says you can't take non-traditional horror characters and make them the bad guys. If there is...well, toss it out the window. (I do it all the time.) Take the image of the child for instance, the purest form of innocence, or so we usually think, and take them and make them into the evil, perhaps even worse then the traditional mainstays we've been talking about. Surprise equals interest and that's what it's all about.

In my own short story "How Blind is Justice?" I throw my own "October Game" but from a different player's perspective. The story centers on Amelia, a little girl living with her deadbeat father and girlfriend, who used some underhanded tactics to get custody of the child. (Bribing a judge with cocaine. Getting pretty dark, isn't it?) It's Halloween night and the wacky father and girlfriend are planning a little party of their own by spicing up the candy with goodies such as red pepper and hot sauce. (Gaining custody of a child out of spite, spiking candy for kids...nice folks, eh?) Amelia, however, is looking forward to a "treat" as her birth mother, seeing as the judicial system has failed them both, told her to be ready to leave for an "unscheduled trip." Regardless of the legal consequences, mother and daughter successfully escape in the early hours of All Saint's Day. The mother is in a panic, but Amelia assures her "It's okay, mummy, they aren't going to wake up for a long while." The mother is quite taken aback by her daughter's calm, but what mom doesn't know is Amelia's Halloween "trick" on her father, stepmother and assorted vagrant party guests. Feeling sorry for all those children who suffered, Amelia spiked the Halloween punch of her father and girlfriend just like they did to the candy...only Amelia's "trick" was less of a silly prank and more of an assurance that her abusive parents wouldn't wake up *"for a long while."* "How Blind is Justice" effectively achieves a happy ending...just in a very dark way, leaving its readers to contemplate what is just and what is not.

Speaking of happy endings, this brings me to another point that drives me crazy. So many writers who claim to enjoy "working dark" INSIST that the good guys always have to win in the end. I wonder what would happen if the readership were actually comprised of some of the creatures we write about, would the concept of a happy ending change? If everything turns out perfect in the end, how is that working dark? And so what if the evil guy wins. Is it game-set-match? Who knows? It's for the reader to decide once they finish your tale from the dark side, and in some stories the happy ending just cannot happen.

The absent happy ending often comes from writers of dark fantasy who find more horror in people we know rather than aliens, demons and things that go bump in the night. Bram Stoker Award-winner Elizabeth Massie, while familiar with the monsters that lurk under beds and in closets, also writes about the "real" monsters among us. In her short story "Snow Day," featured in the anthology *Shadow Dreams*, Massie takes us to a darker side of the unexpected day off from school. We are introduced to Marnie, a shy girl who doesn't wear the latest fashions, never invites friends over to her house to play and always looks forward to school as it is her haven from her mother and stepfather. While Massie never graphically depicts the abuse, the feeling (as I mentioned earlier in this chapter) is clearly conveyed when Marnie's mother (with breath "of ashtrays and alcohol and boredom") says to her daughter "Johnny and me, we love you. We show you we love you, too, in our own special way. You know we love you, don't you, Marnie?" And in the classic style of great ending lines, "Snow Day" concludes with *"And the snow kept up for another ten inches, and school was closed for the week."*

There are writers who enjoy using both medium and dark settings in their "H" to highlight the darker side in a covert manner. An outstanding example of this underhanded tactic is seen in Anne Rice's book and screenplay *Interview with a Vampire.* Here you have two vampires, Louis and Lestat who are opposite in nature. Louis is the vampire with a conscience and Lestat is the cold, hard killer. By having the two contrast each other, it emphasizes their positions. Louis appears as misled, misguided and abandoned in a world he cannot understand. Lestat, on the other hand, cares nothing for the petty concerns that Louis holds dear and mocks him relentlessly. Lestat kills at will and has no remorse. By this stark contrast, the evil in Lestat is brought to the forefront by the benchmark created by Louis. While it appeared on the surface that Rice was hoping to showcase the ferocity of Lestat and, in turn, evoke more sympathy for Louis, the end result was a much different story. Lestat, the darker vampire, became a character in demand, earning him his own book, *The Vampire Lestat.*

The lesson we learn from this? Sometimes it's good to be bad.

*Did you just open a window? No? Then why are you shivering? Do you feel a sudden chill in the room?*

## The Wrap Up
### or How to Dress for Success
#### in the Fantasy World of "H"

Okay now, it's almost daylight, so I need to wrap this chapter up so I can escape to my coffin...

Only kidding. Well, as far as you know.

Besides, you have bigger problems to worry about, that odd dripping sound, a cold draft, a knife being sharpened, the feeling that something is crawling up your leg...and oh did I mention the light bulb just went out? (It doesn't get any better then that!) Anyway, let's do a fast summary for those of you who skipped ahead to see if I summarized at the end, thereby avoiding wading through the several pages of discussion.

(1) What did we seek to accomplish?

We set out to spice up our fantasy writing by using the elements of "H." I think we're past the point of denial so let's just call it what it really is—*horror. THERE! I SAID IT AND YOU DIDN'T EVEN CRINGE—CONGRATULATIONS.* As some of you are already incorporating horror into your work, I offer you new insight on how to use it more effectively. Remember, horror is not only slash and gore, it is the "feeling," and I must emphasize that word, the *f-e-e-l-i-n-g* that the reader receives from the story. We're looking for fear and repugnance, that which gives us a cold slimy feeling deep down inside while smothering the warm fuzzies. But remember, that doesn't mean you can't have fun with this as well.

(2) Types of horror that can be used.

Horror can be divided up into three categories. First we have the light version, where we use elements of horror in a humorous way, pure fun and enjoyment. No punches being pulled on the reader except for the blow to the funny bone. Second, we looked at the medium version best described as controversial, or when horror mainstays are interpreted under a sympathetic light, or when concepts repugnant or morally wrong are suddenly reconsidered. Lastly, we talked about the dark, that which features characters and concepts of little redeeming or socially accepted values.

So there you have it in a nutshell. For those of you that skipped to this summary, you missed some great examples. I suggest you go back and read it! You're only cheating yourself if you don't. Besides, I know who you are and I will find you. (With a name like Ruggiero, you don't think I have connections in the *underworld?!*)

I have conveyed to you my passion towards this misunderstood genre, and offered up some advice on how to incorporate the elements of horror in your fantasy writing. So now all you have to do is get out there and just do it. If you can make yourself laugh, kick up some controversy, or get the goose bumps from your own writing, you can probably make someone else get the same feeling. After all, that's what writing is all about—offering others the same enjoyment.

*Speaking of enjoyment...do you hear the footsteps coming down the hall?*

**EDITORS' NOTE:** *Tony Ruggiero has been a resident of the Shady Oaks Home for the criminally insane for the past* *twenty years. On the publication date of this title, his cell was found empty. He is still at large and considered to be extremely dangerous. His behavior consists of breaking into homes and torturing residents with readings from his collected works. If you should find him on the guest list of your local science fiction-fantasy-horror convention, please approach with extreme caution.*

# Zoinks!
# Like, We've Got a Mystery
# in Our Fantasy:
## MIXING MYSTERY WITH FANTASY

### BY WEN SPENCER

Of the good farmer Kender, all they could find was his severed
leg lying on the roof of his hay barn. At least Shaylaya hoped it
was his; certainly, it belonged to a male, torn off at the hip joint,
still clad in homespun breeches and a sturdy leather boot. But
if it wasn't Kender's, it meant more of her human charges were
missing. There seemed to be no clue to what had killed him in the
blood-splattered barnyard, but it was her job, as Peacekeeper,
to find answers.

So the hunt begins, a murder mystery where the world is not Earth nor all the characters human. Such a hybrid—one part fantasy and one part mystery—is considered a cross genre. By mixing elements of fantasy, science fiction, romance and mystery, it's possible to come up with some very odd beasts indeed.

To write a cross-genre story requires you to understand both genres involved. Each genre has a set of *tropes* or elements commonly found in that genre. Tropes are the bones of the story that identify which genre it falls into. In fantasy, one trope would be that magic is an integral part of the plot, and that without magic, the story couldn't happen. If someone picks up Orson Scott Card's *Ender's Game* and reads it, they will find spaceships, orbital stations and computers that clearly make it a science fiction novel. *Lord of the Rings* clarified many of the high fantasy tropes with magic, swords, dragons and elves.

To gain a good understanding of what the tropes are, and how mysteries and fantasies are put together, it's important to first read extensively. A few dips into the pool will not be enough for you to get past the surface of that particular set of characters, plot twists and writer's style to see the bones. If you don't like that genre enough to read large volumes of it, it's unlikely you will enjoy writing it.

## What Makes a Mystery?

The basic story arc of a mystery begins with a crime and ends with justice being served. This means the crime must be discovered as soon as possible, often in the form of a dead body on the first page. If you indicate that the crime will be revealed eventually, you can delay delving into it. "The crime is coming, wait for it," you say to your readers.

For example, Emma Bull's book *Finder* starts with:

> *I remember where I was and what I was doing when Bonnie Prince Charlie was killed.*

The reader hooked, Bull settles back for a leisurely world building. When we meet her main character, Orient, he's washing dishes. His partner, Tick-Tick, arrives wanting help to find her wrench. Bull uses small events to flesh out her world before Orient stumbles into the main crime. Occasionally she'll remind the reader that some earth-shattering events loom in the distance, but those she holds off until we're comfortable with her world.

While the protagonist/detective can discover who committed the crime before the end of the novel, the action can only continue if the detective then has to prove the guilt, capture and/or punish the criminal.

All other story threads in a mystery are secondary in nature. They can come into the novel at any point and be resolved earlier—or even left unresolved, as in the case of a romance.

In many ways, mysteries are puzzle games for the reader. The writer parades as many clues, red herrings and possible suspects as they can past the reader and dares them to see what is there in plain daylight. Skillfully done, the mystery should end with the reader gasping, "Oh my god, yes, of course! Why didn't I see that?"

## THE DETECTIVE AS THE MAIN CHARACTER

Traditionally, main characters in detective novels are police or newspaper reporters or other people who have good cause to investigate the crime—someone who has a duty or job to do has a built-in cause to continue the investigation when danger arises. Most "normal" people are reluctant to get involved in something that can lead to a bloody end. As an example of a mystery/thriller, *The Fugitive* works because the hero has two reasons to hunt down the one-armed man: revenge for his wife's brutal murder and to clear his name.

A corollary of this is that a reader will disbelieve someone putting themselves at risk for no reason, especially as the danger mounts. Jessica Fletcher of *Murder, She Wrote* would not be believable if she pursued justice after someone gave her a sound beating, blew up her house and threatened to cut off her fingers. Her type of mysteries are call a *Cozy*, a story that involves little or no physical danger to the investigator. Detectives in a Cozy are usually little old women with nothing better to do than stick their noses into other people's business. It is difficult, however, to keep page-turning tension going without some type of risk to the main character. In Cozies, the risk is often to a secondary character that the main character wishes to protect—thus, all the danger is removed and yet the tension remains.

The strength of a mystery is that during the investigation, the main character can step outside his world just to follow a clue. No elaborate excuse needs to be invented to send the characters to places they normally wouldn't go. Therefore, the detective becomes the eyes of the reader going into the unknown. A common practice of mysteries is to use first person, which enhances the reader becoming the detective.

Because of this, it's often best to deliberately choose someone who is out of their element: a blue-collar cop in a high society world, a prince in a ghetto. They're seeing the world for the first time, so they notice all the odd little details that someone familiar with that setting might overlook. They have cause to ask questions like "What do you do for a living? How is that done?"

For a great example of using an outsider as the detective, read Steven Brust's *Vlad Taltos* series. In these, the human assassin acts as the reader's eyes into the powerful and alien Dragaera society. While the main character knows his own world of the criminal underworld well, in most of the novels he investigates the world of the nobles who are strange and unknown to him.

## BACKGROUND AVALANCHE

In a standard mystery, the main character's life is usually lacking in complexity; they fit well in one sentence. Sherlock Holmes lives alone and has one good friend. Nero Wolfe is a recluse whose associate does all the leg work. Nor do these situations change, giving the main characters no reason to discuss their personal lives. Watson does not explain to everyone he meets why he works with Holmes or the interpersonal problems they might be having. The focus is solely on the crime and the various victims and suspects.

However, in the cross genre, the main character's life can be (and usually is) quite complicated; as odd and complex it might be, it's important that it doesn't take center stage while side characters are being questioned. This often leads to repeating information the reader already knows. Yes, it might be important to the plot that the main character is a vampire slayer confusing herself by falling in love with a vampire—but discussing her love life with everyone she meets will probably only bore the reader to tears. "Yes," the readers will cry, "You're conflicted! But what about the dead bodies?" Notice that with both *Buffy the Vampire Slayer* (yes, you can learn from storytelling in television form) and Laurel K. Hamliton's *Anita Blake* series, the main character has two modes. The primary mode is solving the case at hand and nail the bad guy. Secondary—when we have time—the heroines might discuss their relationship with their vampire boyfriends.

They are both reluctant to talk about their odd sex lives and need to be pushed into these discussions.

Part of the danger comes from the fact that background is generally easy to write. You know the main characters well and probably like them a good deal. They can chatter away about themselves quite readily. Background, however, is an avalanche waiting to happen. At every moment, it might cascade into the story and bury the current plotline. This will get worse as you move into sequels. Try to control when and where background moves to the forefront. The important mantra is "Is this important to the story I'm trying to tell now?"

## CRIME LANDSLIDE

Related to the character background avalanche is the crime landslide.

One of the more difficult problems in writing mysteries is how to talk about the crime without repeating everything. The detective has to think about what clues mean, he has to question witnesses and suspects, and he has to solve the crime. If you cover the same ground again and again, though, the reader will become bored. The danger, again, is that the crime is known and thus easy to write about.

One easy way to cut the repetition is during the questioning of suspects and witnesses. Resist the temptation to have the main character explain his line of questioning.

### SOME EXAMPLES OF BAD QUESTIONING:

*"We think that the farmer Kender was killed yesterday. We found a leg on the roof of his barn. No one has seen him since the morning before yesterday. When was the last time that you saw him?"*

*"We found this dirt at the crime scene. A spell revealed that it came from your gravesite. Do you have any idea how it got there?"*

*"Willow told us that Spike was having an affair with Buffy. Giles says you two had a fight over her. Buffy says she saw you in the graveyard after she left Spike. What were you doing there?"*

## SOME EXAMPLES OF GOOD QUESTIONING:

*"When was the last time you saw your neighbor, Kender? Have you seen anything odd lately?"*

*"Where were you the night of the killing? Do you have proof?"*

*"What were you doing at the park the night that Spike disappeared?"*

Think of a questioning as a time to switch the spotlight from the detective to the person he's interviewing. Let the suspect/witness sing, dance, juggle and shine while the detective watches. Typically, a detective will only speak to a witness/suspect once or twice, so there is a very limited window of opportunity for them to spout out their understanding of the universe. If the hero is a wizard who visits the noble castle, the ghetto slums and the dragon heights, he'll see a large slice of your world. If you spend most of the time he's at these locations repeating information that the reader already knows, you'll miss an opportunity to see these settings in glorious detail.

## PACING

All fiction should build tension. Mysteries come with tension built in from page one—a crime has been committed that needs to be solved as people seek to obscure the truth. This tension should escalate through the novel, with occasional small dips in the pacing.

Watch any good action movie and there will be a point when the main character, in the heat of battle, will duck down, panting and sweating, to reload his gun and consider his next move. Without these breaks, the tension reaches unbearable and pushes on through to boring. However, without the escalating tension, the story starts at boring and quickly becomes unbearable, no matter how well-written it is.

The main character solves crimes via observation, investigation, research and deductive reasoning. Each method has its own level of passivity and tension. By interspersing them, you can control the pacing.

Observation and investigation are active and, because they usually require interaction with other characters, they are usually good vehicles for tension. Just because the spotlight is on the side character doesn't mean that they have to be helpful and cooperative, only that they are the center of attention at that moment. Nor does the conflict/tension they introduce into the novel have to do with aggression toward the main character. Tiny Tim, in *A Christmas Carol*, is a pivotal point of conflict; the question of whether he lives or dies causes the tension.

Research is searching archives, reading books and other materials for information related to the case. Because this is often passive, it can be used to slow the pacing down. Small breaks are needed but care has to be taken not to drag down the pace of the story through information dumps.

Resist the temptation to add whole diary/newspaper/book pages to obscure clues. Unless the passage can add tension to the here and now (I put a bomb in your wife's suitcase, your babysitter is a werewolf, and last time we slept together I gave you a sexual disease) treat them as black holes to be measured out with eyedroppers.

## PACING A NOVEL

Because a mystery presents a crime that will be solved by the end of the book, mysteries do not lend themselves to sprawling trilogies. Instead, mysteries are usually a series of related books, each a self-contained story with the same main character solving different crimes.

While fantasy novels are traditionally longer than other genres, chain bookstores are pressuring publishers to limit the length of first novels. Chain bookstores devote the width of one paperback to a new writer's novel—basically how much room it will take up if the novel's cover faced out. This is called *facing*. While the publisher can print paperbacks up to 800 pages in length, only three copies of such a novel can fit on the shelf. This is opposed to a novel that is more the normal length of less than 400 pages, or around 100,000 words which can fit *five* copies. It benefits the bookstores to be able to stock more copies of a book in the same amount of space.

For both of these reasons, you should structure your novel so it can be told in 100,000 words.

As stated before, a mystery starts with a crime—or more specifically, the discovery of a crime. Things have gone before, and the detective is joining a story already in motion that he'll bring to an end. How does this relate to your word limit? By keeping track of your word count, you can plan out the pacing of your novel.

## DISSECTING A MYSTERY

The first part is the discovery of the crime. The villain has painted a picture of betrayal and death. The villain has now hidden the picture away. During the discovery phase, the hero investigates the crime, trying to see the complete picture. It's during this period that the reader is introduced to the hero, the world, the principal players and the laws of your magic and culture. This section should take up the first third of the novel, or roughly 33,000 words.

The middle of the novel is more nebulous. The hero is still trying to uncover the entire picture, but the villain is now aware of his efforts. Both the hero and the villain start to manipulate people and the world around them with goals directly opposed to one another. Rarely at this point do the hero and villain actually come into direct conflict—even if the villain is the hero's best friend. The villain puts things in the hero's path and the hero does his best to dig out the truth. The simple reason for the delay in the confrontation is that it's difficult to bring both together and not trigger the premature annihilation of one of them.

The transition between the first and middle sections is hard to quantify. The largest difference between the two is that during the first section, the hero tends to be in a reactive position. The villain has done something and the hero does not know enough to do anything more than react. He finds the various clues littered about, examines them and tries to move forward, but he can't because he doesn't know enough information. By the middle of the novel, however, he should have discovered enough that he can now make plans. In *The Fellowship of the Ring*, for example, Frodo's flight away from the Shire is entirely reactive. He knows nothing and strives only to survive as he gathers information. It's not until they reach Rivendell that he's learned enough to move from being reactive to active.

If the first two thirds of a novel is the hero trying to uncover the villain's "picture of crime" and then attempting to make changes to it, the last third is a violent fight over the paintbrush.

At round the 66,000-word mark, you should be looking at gathering up plot threads and tying them off. You only have a little over 10-15,000 words to build to the violent climax, another 10,000 for the big bang and then a handful of words at the end for wrap up.

## PLAYING FAIR

Part of the contract between writer and reader in a mystery is that the alert reader will have enough clues to be able to figure out the mystery before the writer reveals who, what, when, where and why through the main character. As a writer, you need to feed the reader clues at a rate that will allow them to know the answer within a page or two before the main character connects the dots for them. This allows the reader to feel smart. Once the reader solves the crime, the clock starts to tick. With each following page that the crime goes unsolved by the characters, the less patience the reader will have for them; *"How could they be so blind?"* becomes *"How can they be so stupid?"* At a certain point, the believability snaps and it's no longer *"stupid characters"*—it's *"stupid writer."*

First readers are invaluable to see if you've managed to pull off this tightrope act. It's important to choose a reader that hasn't heard you plotting out the novel in advance; instead they come at it as totally cold as an average reader. Ideally, they should be both surprised and yet see it coming. (Yes, it is hard to do.)

There are many ways to keep the reader guessing, but it's vital that all the clues are there. True, there are some fine mysteries where the main character discovers something but then doesn't inform the reader until the big reveal. Sherlock Holmes and Miss Marple were notorious for this. I caution against doing this—it's hard to do well and easy to do badly.

As a fantasy writer, your task is even more difficult. If the solution to the mystery is based on magic—a doppelganger, a teleport spell, a magical widget—you need to give the reader everything they need to know to solve the crime. You must create the "laws of magic" for your world, keep within your own rules and explain it all to the reader.

Similarly, if the solution rides on some cultural norm, then the reader needs all pertaining customs to be laid out.

For example, medieval Catholics held being buried in hallowed ground to be vital. A person who committed suicide, however, would not be buried in a churchyard. A devout Catholic of that period might kill to keep secret the suicide of a loved one to insure they will receive a proper burial. For a modern non-Catholic to guess the killer's motivation, this cultural norm has to be discussed somewhere in the course of the novel.

Luckily, there are many tricks to disguising the obvious so you can lay out needed information and yet keep the reader guessing up to the end.

## PLANTING CLUES

There are two types of clues: *visible* and *invisible*.

*Visible clues* are the ones that the main character uncovers and the reader immediately recognizes as possible clues. A key. A letter. A weapon. They gleam on the page, bright with the promise of their ability to shed light on the mystery.

Visible clues work best if you use them to play connect the dots. This visible clue will take the main character to this place. That visible clue will force the main character to talk to those people. So obvious is their nature as a clue, their strongest ability is to tie the story together. You can scatter the witnesses and invisible clues to all corners of the world, and the visible clues will drag the detective out to those places.

Once introduced, though, a visible clue cannot be ignored. It must be dealt with. An old rule of writing is that if you wheel a cannon onto the stage in act one, you must fire the cannon by act three. The same holds true in mysteries. If you establish a clue, it must lead to something. A key doesn't have to unlock a door, but it should matter somehow in the plot.

This is not to say that visible clues have to be immediately understandable. They can be obscure, such as a set of numbers on a scrap of paper. What do they stand for? Neither the reader or the main character has to know right away.

*Invisible clues* are those that are part of the landscape. The reader and the detective takes them in with a casual sweep of the eyes, but their significance isn't realized until later.

### EXAMPLE OF INVISIBLE CLUE:

> *"The flashlight is dead," I called to John. "Where do you keep the batteries?"*
> *"In the frige."*
> *There wasn't enough in his refrigerator to feed an ant colony; judging by the contents he existed on cereal and Chinese take out. I moved a nearly empty carton of orange juice aside and found the batteries.*

Later in the story...

> "Can I have something to drink?" she asked.
> "Doubt it." I opened John's refrigerator and checked the cartons by weight. "There's a little milk in here, and a good bit of orange juice."

The invisible clue is that "nearly empty" orange juice has now become "a good bit," and the hero is about to unknowingly poison the female visitor. It is fairly obvious in this example since everything else has been eliminated, but tucked into a full story it vanishes neatly.

Invisible clues are much harder to juggle since you need to make them stand out enough for the reader to notice and yet not pay attention to them. A common mistake is to stress the invisible clue too much, calling attention to it.

One way to deal with invisible clues is to make your main character someone that notices and remembers details. This seems counterproductive. What in fact happens, though, is that they detail out everything. It is easier to slip in important clues when they list out exactly what they order for dinner, what clothes another character is wearing and all the cards played during a trivial card game.

A second way to keep invisible clues from leaping off the page is to write the scene without the clue present. This keeps you from centering on what isn't supposed to be noticed. After the scene is finished, go back and insert the minimum words possible.

### EXAMPLE OF A BADLY PLANTED INVISIBLE CLUE:

> "What a mess," she sighed looking at the cluttered office. Paper, books and bills were piled high on the desk. What a packrat Marge must have been—she even had a badly stained teddy bear; it wore a black leather biker coat with "Dog Warrior" stitched over a picture of a snarling wolf.
> She was still sorting through the mess when Tee stuck his head into the office. "Find anything?"
> "No, there's nothing unusual here."

### EXAMPLE OF A FIXED SCENE:

> "What a mess," she sighed looking at the cluttered office. She settled into the chair and started to dig through the objects piled

*on the desk. What a packrat Marge must have been! Turtles*
*marched across the top of the monitor. Under a layer of paper,*
*she discovered a small ceramic piggy bank with "baby's first*
*bank" written in pink, a beanbag lizard, a silver bracelet and*
*dozens of pens in a rainbow of colors. A small leather change*
*purse held Canadian coins, a diamond ring and what looked to*
*be a cat's tooth. Signs of sloth were everywhere, from a five-*
*month-old bottle of antibiotics with six pills still inside, to a*
*stack of five unopened electric bills, the last one marked "shut*
*off notice."*

  *"Sooo," she sighed to the teddy bear in a biker's jacket perched*
*on the corner of the desk, "You saw everything—what were the*
*thieves after?"*

Notice that the main character paid attention to all the objects in
the room; she is treating everything as a possible clue. With such
even treatment, the teddy bear blends into the background. Once the
significance of the bear is realized as a clue, the main character can
examine it closer. Also notice that we get a better insight into the
owner of the desk in the second example.

## MOTIVATION

The game of "Clue" presented a murder in a neat little package—
Colonel Mustard in the library with the candlestick. It ignored the
most important part of a murder—*motivation.* Why did the culprit
actually commit the crime? This is an important part of creating a
"crime picture."

Too often in fantasy, the motivation presented is simply *"They are
evil."* Dark lords, evil incarnate and gods of void abound in hordes. The
hero fights against "faceless minions" until he takes on Evil itself.

A strong mystery, however, needs named suspects. It needs Colonel
Mustard, Miss Scarlet and Mr. Green to confuse the trail and muddy
the waters and, in the end, be brought to justice. Yes, they can be
working for Evil—but why? If Evil rang your doorbell today and asked
you join the cause, what would be your motivation for betraying all
you presumably hold dear? Fear for your life does qualify as a good
motivation here.

Remember that mysteries are puzzle games. The readers wants to be
able to figure it out but at the same time they don't want the solution
presented to them on a silver platter. The writer must present all the

clues, but he's allowed as many tricks as a street magician to keep the reader guessing.

## LOADED DECK

The first trick is to present a number of suspects who all seem guilty. All the suspects have good reasons to see the victim dead, steal the priceless object or plot to take over the world. Often, as evidence is uncovered, one suspect will appear guiltier than the rest until the next clue moves the suspicion to another person.

For example, Lord Dar'kain is dead. His brother wants his estate. His wizard is acting suspicious and possibly practicing dark arts. He beat his wife regularly. His daughter lived in fear of him. Which person actually killed him?

In this scenario, the detective weighs opportunity. The suspects give reasonable explanations about where they were at the time of death, and the detective must cross-check this information, thereby eliminating possible killers.

Often in these types of murders, where the victim is evil himself, the person most likely to be found guilty and punished is the most likeable of the suspects. For example, Dar'kain's beautiful young daughter has been framed and will be put to death if the true killer is not found.

A variation of this is when the victim seems to be loved by all. Often in this case, no one can prove their whereabouts, and the investigation becomes focused on uncovering hidden motivations.

## HANDLING LARGE NUMBERS OF CHARACTERS

Whereas detectives of the mystery genre are usually lone lawmen, the main characters of fantasy are usually part of an ensemble cast. Add in a loaded deck of possible suspects, and you have a large number of possible characters in any one scene. Worse, certain stock fantasy situations mandate a crowd; the standard meeting with the country's ruler—a king, queen or emperor—will probably include guards, advisors and various members of the court.

Two characters, however, are the optimal number in any scene. A person by himself is limited both in conflict and dialogue. With two characters, dialogue is now possible. The number of conflicts expands from two (internal and man vs. nature) to countless; they can include anything from sexual tension to deadly violence. The rhythm of dialogue that best reflects conflict is the tug-of-war between two people. The addition of just one more person disrupts the focus and power. The discussion is no longer give and take. The attention of the characters and the reader is no longer a bright spotlight that bounces back and forth. One best-selling mystery writer went as far as to advocate making it a writing rule: there shall be only two characters in a scene.

As stated before, you want suspects/witnesses to be in the spotlight. It is possible to present a one-on-one conversation in a crowd. This will keep the power of the scene from being diluted.

The easiest way separate out two characters is with a delay/shuffle. A typical scene in fantasies is the gathering of the ensemble. This overloads the reader with names, physical traits, and personal details.

Instead of the main character encountering everyone at the same moment, stage mini-scenes. Delay new characters from arriving until the present character talks, then shuffle that person off to make room for the next arrival. Done quickly, it seems like an encounter with a mass of people but in truth, is a series of meetings.

### EXAMPLE OF OVERLOADING:

John turned the corner and ran into a tall warrior, a man in black robes, and a slim girl all in leather.
"Who are you guys?" John asked.
"There he is!" the man in robes cried. "I'm Devo!"
"I'm Lankin, come with us if you hope to live," said the warrior.
"Geez, you're scaring him," said the girl. "I'm Suzzie."

### EXAMPLE OF DELAY/SHUFFLE:

John turned the corner and collided with a tall warrior.
"Who are you?" John asked.
"My name is Lankin," The warrior put out a hand, challenging John with his eyes to take it.
John extended his own hand reluctantly. The warrior's fingers felt like steel bars wrapped around his, firm but painless. "What do you want?"
"Come, the others are waiting, and there's no telling the mischief Suzzie will get into if left idle too long."

*Placing a massive hand on John's shoulder, Lankin half-dragged John down the street and into a dark alley. For a moment John thought the alley empty, then a man all in black mage robes stepped forward, separating himself from the shadows.*

*"Here he is, Devo." Lankin released John. "I'll go arrange the horses."*

*With that, Lankin loped back down the street.*

*"What do you want?" John asked the mage.*

*"You're in grave danger." The mage's eyes gleamed in the darkness. "You must come with us if you wish to live."*

*John rubbed at his shoulder and used the movement to glance back, seeing if he could bolt without being caught. Was there someone standing at the mouth of the alley, or just a trick of the light?*

*"What are you talking about?" John asked to cover his uneasiness. "Does this have to do with the killing in Market Square?"*

*"Ahhh, he's a sharp one." A woman's voice lilted out of the darkness. "You're doing nothing but scaring him. Do your warding thing and let me handle this. It needs a woman's touch."*

*Devo snorted but stepped back, becoming one with the shadows again. "Five minutes, Suzzie, and then we must go, if we're to stay ahead of them and uncover the truth."*

*The woman came to John's chin—lithe, young, dressed all in bright patches. "It's like this, John—sometimes in life, you're the cat, and sometimes you're the mouse. Tonight, you're the mouse."*

Another way to keep the focus on the witness to surround them with spearcarriers—the nameless people that stand in the corner and come with the understanding that they will not speak unless spoken to. This, in the case of kings and generals and such, can be quite literal. A sleeping/unconscious character can also fall into this category of present but silent. Combined with a delay/shuffle, it is possible to interview the heads of state surrounded by their court and still keep the conversation one-on-one.

## DIALOGUE WITH MULTIPLE CHARACTERS

Unfortunately, sometimes you must have more than two people speaking. In these situations, all dialogue must be tagged to avoid confusion of who is speaking.

## EXAMPLE OF MULTIPLE CHARACTERS HANDLED BADLY:

> *Jomn and Maarc came to see Peat that afternoon.*
> *"Something must be done," Jomn cried.*
> *Peat nodded in agreement. "I know, I know."*
> *"No, you don't know."*
> *"We're in danger of being discovered here!" Maarc shouted.*

Who said, "No, you don't know?" Reading closely, you can tell Jomn did, but there is a moment of confusion. Anything that confuses the reader long enough to pull him out of the flow of the story must be avoided. Tag all dialogue. "Said" is nearly invisible and can be used anyplace it might be otherwise unclear who is talking.

## GOD IS IN THE DETAILS

In mysteries, characters *must* lie—otherwise the detective wouldn't have to investigate and the crime would be quickly solved. The truth often has to be hidden in the way they say things, so care has to be taken in being as precise as possible. Bad dialogue can sink a mystery.

Avoid adding adjectives to your dialogue. The words of dialogue themselves should indicate the tone of speaking:

> *"Hush, quiet as a mouse."*
> *"No!"*

If the words themselves don't hint at the emotion (level) of the speaker, then actions can be added which will have more impact than a descriptor added to the tag:

> *She put her mouth close to my ear, her words a tickle of a snake-tongue against my flesh. "Hush, quiet as a mouse."*
> *Denial burst out of me, as if all my being roared against the possibility. "No!"*

## CROSS-GENRE MARKETING

While it seems logical that if you write a book that satisfies two genres, it would sell well for both, in truth, it rarely does. While some fantasy readers can be narrow in their selections—only reading high fantasy or epic fantasy—most are open-minded avid readers. They not only read fantasy, but science fiction, romance and mystery. Mystery readers, however, are more often very narrow in what they will read. Those that like police procedurals usually will not read a Cozy, and vice versa.

Technology is blurring the line between what we can do now and what we might be able to do in the future. Because of this, a science fiction/mystery mix has a better chance of selling to mystery readers. In fact, SF novels are starting to win mystery awards.

Donald Maass of the Donald Maass Literary Agency says, "While there are plenty of fantasies with detective protagonists, the reverse is not true in the mystery field. Just go into any mystery bookstore to look for a wizard detective, or similar. You won't find them. I think that is because crime fiction fans are grounded in the real world. I know, I know...that hardly seems possible when one considers how cute and cozy some of those novels are. (I mean, what is cute about murder?) Nonetheless, I believe it is true: generally speaking mystery fans want their mysteries straight, with no magic rings, elves or dragons."

Your audience will be the avid fantasy readers that enjoy foremost a good story. They will be delighted in a tale that mixes in the elements of two of their favorite genres. Ultimately, though, you must write the story to please yourself. If you love both genres, then writing a cross-genre book is its own reward.

# It's Only Sex, For Crying Out Loud:
## INCORPORATING ROMANCE AND SEX IN FANTASY

### BY JEANINE BERRY

#### INTRODUCTION

Sex and magic. What a combination. But will it work in a fantasy novel? For that matter, do the characters in a fantasy novel ever *have* sex?

For a long time, it seemed the answer was no, or at least, not in the story. Maybe a sexual relationship between consenting adults was part of the "happily ever after"—after the prince had won the princess, the kingdom was safe and the last page was turned. But within the pages of the book, the closest thing to sex was a chaste kiss between the hero and the heroine, usually in the closing scene.

Apparently, none of the heroes in a fantasy novel had time for any sexual adventures. Oh, sure, the scantily-clad maidens common on many fantasy covers might have promised a more sensational read. But when you got inside the book, the heroes were too busy slaying dragons, fighting evil wizards and saving the kingdom to notice how provocatively the heroine was dressed. Occasionally, the maiden, who more often than not turned out to be a princess, came along for the ride. At the end, the hero/prince declared his love, while the princess blushed becomingly. If we were really lucky, we might be invited to the wedding, which took place with pomp and ceremony. Then, just as some of us thought we'd finally gotten to the best part of the book, the couple stepped into the bedroom to start their life of wedded bliss together, the door swung firmly shut and the story was over.

Today, things have changed. In part this change is driven by a need every bit as basic as sex: the need to make a buck. In today's tough, competitive market, a book has to sell well or an author's career is quickly over. This gives the marketing department an influential voice in deciding what books are published. For the moment at least, many marketers are clinging to the truism that "sex sells." Romance, with varying degrees of heat, has become acceptable in fantasy.

Whether or not fantasy readers want a great deal of sex in their stories might still be debatable. Purists can argue whether this trend is aimed at the diehard fantasy reader or at drawing in new readers, perhaps from the world of romance. But whether or not traditional fantasy readers want more romance and sex in their novels, the market has moved in that direction. This gives fantasy writers more freedom to write a story that explores the complexities of adult relationships, including love and sex, but it also makes their task more difficult. When you add love and sex to fantasy, you need some magical skills of your own to pull it off.

## Do Fools Rush in...to the Bedroom?

At first glance, these changes seem exciting. Publishers are launching new lines and boasting they will combine fantasy and romance. New readers, many of them female, are discovering the realm of fantasy, drawn by this explosive combination. These readers feed the hunger for more fantasy stories with an element of romance and/or sexuality. It looks like a growing market.

But this trend is also a symptom of a problem. The market for books overall is shrinking. Even established, best-selling authors must battle to keep their sales up. Is love and sex in fantasy simply a "hot" trend that will soon pass as the market for sexually-oriented material becomes totally saturated? Should you as a writer embrace this trend, and if so, how far should you go?

In real life, love and sex can be a dangerous minefield: explosive, unpredictable, loaded with traps for the unwary and downright earth-shattering in impact. And the same can be true when adding the ingredients of love and sex to a traditional fantasy novel.

This chapter will help you through the minefield. We'll take a look at the historical perspective to see how writers in the past have handled this kind of material. We'll examine the work of three current writers on the cutting edge of this trend: Angela Knight, Jacqueline Carey and Catherine Asaro. These authors have graciously agreed to share their expertise with you. And we'll also get into the nitty-gritty of technique with a discussion of various approaches to writing about sex.

## A CHANGING TRADITION

Modern fantasy's popularity started with the *Lord of the Rings* trilogy. Today, *LOTR* remains an excellent example of a traditional fantasy. J.R.R. Tolkien's landmark work consists of three weighty volumes and hundreds of thousands of words. You might think the length alone gave Tolkien plenty of room for a love story, especially with all those very sexy elves involved.

But Tolkien wrote high fantasy where the quest is the vital thing. His stories were grounded in old traditions. The main plot centers on the heroes (all guys, mind you!) and the destruction of the Ring. The love story between Arwen and Aragorn is a minor subplot at best, spiced with a side serving of unrequited love on Eowyn's part. During the course of the books, Arwen and Aragorn's love consists mostly of yearning from afar, and while the two lovers are united in the end, we hear nothing of their physical passion.

When it came time to make *LOTR* into a movie, the producers took note of this lack of romance. While there wasn't much they could do about the missing sex, they did add a large number of scenes filled with longing looks. I'm sure the adults in the audience guessed what Arwen and Aragorn were longing for!

Without a doubt, the *Lord of the Rings* trilogy is a monumental achievement. Tolkien created a richly realized fantasy world with a complex history, multiple races and hundreds of fascinating characters. So perhaps it was too much to expect him to revolutionize the treatment of sex in fantasy as well. Indeed, such an approach would have been totally out of place in his day. The sexual revolution was still in the future.

After the publication of the *Lord of the Rings* trilogy, the majority of fantasy writers followed in Tolkien's footsteps. Traditional fantasy is based on the story of a quest. It focuses on high ideals, sacrifice and self-control—themes not conducive to uninhibited sexual scenes.

Sex was also usually a missing ingredient in another staple of the fantasy genre—the story based on some magical power. The theme of power in these stories centers on the magic, not on that other notorious source of power, sex. Indeed, in many of these novels, such as the *Merlin* series by Mary Stewart, or the first of the *Witch World* books by Andre Norton, the hero or heroine will lose their magical powers if they have sex. Once again in these books, fantasy tapped into the tradition of the "pure" hero, a hero who avoided contact with women or sex.

Certainly, you could find some faint traces of romance in a fantasy book. The hero needed to receive a prize once he completed his perilous quest, after all. Often, his reward was the pure love of the chaste heroine. But in the vast majority of fantasy books the romance, if there even was one, was relegated to a subplot. It might be there, but it was overshadowed by more important events. Romance, in the sense of a story focused on the evolution of a passionate relationship between two adults, didn't exist in fantasy novels. Neither did sex itself, despite the fact that sex is the driving motivation behind much of the activity in the real world.

But while fantasy writers were busy exploring imaginary worlds, times were changing in this one. For one thing, the sexual revolution brought a new openness about sexual matters, and that led to changes in the generally accepted community standards on what could be put into print. But other things changed in the world of publishing as well.

## THE IMPACT OF ROMANTIC FICTION

Foremost among these changes was the burgeoning popularity of the romance novel. This amazingly successful genre proved that there is a huge audience of women readers, and that they are hungry for stories about relationships between men and women.

Of course, romance is an entirely different genre than fantasy, and therein lies some of the problems that arise when attempting to combine the two. Romance readers have clear expectations of a romance book. The Romance Writers of America, the premier organization for romance writers, has outlined two elements—a central love story and an emotionally satisfying ending—as the crux of their association's official definition of a romance novel. This is quite different from a fantasy novel, where the love story is traditionally a subplot and the emotionally satisfying ending is not guaranteed. In fact, in some fantasy circles the "happy" in happy ending is sneeringly referred to as the "h" word!

The marriage might be an uneasy one, but it was consummated nonetheless. As romance writers attempted to meet the ravenous demand for books, they began to incorporate fantasy elements into their plots. Their books included popular themes such as magic, elves, shapeshifters and wizards. "Otherworldly" elements such as mystical creatures, ghosts and characters time-traveling between historical or pseudo-medieval periods via portals, genies and bewitched amulets, began to appear in this radical approach to the romance novel. These books proved so popular that the RWA now recognizes them as a subgenre of romance that directly pertains to fantasy: the paranormal romance.

And so the effort to combine fantasy and romance was under way.

Clearly, romance writers have made a huge impact on expanding the audience for popular fantasy. But the changes they started didn't stop with a new emphasis on romance. As these writers continued their quest to spice up their work for readers, they added more and more sex to their plots. This trend, which started with historical romances (known in the trade as "bodice rippers"), eventually spread to the fantasy romances as well. When writers started combining romance, fantasy and sex, a whole new realm of possibilities opened up.

## The Old Meets the New

You may have come to fantasy as a result of reading paranormal romances, or you may be part of the more conventional fantasy tradition. But you've certainly noticed that fantasy and romance have gotten into bed together. Whether this trend will continue, or whether fantasy readers will grow tired of the relationship and demand a return to old formulas, remains to be seen. The paranormal enjoyed a brief flurry of popularity a few years ago before sinking back into relative publishing obscurity. Yet rather like the vampire that is such a popular character in these books, it's risen once more from the dead and become a hot commodity.

Several new lines have been started specifically to support books that combine fantasy and romance. These include the new Luna line and Tor's paranormal line.

The Luna line was intended to deliver "a compelling, female-focused fantasy with vivid characters, rich worlds, strong, sympathetic women and romantic subplots," according to their original statement. Tor's paranormal romance line was created in response to a huge call from readers for more romance and fantasy, according to the line's editor. Tor's guidelines state, in part: "Each novel should include at least two main plot elements: one, the romance and the conflict inherent in that; two, another significant conflict. Both storylines should be crucial to the overall novel, and the romantic elements should make up no more than half the entire story. ... We are open to non-traditional romances (i.e., multi-racial, multi-ethnic, religiously diverse, non-traditional gender/sexual orientation, etc.), as well as traditional ones. We are open to very erotic works as well as less graphic ones; in any work the sex and romance should be believable and rational and well-suited to the story."

Today, fantasies at your local bookstore will range from the traditional to the erotic. In the latter category, one of the newest publishers to gain recognition from the RWA is Ellora's Cave. Commonly known as EC, Ellora's Cave is an erotica publisher that is notable for publishing many first-time authors. EC publishes novels that combine romance and hot sex. They've named their new genre "romantica.™" As of this writing, Ellora's Cave is actively seeking more fantasy novels that include romance and hot sex.

## Time to Send the Computer up in Flames?

If you have a story that combines fantasy, romance and sex, the market is more open than ever before. But it's also more important than ever to pay attention to a publisher's guidelines. Each publisher looks for something specific to set their line apart from the others.

In general, most fantasy romances and paranormals are still published by romance publishers. And most fantasy publishers still want the romance and sex to be a subplot, with the main story centering on some other strong conflict or motivation. If you, as a writer, decide to aim for a traditional fantasy market, you will be juggling two often difficult and sometimes opposing goals. You will need to keep your story moving forward in the main story arc with the necessary pacing and development. At the same time, you'll need to make room for all the complexities that romance—and sex—bring to our lives.

Incorporating romance and sex into a fantasy adds a new set of complications. Romance and fantasy are fundamentally different. Romance focuses on relationship; fantasy focuses on plot. Your task is to combine the two. You'll have two main characters to develop, not one. Keeping the book focused can become a struggle as a third element—the relationship itself—always looms in the background ready to take over the story. You need to develop the romantic elements and at the same time keep the story moving. It's a tough job.

As fantasy writers strive to include romance, they will find some hidden landmines strewing their path to success. Remember all those readers who came to fantasy by way of romance? They expect fantasy to abide by some of the rules of romance. You can certainly choose to break these rules, but it will be at your peril.

Most of these rules are unwritten, but are well-known among romance writers. Let's consider just a few.

**THE HERO AND THE HEROINE MUST BE LIKEABLE.** The reader wants to identify with these people and their relationship. In general, a romance reader wants the hero to be an alpha male—a strong, commanding take-charge type, assertive but not arrogant, and most of all protective of the heroine. At the same time, the heroine should be intelligent and independent as well.

**THE HERO AND HEROINE MUST BE ATTRACTED TO AND HAVE SEX ONLY WITH EACH OTHER.** Romance readers want romance and that means two people who are faithful to each other. This is a case where you must know what you are writing. If you aim at the romance audience, you will disappoint your readers if the lovers are not true to each other.

**KEEP THE EMOTIONS INTENSE.** When writing romance, you are dealing with the oldest plot of all time, going right back to the Garden of Eden and Adam and Eve—boy meets girl. The outcome is a given. What the reader wants to experience is the thrill of the hero's and heroine's emotions as their romance develops.

**HERE IS THE MOST FUNDAMENTAL ROMANCE RULE OF ALL: YOU MUST PROVIDE THE READER WITH A HEA, OR HAPPY-EVER-AFTER ENDING.** Romance writers break this sacred rule at the risk of ending their careers. Happy ever after has never been an expectation in fantasy, where anything can and does happen, but if you are going to attempt to combine fantasy and romance, I strongly suggest providing one.

## COMING TO GRIPS WITH SEX

As a writer, I've participated in many book discussions. Over and over I hear readers make the same complaint: They want more depth and emotion. Young and old, if they relate passionately to a character, they want to know about all aspects of that character's life. Certainly, sexuality is a vital part of human life. Our sexuality strips us down and exposes our most intimate secrets and desires. In the same way, writing about sex can seem like personal exposure the first time you try it.

Writing about sex isn't as simple as it may seem at first glance. The key to a good sex scene is that it must belong in the book. If it's been added merely to titillate your readers, they will be able to tell. But if it advances the story and deepens our knowledge of the characters, it is sure to grip the reader. As a writer, you must make your sex scene far more than a momentary diversion. Such scenes have the potential to be engrossing on nearly every level: physically, mentally and emotionally.

Not every fantasy novel will touch upon sexual matters. Tolkien's writing reflected the times in which he lived, but even today I suspect he would make the same choices. Other fantasy novelists are renowned for a lyrical voice. In books such as *The Last Unicorn* by Peter Beagle, the whole story hinges on the delicate interplay of poetry and magic.

These are ethereal, otherworldly novels where physical passion seems out of place.

So, how do you judge if your book is one where a sexual encounter is really necessary to the plot? One way to start is to read books that do combine fantasy and sex. I recommend reading *Kushiel's Dart, Kushiel's Chosen* and *Kushiel's Avatar* by Jacqueline Carey. Include Wen Spencer's *Tinker*, which demonstrates a seamless incorporation of romance, sex and action, and *Captive Dreams* by Angela Knight. Then, ask yourself these questions:

> *Does what happen between the characters as they make love advance the storyline?*

> *Does the sex illuminate some facet of their character that's pivotal to the story?*

> *Will the intimacy of sex provoke a revelation between them that might not have come otherwise?*

> *Will some plot point turn on the trust created by this mutual sharing?*

> *Will some conflict be born from what they discover about each other?*

These are all good reasons to include a sex scene. On the other hand, if you could remove this scene from the book and nothing would change in the plot, it's simply gratuitous.

Speaking of gratuitous sex, what of those people that equate sex with pornography? The U.S. Supreme Court justices may know it when they see it, but for the rest of us, it's probably true that we each have our own viewpoint about when an author might have crossed the line between sensual writing and pornography.

As a writer of some very erotic SF and fantasy myself, I've had an opportunity to discuss this subject with quite a few erotica authors. Most will tell you that it's pornography when it's about sex, sex and more sex. In pornography, sex is the whole point. People reading pornography just want to read about sex.

In erotica, on the other hand, the author is telling a story, and the sexual experience is a part of that story. People reading erotica want to read about a sensual relationship between two characters who matter to them. In pornography it really doesn't matter who's in the bed and why as long as they get there fast and stay there for a long time. In erotica, it does matter. And they don't even have to get there until the last page—the sensual journey, the growing erotic awareness between the hero and heroine, is what the reader craves.

In my own career, I've combined both sex and SF and sex and fantasy. Although my *Sex Gate* series (written with Darrell Bain) is SF, it's a good example of making the sex integral to the story. The first book of the series, *The Sex Gates*, was an immediate success and I took a bit of teasing from other writers who suggested this popularity was due to the word "sex" in the title. But readers are far more sophisticated than that. If the only thing the book had to offer was a word in the title, it would have been a flash in the pan—and deservedly so. Instead, *The Sex Gates* offers an idea that readers found compelling, but an idea that could not be divorced from sex. In the book, thousands of mysterious gates appear on Earth one day. If you go through one, your sex changes. You also emerge young and cured of any diseases you may have. But there's a catch—you can only go through once.

In my fantasy *Dayspring* trilogy, the sex scene doesn't occur until almost the end of the third book, *Dayspring Destiny*. Yet this scene is crucial to the denouement of the story. The heroine, Elinna Serru, is a Master of the House of Lohenrin and a fiercely independent woman who has taken on the heavy burden of trying to save her world from impending doom. Despite her great Power, she is failing at this task. Then, at a point of despair, she has a dream of an alternate reality. She sees the future as it would have been if she had chosen to accept the love offered to her years ago by the Inheritor, Mesor Tethays. In this future, they would have combined their powers and found the way to save their world.

As soon as she wakes from the dream, Elinna rushes from her bed to the palace where Mesor is sleeping. Praying it is not too late to create that future, Elinna slips into his room and wakes him. With her khi power, she is able to share the dream with him, mind to mind. Then comes the moment of truth.

*Mesor leaned toward her, his breathing harsh. "You will share your life with mine? You will not run away when the Power calls or some demiurge beckons or some crisis demands the wisdom of Elinna Serru to solve it?"*

*She sat up straight on the bed and put both hands over his heart. "I swear. The world may perish but I will not again leave your side. Whatever life brings from now on, we will face it together as we did in the dream."*

*She saw his teeth flash in the moonlight, saw hope win the battle and shine from his face. "I would love to make your dream become real, Elinna. That is, if I am not dreaming myself even now."*

*"Is this a dream?" She leaned into him again, searching for his mouth. His arms went around her, gathering her close.*

The sex scene that follows portrays an act of complete surrender. In this instance, their sexual union is a symbol of Elinna's deep commitment to follow the revelation she has received and change her life, so that a new and hopeful future can be born.

## I've Got Them in Bed, Now What?

You're all too familiar with the moment. Someone asks you what you do. You reply that you're a writer. They nod and inform you that someday they're going to write a book too. Everyone thinks it's easy to write a book, right up to the moment they try. In the same vein, most writers think it's easier to write romance than other kinds of stories, until they try. And I'd venture a guess that everyone thinks it must be pretty darned easy to write about sex. Hey, just write down the words "breast," "nipple" and "naked." Congratulations—you're halfway there! But a truly erotic sex scene is far more complex than that.

Simply put: Having sex is fun! Writing a sex scene can be fun, too, but it is also hard work. The sex part is simple. Most people discover how that works at an early age. The writing part, though, can get complicated. You will be portraying two beings (human, elf or otherwise...) interacting at their most intimate level. You must meet the reader's expectations for passion, romance and drama. You must create a scene that is intense, emotional and sensual. You must remember to include motivation and conflict. More than ever, you will need to set the scene and then evoke all the physical senses to make it real.

In *Morevi: The Chronicles of Rafe & Askana*, authors Tee Morris and Lisa Lee create a rich and almost magical garden outside the royal palace as the setting for the start of their love scene.

> And like a girl void of all decorum, she danced lightly over the grass, keeping time with the far-off music of Palace minstrels and English sailors ... two cultures merging through joyous music. The sounds of music, laughter, and mirth reached them in this courtyard attached to the Palace. Yet it seemed shut out in his haven of cool darkness, out of place with the fragrance of greenery and nightblooms. He watched her dance in the light of the twin moons, completely surrendering to the song of two worlds.

Don't stop at touch, include smell and taste too. Take the extra time to set the scene, to create an atmosphere suitable for romance or eroticism or a dangerous liaison. Let the setting help to convey the mood of your story. One advantage of fantasy is that you can employ some truly exotic settings for the romantic interlude, from castles to palaces to a magician's lair.

As your characters approach each other in the mating dance, they will take certain physical steps that reflect their deepening intimacy. In our contemporary human society, researchers have spent a great deal of time studying these steps and have determined they usually occur in a ritualistic sequence. They start with the first look at the other person, and advance to eye contact, then the first touch, the first kiss, and eventually full genital contact.

Writers were quick to recognize the value of incorporating these steps into a scene as it grows progressively more sensual. Linda Howard, a best-selling romance author, has provided a detailed outline of the steps to intimacy. You can find it on her web site at http://ourworld. compuserve.com/homepages/ajax21/writer/12steps.html.

In your fantasy novel, you are free to change this formula into whatever your imagination can conjure up for an alien culture. Humans are attracted by sight, but in my most recent erotica fantasy romance, the hero and heroine are instead drawn to each other by scent, hence the title, *Scent of Magic*.

Whatever your choice for the stages of arousal, be aware it is a process and that mental sex always comes before physical sex. Sexual tension in any story is a result of the mounting awareness and increasing curiosity between the hero and the heroine. All the senses must be engaged and explored. Sight and taste and smell must all play their part in the arousal of love. For instance, in *Morevi*:

> *The sensation of her weight against him, the strange feel of her arms around his waist, made his breath catch in his throat and his heart knock against his ribs. A woman like any other? Rafe smiled, enjoying the scent of her perfume. No, never, not you, my Queen. Her veils fluttered against his hand as he touched her hair lightly. Soft, silken.*

So far, we've set the scene, we've engaged all the senses, and we've deepened the intimacy. Now it's time for some action. As a writer you should be aware that the days when you can excite the reader by describing a simple sex act are long gone. Erotica writers have a term for what would be considered normal sex in most circles—a man and a woman in a bed in the missionary position. They call it "vanilla sex." Nowadays, vanilla is dull. You need to spice it up!

One way to turn sex from vanilla to spicy is by setting it in an exotic location. Forget a bed. Try the bathtub, the shower, the beach by the ocean, under a waterfall, or—why not?—even on the back of a dragon in flight. Let your imagination be the limit. Add unusual attire, sexy lotions, and exotic, perhaps even magical, sex toys. It all adds to the sizzle.

Red-hot emotional intensity is the final ingredient needed to set your pages on fire. The emotions that surround sex strike at our deepest needs and desires. If you can evoke those emotions, you will hold your reader enthralled. What makes a sex scene exciting is not the actual physical actions of the characters, but their emotional interaction, which reaches its strongest, most revealing peak during the openness and intimacy of the sex act.

Your readers want that emotional experience. They want to vicariously share the feelings going on inside your characters. They want to soar on the wings of love and desire, to writhe in the consuming fires of hatred, or to tremble with hope, to taste all the myriad of emotions that propel us into someone's arms. Those emotions are what are driving your story forward, and the reason for being in this bedroom should be because the sex scene will illuminate them.

Keep repeating this magical mantra to yourself: emotion, emotion, emotion. How do you create emotion in a sex scene? Emotion comes from tension and conflict. When your hero and heroine go to bed together, something needs to be at stake. Make the sexual act a magical catalyst that will change everything and your reader will be glued to the page.

The final key ingredient of great sex is conversation. When you're writing about the love relationship between two people, dialogue becomes a key way to portray their characters. People talk in bed and what they say is usually quite revealing. Dialogue during sex can be seductive, tender, touching and even downright funny.

## THINGS TO AVOID DURING SEX

We've all seen the sex scene. The hero finishes, lights a cigarette and asks: "Was it good for you, too?" That phrase has become so much a cliché that's it's almost a joke. Here are some other clichés to avoid when writing about sex.

**PURPLE PROSE.** Call it a cliché, or call it just plain bad writing, but purple prose should be avoided. What is purple prose? It's overblown language to describe things for which there are perfectly good words. Clichés like "the rod of his desire" or "the moistened petals of her sweet passion" are dangerous to use unless you want the reader to start laughing at your scene.

What words should you use? To some extent that will depend on your personal taste and the guidelines of the market you are targeting. Some writers use good old everyday terms for various body parts. Fantasy writers sometimes get away with inventing a term. It's also acceptable, and perhaps even preferable to a lot of readers, to simply say something like: "Melting into his arms, she grasped him." The reader is more than capable of figuring out where she grasped him.

**GOING TOO FAR.** How far you go in describing certain sexual possibilities will depend on your characters and their interactions, but you should be aware that readers do react strongly to some scenarios. Unless the story absolutely demands it, think long and hard before putting in any excessive violence. As for rape, once a staple of the romance novel, this act is abhorred in real life, and writers now avoid it in the pages of a book as well. There may be a reason for an exception in your story, but remember, the reader will need to be convinced of that reason.

**MORE POLITICAL CORRECTNESS.** The realities of life do have a way of intruding, even into fantasies. Sex can transmit disease, and sex can result in babies. Well, maybe not on your fantasy world ...but these are issues you should at least think about. People have become more aware of their responsibility to society, and they like their characters to be aware too.

**HEAD HOPPING.** Head hopping is moving from one character's viewpoint to another's. Writers differ on how much head hopping is too much. As this is being written, the current style favors one deep point of view in a book. In romance novels, generally, there are two points of view, the hero's and the heroine's. But some writers still use multiple viewpoints. Regardless of your preference, the bedroom is not the place to the switching back and forth. When you come to the love scene, you want intensity and intimacy, and that means picking one point of view and staying there.

**THE PHYSICALLY IMPOSSIBLE.** All right, maybe it is a fantasy, but some things just plain aren't possible. This is where you need to do a little research (or have a really good imagination). Can two bodies actually do this? Remember, your readers will be picturing it, and you do not want them to stop and say, "Wait a minute..."

## ONE OTHER PROBLEM

There's one other problem you might encounter when you start to write your sex scene: You might suddenly picture your mother reading this steamy, edgy interlude of yours.

Seriously, the thought of what your mother will think, what the neighbors will think or—horrors—what close friends will think has probably stopped more erotic passages from being written than anything else. It's also the reason that many writers choose to write their more erotic novels under a pseudonym. Writers know that a publisher will make every effort keep their identity secret if that is their wish, but these things do have a way of slipping out over time.

Besides your worries about what others might think, there is one other valid reason for considering a pseudonym if you plan to write fantasy romance or erotica. Many writers pick a pseudonym as a way of keeping their fantasy romance or erotica distinct from their more traditional works. They may not even try to hide who they are or that this is a pen name. You've probably seen something like "famous writer" writing as "not so famous writer" on the cover of a book. The pen name, in this case, serves as a device to let the reader know what they are getting when they buy this particular book. A reader might love your traditional fantasies but balk at something a little edgier. The pen name is a way to warn him or her away from that particular book.

## DON'T TAKE MY WORD FOR IT:
## CONVERSATIONS WITH THREE AUTHORS
## OF FANTASY AND ROMANCE

By now, the diversity of the expanding fantasy genre should be obvious. To explore this diversity further, I contacted three very different authors who agreed to share their perspectives on combining fantasy, romance and sex.

### ANGELA KNIGHT

Angela Knight describes herself as a romance novelist at heart, but her published books include fantasy and SF themes. She is a good example of a writer who has achieved success with incorporating the elements of many genres into her work.

**JB**: *What is your history in writing fantasy and romance?*

**AK:** *In 1996, I saw a flyer for Red Sage, a small press publisher who publishes a romance/erotica anthology called* Secrets. *I ended up submitting four stories to Red Sage over the next several years. Cindy Hwang at Berkley started reading* Secrets, *and liked my work. So she e-mailed me and asked if I'd like to write for Berkley. Well, the answer to that is self-evident!*

**JB:** *Why do you think there is a trend to include more sex in fantasy and SF?*

**AK:** *There does seem to be more erotic stuff in SF and fantasy, possibly because the SF audience is growing. It's no longer just the stereotypical thirteen-year-old male audience who think girls are icky.*

**JB:** *Given the growing popularity of this combination, what advice would you offer for those considering straddling genres themselves?*

**AK:** *The focus of the story is always on the romance, because that's how the publishers want it. And that's how I want it. For me, sex and romance are the core of whatever story I do.*

**JB:** *Who are some authors you recommend when it comes to writing romance and sex into science fiction, fantasy, and horror?*

**AK:** *Laurell K. Hamilton. Sherrilyn Kenyon is doing some cool stuff. I also really like Tanya Huff, Jim Butcher and particularly Wen Spencer, who wrote the most kickass SF novel I have ever read,* Alien Taste. *Reading that thing, I kept flipping the pages saying, 'Where is she going with this?' There's a series of those books now. And I like Charlaine Harris too:* Living Dead in Dallas *and* Club Dead. *Good stuff.*

## JACQUELINE CAREY

Carey is the author of the acclaimed *Kushiel* series: *Kushiel's Dart, Kushiel's Chosen* and *Kushiel's Avatar.* Her trilogy combines complex historic fantasy, elegant writing and lush sensuality.

**JB:** *How did you get started writing fantasy and how difficult was it to get your first book published?*

**JC:** *I started writing a fantasy novel when I was sixteen years old and bored in a high school class. The novel spanned several generations, and was quite thoroughly awful, but I got hooked. After college, I began writing in earnest. I actually have a couple of unpublished novels I wrote prior to* Kushiel's Dart. *It took ten years to hone my craft and develop my creative voice. It's rewarding, but it's not easy!*

**JB:** *Your Terre d'Ange trilogy is groundbreaking in incorporating such lush sensuality into a fantasy story. To what do you attribute the popularity of this series?*

**JC:** *What I hear most from readers is that they love the books because they're the whole package: epic plots, intrigue, adventure, sex, romance, faith. There's a lot of fantasy that contains several of those elements, but not all of them. The sexual theme is definitely a significant component of their success. A lot of readers who came into the genre in their early teens have grown up and are looking for work that reflects a more adult sensibility, one that incorporates sex as an integral part of the human experience. And my heroine, Phèdre, is a female character who very much owns her own sexuality, which is still relatively uncommon in the genre.*

**JB:** *What do you see as the advantages of writing fantasy or SF that includes frank sexuality?*

**JC:** *I'd advocate in favor of artistic reasons. Incorporating frank sexuality can be incredibly powerful and rewarding, making your characters and their experience richer, deeper and more* resonant. It's very hard to write for the market and try to take advantage of a trend, because it's always shifting and impossible to time. And if your heart (or other parts) isn't in it, it's going to show.

**JB:** What are some of the disadvantages of including frank sexuality in your work? Do you feel it limited your acceptance, labeled you or led to any adverse reaction?

**JC:** Adverse reactions have been limited, for which I'm grateful. In commercial terms, the main disadvantage is that including graphic sexual content means sacrificing marketing to young adult readers, many of whom are avid fantasy fans. I always try to make it clear that the books are R-rated. I might have read them at fourteen, but I'm not going to tell anyone else to!

**JB:** Do you see the inclusion of sex in fantasy as a growing trend or something that will continue to be rare?

**JC:** As of this writing, it's definitely a growing trend. Paranormal romance is booming! So while I don't recommend writing for the market, unless it's what you want to write anyway, I don't see it going away any time soon.

**JB:** Who else do you see as a trendsetter in this field of sex and fantasy?

**JC:** There are seminal works in the history of the genre, like Samuel Delaney's Dhalgren and Michael Moorcock's Gloriana. The rape scene in Stephen Donaldson's Lord Foul's Bane was shocking at the time, both for its content and the nature of his anti-hero protagonist. In more current trends, George R. R. Martin's epic fantasy series incorporates a frank sexual element. Guy Gavriel Kay's work isn't as overtly sexual, but it's beautifully romantic. In science fiction, Catherine Asaro comes to mind, and Laurell K. Hamilton's horror/paranormal romance books have a strong erotic component.

**JB:** Any final advice about writing sex scenes?

**JC:** Writing effective sex scenes is about more than a working knowledge of the plumbing, so to speak. It's about the emotional and psychological state of your characters. That's where the real impact lies, and it's important to keep sight of that fact.

## CATHERINE ASARO

Catherine Asaro is a Nebula-award winning SF author and the creator of The Skolian Empire. She was chosen as one of the authors who launched the new Luna line with her fantasy novel *Charmed*

*Sphere.* This delightful tale of the magical land of Aronsdale features not one, but two romances.

**JB:** *Traditionally, fantasy (or SF for that matter) has not emphasized romance or sex, but that seems to be changing with a new generation of authors. What do you see as the trend in this area at present?*

**CA:** *The fields of science fiction and fantasy have been diversifying a great deal, and I expect that will continue. Magazine and book publishers are more willing now than in the past to publish fiction that includes intimate scenes. Love and intimacy, both emotional and physical, are fundamental to what makes us human, so I'm not surprised to see more development of those themes in the genres of science fiction and fantasy. Science fiction isn't about science and technology so much as how they affect people. The same goes for fantasy; it is about how the magic and mythology affect people more than the magic itself.*

**JB:** *SF has rules, fantasy has rules, and romance is a genre all to itself with its own rules. What advice can you give to an aspiring writer about combining them into one book and what pitfalls should they avoid?*

**CA:** *I would suggest that writers who want to combine two genres (SF and romance or fantasy and romance) read widely in both.*

*For romance writers who would like to do romantic SF or fantasy with an SF/F house, books I would suggest include the following (but certainly aren't limited to just these):* Forgiveness Day *by Ursula Le Guin,* Archangel *by Sharon Shinn,* Cordelia's Honor *by Lois McMaster Bujold,* Knight Errant *by R. Garcia Robertson,* Jaran *by Kate Elliott, and* The Sun and the Moon *by Vonda McIntyre. Of my books,* Skyfall *is one of my better SF romances.* The Quantum Rose *is also good.*

*Mercedes Lackey and Ann McCaffrey are also two excellent authors to read. Among the books I would suggest for science fiction and fantasy writers who would like to write futuristics or fantasy romance for a romance house:* Body Electric *by Susan Squires,* The Bride Finder *by Susan Carroll, Susan Grant's* Star King *series,* Heartmate *by Robin Owens, and* This is All I Ask *by Lynn Kurland.*

*The above is by no means an exhaustive list of books. I will surely think of another ten excellent examples as soon as I send this to you.*

*Pitfalls to avoid: For SF and fantasy writers seeking to cross over to romance—the whole point of romance is how the lovers*

*work out their difficulties and achieve a successful relationship.
Leaving out that ending would be like writing a mystery and
leaving out the solution to the mystery. To reach the romance
audience, the story must have a happy ending.*

*For romance author seeking to cross over the SF and Fantasy—
no purple prose. It is the kiss of death in SF and fantasy. Build
your world and culture with care. If the world is exactly like
Earth in terms of gravity, atmosphere, and so on, have a good
reason (e.g., it was terraformed for human settlement). If you
have a galactic civilization of humans, it should have a believable
history. SF and fantasy don't usually have detailed sex scenes
unless the intimacy itself is crucial to the development of the
science fiction or fantasy themes of the book. However, it is no
longer necessary to "turn off the light," either.*

**JB:** *How would you describe the combination of romance
and fantasy/sf in your work?*

**CA:** *The Charmed Sphere, my first book from Luna, has a
strong romantic plotline. It isn't pure romance; the story includes
other plotlines as well. My novella Moonglow in the anthology
Charmed Destinies is primarily a romance.*

*The amount of romance in my SF books varies a great deal.
The most romantic are probably Skyfall, The Quantum Rose,
Primary Inversion, and Catch the Lightning.*

*For me, romance adds depth to a story and the development
of characters. I love both writing and reading the genre.*

My thanks to Knight, Carey and Asaro for sharing their experiences
for *The Fantasy Writer's Companion.* And now...

### RESPECTING YOURSELF IN THE MORNING

Your sex scene should serve as the doorway to a new country. We
acknowledge this when we speak of sex in marriage as a commitment.
Like books, relationships have an arc and a changing point, and
the first sexual encounter between two people is always a crucial
changing point. For some relationships, it spells the end. The goal
was to achieve possession of the other person and it's now been
reached. The relationship may continue for a while for pure pleasure,
but it's basically over. But in most cases, the first sexual encounter
is a doorway into a deeper union. In the marriage ceremony, we
hear that the two have become one, and the same is true in a sexual
encounter. Insofar as this may signal the merging of two goals into
one—or conversely may bring to light how impossible it is for these

two people to become one—this encounter can serve as a crucial dramatic turning point of your story.

The door is open…and the bedroom awaits. Fantasy has grown up and joined the adult world.  If you have a desire to combine fantasy and romance, your choices range from traditional fantasy to the new genres of fantasy romance and paranormal. Chose your favorite brand of fantasy, add some romance, heat to a comfortable temperature and enjoy!

## ONLINE RESOURCES (THAT DON'T ASK YOU TO PAY $19.95 A MONTH!)

If you want to try your hand at a fantasy that is outside the traditional bounds, these are some places to find out more about the world of fantasy romance, fantasy paranormals and fantasy eroticas:

PARANORMALS: Some paranormals emphasize the romance and some emphasize the fantasy elements of the plot. Variations are as vast as the many authors involved. I recommend a visit to this web site where you can read a number of definitions written by noted authors of the genre

http://www.writerspace.com/ParanormalRomance/Paranormalromance.htm

If you are just starting out in the field, here are several links to articles that discuss specific aspects of writing a paranormal romance

http://romance-central.com/Workshops/paranormal.shtml
http://www.hodrw.com/writingtheparanormal.htm
http://www.bibliora.com/P5_0502/html/pnr1.html

To check out some of the current writers of paranormal romance visit this list at the Paranormal Romance Readers web site:

http://paranormalromance.writerspace.com/AuthorSites.htm

This same site also reviews paranormal books. You can find the home page of the site at this URL: http://www.writerspace.com/ParanormalRomance/

The Romance Writers of America have a chapter devoted to futurist, fantasy and paranormal. Their site is at http://www.romance-ffp. com/. The mission of this chapter is to promote excellence in romantic, futuristic, fantasy, time travel and paranormal fiction, to help writers become published in the genre, to provide current information and continuing support to the writers in the romantic, futuristic, fantasy, time travel and paranormal industry.

**FANTASY ROMANCE:** Both Luna and Tor have launched new lines that combine fantasy and romance. In addition Dorchester Publishing has a line of futuristics, time-travels and paranormals.

Luna's Web source: http://www.hotkey.net.au/~melinda1/Luna. htm

Tor's Paranormal romance Web source: http://www.tor.com/ paranormalromance.html

Dorchester's Web source: http://www.dorchesterpub.com/ guidelines_01.htm

**FANTASY AND EROTICA:** This is currently a hot market in the eBook world. Some of the noted publishers of fantasy erotica:

Ellora's Cave: http://www.ellorascave.com/
Ellora's Cave is actively seeking paranormal and fantasy romances. Check out their guidelines for sexual content.

Extasy Books: http://www.extasybooks.com
Extasy actively seeks fantasies and paranormals. They look for solid plots, well-developed settings and characters that are fully three-dimensional.

Liquid Silver Books: http://www.liquidsilverbooks.com/
They are looking for erotica paranormals in full-length novels of 45,000 + words and 25,000-45,000 in novella length.

PEACE THRU
SUPERIOR FIRE POWER

# Princes, Politicians and The People's Voice:
## GOVERNMENT AND SOCIAL STRUCTURE FOR FANTASY REALMS

### BY ERIK AMUNDSEN

Karsh the Innkeeper, as we come to know him in Peter S. Beagle's *The Innkeeper's Song*, is angry. He finds himself a common man caught up in the ebb and flow of forces and disasters beyond his control, and he doesn't like it. Between arrogant, possibly violent and possibly insane guests, the assassins sent to kill those guests, the near death and transfiguration of a wizard into a demon, and the loss of his pigeons, he's had a rough time of things. One day, he promises himself, he's going to walk up to the Black Castle and ask the king, or the queen, or the elected council, or the military junta, or whoever is in charge why his life absolutely must be so difficult. He has no idea who is in charge, and doesn't really care, he just wants them to hear what he has to say.

## ASKING THE BIG QUESTION:
### FIRST STEPS IN CREATING GOVERNMENT

If *"What's for dinner?"* is the first great question humans face, the second is *"Who's in charge here?"* The need for hierarchy, a place for everyone and everyone in their place, is far more pervasive than most folks would like to admit. Even though Karsh has no earthly idea who it is that runs his country, he believes that he lives in a country and there is *someone* running the show. People need someone above them and someone below them in order to function. Rule and government are key elements of any setting. Even in small, informal groups, you will see an individual name him or herself as "leader." With larger alliances, it's necessary to have a chain of command in order to get things done. The larger the group, the more complex and explicit that chain of command needs to be. Whether the government is the distant conjecture of an irate innkeeper or the focus of wars and assassination and shifting alliance, such as you'll find in George R. R. Martin's *Ice and Fire* series, it is a sure indicator of the complexity, sophistication, values and culture of a place and time. How the ruler, the law and the people interact is a necessary element of the creation of a culture and understanding how they interact brings a deeper note to your world and your writing.

The government of your fantasy work will largely be back-story, and most writers have issues with how much of it to include as their heroes go off on their heroic business. Robert Jordan, in the *Wheel of Time* series, gives you the whole history, with all the practices and intricacies of his governments, in excruciating detail. If you have multiple thick volumes to fill and a patient reader base, feel free. If not, you'll want to restrain your background, however clever or well-reasoned. Mark Helprin, in the book *A City in Winter*, gives us the Usurper, who stole the kingdom from the rightful king and queen, has literally unlimited soldiers, and rides around the city at night to kill anyone he finds in the street. We don't know how he runs the country, how he obtained the throne (though you assume it was his soldiers), or even how he feeds those unlimited supply of troops. He's simply a bad man, his government is simply a bad government, and it only serves to provide an almost insurmountable trial for the girl who will grow to win back the land and become queen. If the story you wish to tell is iconic and doesn't spend a lot of time contemplating the whys and wherefores of the actions, you can get away with a marginally developed government. Once you start explaining why the things in the land are the way they are, you'll want to have more development and thought on your government.

Real governments are incredibly complex; they depend on millions of variables and often hundreds or thousands of years of history, tradition and precedent. If the government in your story is young, it may not be fully settled and formed. Divisions of power may not be completely hashed out, lines of communication not fully established and alliances untested. In Martin's *Game of Thrones*, the new dynasty brought with it an uncertainty as to who each of the great families could trust; they knew who their enemies were, but not their friends. If the government is in its prime, with many years and success behind it, there is bound to be intrigue and maneuvers as the major players in that government vie for a greater portion of that success. In the Arthurian legends, Morgan LeFay and Mordred scheme to take the glory of the kingdom that redeemed the land and recovered the Grail. If the government is old, many of its driving forces may have lost all practical meaning and all but faded from memory; they may not, however, have lost any of their power. Life in Mervyn Peake's *Gormenghast* was controlled by a complex set of rituals and precedents whose significance had been lost under the dust of centuries, but held the Groans and their vassals firmly in its grasp. Why would a writer, you ask, spend time on creating something so complex and labor intensive as a living government, when you can let it do its thing while the heroes do theirs? It's easy enough to let the government be something that only serves to give venue to innkeepers' complaints, or the wise old king to hand out quests to the earnest young knight (Sir Gawain and the Green Knight, anyone?) but most fantasy stories center on a climax that is just as much historical as it is dramatic. Heroic fantasy, in particular, draws much of its tension and conflict from how the heroes and villains change their world. Robert E. Howard's Conan goes from being the insignificant enslaved sole survivor of his race to a fearsome, mighty king. Your story will likely change its world, and one of the easiest ways to gauge and illustrate these changes is in the government; the old king is assassinated, the false king deposed, the realm invaded by hordes from the north. All the dominoes you set up are going to come tumbling down. It's the literary equivalent of building a huge, beautiful sand castle and kicking it over as you leave the beach; the satisfaction of watching it all go down in flames is worth the setup. If you've done your job, the reader gets to share in that joy.

## NOT A STUFFED TIGER:
### HOBBES, LOCKE, ROUSSEAU, HUMAN NATURE AND A "NASTY, BRUTISH AND SHORT" LOOK AT THE SOCIAL CONTRACT

Governments are a product of their people. So before you delve into the halls of power, take a look at the hands that built them. The assumptions you make at this level about the nature of your people are going to form the foundation for the ale hall, castle, palace or forum. Write down a paragraph or two on the "national character" of your people. The people Tolkien's Rohan are proud and independent, mobile and loosely organized, while those of Gondor are more centralized, dutiful and metropolitan. When dealing with more than one culture, this becomes more important; in our world, for instance, Russians and Americans are quite different, but Canadians and Americans are fairly similar. Understanding the differences between cultures mean a lot to how they and their governments interact. You may also want to jot down some of your assumptions about human nature for reference. In this case, human nature refers just as easily to any speaking creature you throw into the story. Tolkien didn't call elves, dwarves, men and hobbits the "kindred races" for no reason; while they were demonstrably quite different, they were enough like one another to live together and band together to save their world. There is, however, something to be said for approaching your humans the same way you would a new race that is unique to your writing. If you introduce them, if only to yourself, as thoroughly as you would a brand new race, you will understand them as well, care for them as much, and be able to write them as vividly and well. They won't be boring, either for you or your reader.

From the history of our world, we can drag up any number of historical and philosophical models on human nature and what it means to govern. I'm going to use three that are related, sequential, and most likely to be relevant to the vast majority of modern popular fantasy. I give you Hobbes, Locke and Rousseau.

In historical order, Hobbes goes first. Hobbes had a very dark view of humanity; to him they are selfish, murderous savages that need iron laws and swift, sure punishment to prevent them from destroying one another. Most writers have Hobbes in mind when they write their "evil minion" race or culture. Like the rat creatures in Jeff Smith's *Bone* comics, they are often animalistic in appearance to match their nature. The rat creatures provide a wonderful illustration of Hobbes's thoughts on human nature. With the general shape of large, round faces rodents, they are bestial, skittish, stupid, reflexively ambitious, servile to anything stronger than they are, and predatory toward anything weaker.

Next, we come to Locke, whose view of humanity is decidedly neutral. To Locke, humans begin as blank slates, and their environment and choices shape what they become. Human nature is neither good nor bad, save what the individual makes it. This is, in a way, the "default" setting for most races and cultures in fantasy; without making any moral assumptions about the nature of the people, it frees the writer up to create the good, the bad and the ugly as the story demands. Mark Oakley's *Thieves and Kings* series illustrates a wonderful society based on this assumption. Much of the population of Oceansend follows the wicked prince and the witch who backs him but many do not, and quietly resist the change he works on their city and nation.

Finally, we have Rousseau. Rousseau believes that people are inherently good, and that their environment and the demands made on them by society inexorably poison "civilized" people, making them selfish, suspicious and cruel. He celebrated the idea of the "noble savage," a person unconstrained by the shackles of a complex society, who lived in pastoral or bucolic simplicity. Tolkien's hobbits are an excellent example of somewhat advanced noble savages. They live close to and in harmony with nature; they are simple folk, and good-natured. They are not ambitious or cruel, or crave power, which is why a handful of them were the only ones capable of destroying the One Ring.

From Hobbes, we get the concept of the Social Contract, upon which Locke and Rousseau added their opinions and critiques. In brief, the Social Contract states that subjects consent to the dominion of the ruler, following the ruler's commands and supporting the ruler through taxes. In return, the ruler protects the subjects from foreign threats via an army, and from internal threats via laws and law enforcement. The basis of the Social Contract is really no different from a mafia protection racket: do as you are told, and the rulers will protect you from each other and outside threats, *capisce?* Hobbes believed this arrangement was both positive and necessary, as without it, humanity would spiral into cannibalistic chaos. Locke saw it as largely positive, and probably necessary, though he sought a better balance between the rights, duties and privileges of the subjects relative to their rulers. Unlike Hobbes, he believed people could handle it, and didn't think that any ruler, however cruel and awful was better than no ruler at all. Rousseau thought the Social Contract was negative and destroyed the inherent goodness of the individual; it put all the Pippins in the world into Gondor and Denethor's dubious care.

The relevance of all this to the writer is in the fact that different governments are appropriate to different models of human nature. As a writer, you're not allotted a single model, either; Tolkien uses all three and then some. The orcs, who represent the worst in human nature, are Hobbesian. They need Sauron and Saruman to keep them in line. The men and dwarves are more in tune with Locke's vision. They can be good or bad, but they are, in the end, themselves, and do as their choices and environment lead. The hobbits, though probably not what Rousseau had specifically in mind, are his noble savages. Some of them can be officious, suspicious and disapproving (like Bilbo and Frodo's relations), but they're good people, and could not be otherwise. Tolkien also employs the enlightened post-human elves, who maintain their goodness despite having a highly developed society; they chose their rulers because those rulers deserve to rule, and they do a very good job of it, thank you. Allotting the orcs the government of Gondor would lead to the whole place going up in flames in a week; allotting it to the hobbits would make them miserable and ultimately destroy them.

## SOMETHING SHORT ABOUT RACE

Most nations are composed of more than one culture or race. Which one started the nation, how the others came to be part of it, which one(s) have the most power and how they see one another are all questions that need to be answered. Some cultures are together for such a long time that their differences are thought of as local customs and eccentricities, nothing more. In most nations, the largest group in terms of population holds the power of the majority. This is not always the case, and it can just as easily be a minority population that controls the nation. Martin's Valerians were an ethnic minority, originally of three, that ended up ruling the land (the fact that they had dragons probably had a lot to do with it...). The latter case is going to be a lot less representational, if representational at all, than the former. Also, if there is hereditary nobility, they are likely to over time view themselves as a race apart from their subjects.

Compatibility of two cultures within a single nation can be seen through language, physical appearance and cultural practices. *Language* is a huge barrier between two cultures that do not share it, and stands as the most important point of distinction. Most nations have an official language. Those who do not speak it are marginalized from most of the functions of government and the national society. After language comes *physical appearance,* which is important enough in our world to form the basis for our conception of race. Only in very cosmopolitan societies do people of radically different appearances interact widely among one another. Finally, various *cultural practices* face the threat of being poorly understood by a nation's majority. Any of these can be basis for discrimination and racism, prime sources of conflict.

Tolkein and his thousand imitators give us the wonders of the interactions between elves and dwarves. Both races are essentially good. Both races want essentially the same things: mostly to be left alone to do their respective things. Both races will show up on the same side of the field on the day of doom when the dark whatever threatens to cast his shadow over the whole land. Neither race can abide the other's presence for more than ten minutes without necessitating a third party pulling them apart.

Add to this the fact that most fantasy settings feature members of different species and the thorny issues that bubble to the surface include genetic compatibility (whether or not members of the two different "races" can have children), relative supernatural aptitude and the overall attitude concerning the blending of a race or species.

A racist society that views interracial union with terror and disgust may find a compatible race just as alien, and half-breeds abominations because they are impure. The recent film *Underworld* based its entire premise on the Vampire's reaction to the possibility of a cross between their kind and the Lycans. Relative supernatural aptitude can get to be a sticking point as well, especially if those who have the greatest supernatural power do not also have the temporal power. Supernatural abilities are, by nature, poorly understood and feared by most people. That fear of the unknown leads to lynch mobs, riots and repressive legislation. J.K. Rowling points to that interaction as a reason for the separation of her wizarding society (who, especially if they are nasty folks like the Malfoys, view themselves as a separate species) from the Muggles.

When fitting the people to a government ask yourself what kind of government would your people make. If you already have the government and not the people, ask yourself what kind of people would make this government. You'll want to determine the nature of the Social Contract in your story's government: i.e., what the roles and rights of each side happen to be. Then you need to determine how the government and the subjects each discharge their responsibilities and take their privileges. Decide if you're going to believe it, for the story, and remember that there are also differences. Countless would-be tyrants only learn that while common folk are often regarded as cattle or sheep, they are not always easy to herd. This usually comes to them as their palaces burn down around their ears. People have to want to be herded before you can get them in order. When writing up your Social Contract, remember that it has to be one that the people, at one time or another, agree to sign.

Most common folks never realize this. The rules that define and motivate their society may be centuries old by the time they're born, but they all boil down to the Social Contract. It's a pretty simple contract for simple governments, but in more complex societies, you may see more responsibilities and privileges allotted to each side. For example, the subjects may gain representation in exchange for their participation in the government, perhaps through voting or mandatory military service.

## TELL ME ABOUT THE RABBITS:
### SOCIETY BUILDING FOR LAGOMORPHS

I've spent a little time telling you why humans are not like other animals, but if you want a good example of group dynamics in action, the founding of a community and communities in conflict, the best place to look is in a rabbit warren. Richard Bach's *Watership Down* shows the founding of a new community and the formulation of its rules, jobs and functions. The ways that different individuals have different forms of authority. It's also a strong example of government based on Locke. The rabbits in *Watership Down* survive through cooperation that creates the government of the warren rather than the government creating the cooperation. Among the rabbits, you see the early stages of society building, how roles are apportioned, and how leadership is, contrary to what Hobbes would have us believe, divided among the rabbits. Bigwig is the strongest rabbit, physically, but he couldn't create a society with his strength. Hazel is a charismatic leader, but his charisma wouldn't have swayed many other rabbits if Bigwig hadn't lent his strength to it. Neither of them would have left their old lives if not for Fiver's visions and intellect; then again, for all his brains, Fiver was not strong or charismatic enough to do the work on his own. Furthermore, Bach pays attention to how each rabbit contributes something to the warren, without which none of them would survive. The attention to detail he shows and the strength of his logic is particularly successful in the fact that, a short way into the story, you forget you're reading about rabbits.

While human societies never seem to work even as smoothly as the rabbits' (and it's not *that* smooth), there are elements of that cooperation and generosity. Sometimes, we're not as good as the rabbits or as bad as orcs. Sometimes we're better than the rabbits and sometimes we're worse than orcs. This is what makes us interesting, and it's that interesting edge that we as writers should be exploiting. Hobbes, Locke and Rousseau provide a spectrum of different models for interaction. When writing up your government, feel free to mix and match; life is more complex than philosophy, and, in an imaginary world, likely with magic and legendary creatures, you need to keep as much of that sense of life as you can in order for the reader to keep their disbelief suspended.

Much like the rabbits, human societies tend to start as *tribes*, with a small number of people and a fairly simple idea of government. It is far easier to run a group of two dozen families based on tradition, mutual agreement and occasional meetings among the old folk than it is to run a group of two hundred. Tribes are like families and their politics are similar. Tribes are often mobile, which often suits the heroic quest motif in fantasy. Writing your society as a tribe is useful when you want to show just how much your hero is like his or her people. Despite being the last of the Cimmerians, Conan's exploits, especially in his younger days, show the culture and the tribe living through him. If your story is mobile, has a lot of important characters that work and live together, and involve any sort of beginning of something larger, you might want to write with tribes. Tribes aren't done nearly so much as kingdoms. In a crowded fantasy market, there are practical advantages to writing them and doing it well.

As a society grows in population, it's going to need more resources. There are going to be more people who do not know or feel attached to other members of their society. There will also, undoubtedly, be more "bad apples," be they thieves, bandits or rabble-rousers. At some point, society will need warriors in order to secure new resources (often by taking them from other societies), protect their growing tribes, and enforce tradition. As populations grow, the ability for the elders to sit in solemn judgment over every dispute or sin is going to decrease as there will be too many grievances to hear. The society will need to develop a more impersonal and explicit form of government in order to continue. This is also the point in the society's development where you are going to have a separate warrior class.

Since the Social Contract entails at least two different responsibilities for government, protection from outside threats and protection from inside threats, governments adopt a number of functions. You'll need to jot down how they would go about both and what they need in order to do it. These functions may be considered separate entities (as in most modern Western Governments; Canada or the U.S.) or not, as needed. The larger and more complex the society, the more likely it is that these functions will develop into separate entities. Protection from external threats requires some form of military. In the earliest complex societies, the government and the military were one and the same. Completely peaceful or pacifistic societies never develop much complexity that has precedent in our world, which makes it both open territory for your imagination and very difficult for the reader to grasp. Militaries need soldiers, supplies and a reliable apparatus of gaining both. A simpler society, like that of the rabbits, may stop there, leaving the laws and public welfare over to local leaders, as long as the ruler has enough warriors on the field and enough revenue to feed, clothe and equip them. Protection from internal threats, most likely, falls to the same group of warriors, or there may be a specific constabulary that grows out of the warrior class for policing.

The individual settlements at this point in a society's development may still be tribal in nature. You can have a nation of tribes, an affiliation of warlords, or a feudal society with ring-giving lords and their hired spears. These societies are the simplest that involve many different localities. Probably the most well-known example from historical literature is the world of *Beowulf*; and the most well-known from modern fantasy is Tolkien's Rohan from *The Lord of the Rings*. In both cases, the settlements are fairly small, the government is primarily local, though both Hrothgar and Theoden have the ability to call on allied lords to lend soldiers for their battles, and control larger areas than they could on their own.  The advantage of writing this sort of society and government is that, like a tribe, it is still pretty flexible and individualistic, but is more complex and sophisticated than a tribe. Sophistication breeds intrigue, and nations such as this provide a lot of latitude for how much intrigue you'd like to put in to the nation. Crichton's *Eaters of the Dead* provides a taste of what can be done in this direction with the conflict between the thirteen warriors dispatched to fight the eaters of the dead, and the faction headed by the son of the lord they're aiding.

At some point, a feudal system is going to become inefficient. Once there are too many local lords for a ruler to know them all, the ruler is going to want to make things still more formal and explicit. Codes of law are created and established, some level of bureaucracy develops to accommodate the collection of revenue, the enforcement of laws and the movements of the military. Power becomes more central, whether focused on a monarch, an elected ruler or a council. An elite class develops from (usually) the landowning and military classes. In the Arthurian cycles, you can see the difference between Arthur's knights and his father's. Uther Pendragon was a conqueror and focused on having a military class that could wade in an awful lot of gore. Arthur, of course, had knights like that, such as Lancelot and Percival, but he also had Gawain and Galahad who were (when gore-wading wasn't in the offing) also courteous, virtuous and noble. Even Arthur's hardcore gore-waders had some level of gentility in them that Uther's men largely lacked. The reason was that Arthur needed his loyal knights to represent him and his kingdom (both the might and the virtue) when they went to deal with the lords and commoners in the land. Here is where the iron fist puts on the velvet glove. The centralized monarchy is the staple of both the European Middle Ages and in commoditized fantasy. As it develops, the elites think of themselves more and more a breed apart from their people, interesting codes of conduct develop, and intrigue starts playing a major part in the halls of government. Martin's *Ice and Fire* series hinges on such complexities. Also, as authority becomes centralized, laws become centralized as well, and legal codes and practices are generally developed. In some cases, separate judicial and legislative entities may appear in the government. Tradesmen may begin to band together as well, into associations or guilds. These guilds are not yet a direct part of the government, but may, through judicious application of the golden rule, become so in the years ahead. The centralized kingdom is the most common form of government you're likely to find in fantasy, be it the fairy tale kingdom, the vast conquering empire, the land of the evil dark lord or Tolkien's Gondor.

The joys of writing this sort of government are summed up in knights and intrigue. A ruler can no longer rule this nation through force and oaths alone; he or she's got to have other ways of holding the country together. This is where you come in. Decide what the heretofore strengths and weaknesses of the nation have been. The ruler will need to use the strengths to shore up the weaknesses. Arthur's Britain was composed of dozens of fractious, bickering tribes that seemed to have little unity or sense of purpose, but Arthur had excellent fighters at his command. The solution? Make these knights a shining example of what a Briton is supposed to be, make them something for all the bickering tribes to want to emulate. If you have been following, creating your people based on their natures and character, tied your government to a consistent logic, and addressed the nation's strengths and weaknesses, you should have no problem coming up with an artful and creative solution that allows the country to unite under your ruler.

## Face the Nation: Character and Direction

The people create the government but the government, once created, is a lot like Frankenstein's monster without the brain. It needs a personality and a guiding force in order to truly live. This part of creating the government is familiar to most writers since at this point you are creating a character. Your government, as you may have gathered, is a character in itself, though it doesn't usually have a very strong character of its own. It's important, at this stage, to concoct the character of the ruler. The ruler is not necessarily the king or queen or chieftain or president. The ruler is the person who actually runs the country. It may be a single person, a group or several factions fighting over control. Who or whatever actually rules the country provides a major portion of the nation's character. Arthur's Camelot goes through its birth, growth, glory, decline and death right along with its king. Roland the Good, in Stephen King's *Eyes of the Dragon*, is a good man, but a simple one, more like his subjects than a king ought to be, and not much of a match for the machinations and plans of his magician, Flagg. Roland's people liked him, but there was not a lot of respect; and as Flagg's plans bore fruit, they grew to resent the dark, repressive direction the country was taking. Lackey's King Randale of Valdemar, likewise, is a good man, and stronger and wiser than Roland, but does not always understand the stakes in his decisions, and, as such, the forces of evil spread in his kingdom, killing off all the Herald-Mages before they're driven out. Denethor as Steward of Gondor is a good ruler, but the job of ruling Gondor at the end of the third age is too much for him, and he drives himself mad trying to rule a country that only the rightful king can. Creating the ruler is no different than creating any other character with the single exception that the ruler should be a fairly well-developed character, regardless of how many lines of text he or she gets. The process gets more difficult when you apply the character to the government. This requires a little thought exercise. Imagine what the ruler's choices and concerns would have been to this point and then how the culture and people would react. What would they think about the ruler's decision? What does the ruler need to get his or her will done? How might these decisions change the government, culture and land?

You'll need to know the ruler well, since their character is going to be reflected in the character of the nation: a good example is C. S. Lewis' Narnia under the White Witch, where it is always winter, but never Christmas. In Beagle's *The Last Unicorn*, the land King Haggard rules is said to have been green and good up to the moment he touched it, tainting it with his joyless cruelty and the power of his servant, the red bull. Nations tend to get the government they want and deserve, and as the society affects the power structures, so too do they affect the society. If a government is less organized, the people will form tribes, sticking close to their home concerns and needs. If the ruling body is brutal and repressive, the people will be suspicious of outsiders and silent out of loyalty. If the government is very complex, full of intrigue, people are likely to be well educated and ambitious, vying for positions of power. Any of them are interesting to write, just keep it consistent, and you won't lose the reader.

## A Bug's Life: Factions within a Government

Government is, like all other elements in your story, what you make of it. In recent years, fantasies that involve complicated, convoluted intrigues and power struggles have become popular and successful. They aren't, unfortunately, that easy to do, or to have justice done to them. If you want to write a tale of political intrigue and backstabbing, this is where all your background work on your government structure pays off. Following this chapter, you should have some idea of how governments are founded, who has what kind of power, how they interact, and most importantly, how your characters fit in that interaction. Now, create factions! Remember that governments cannot rely on the will of one person alone, and the more the society grows, the more opposing factions emerge and the more distinct they become from one another. This is your jar, and you get to create the bugs to drop into it, to see which one eats the other. Like insects, political factions have their different parts, and each faction believes themselves superior to others. They also want the same things: territory, resources and protection from their enemies.

The noble houses of Martin's *Ice and Fire* or Frank Herbert's *Dune* (not technically Fantasy, but worthwhile for the backstabbing) provide a lot of the inspiration for the insectile image. It's not a big stretch to imagine the Lannisters or the Harkonens as things you'd best shake out of your boots when sleeping in the desert. Beyond that, it's really important to think of each faction as a character independent of its components. In China Mieville's *The Scar*, the ridings of the Lovers or the Brucolac had their own movements, independent of their masters. Factions are living things and they grow and change on their own as they make their way through the halls of rule and justice.

FACTIONS HAVE A HEAD: the brains of the operation. In Mieville, these are the Lovers; in Martin, usually the heads of the houses; in Herbert, it's Leto Atriedes and Vladimir Harkonen. These folks are who you want to spend the most time developing. The head of the faction determines what to do with their followers, what their agenda is and how to go about getting what they wants. You should know these leaders well. You need a complex person to carry out complex machinations, plan strategically to get what they want and know exactly why they will win their ultimate goal. The heads may be open or secret, but they are the most important part of a faction. Without them, the faction dies.

THE FACTION WILL HAVE EYES AND ANTENNAE: spies, informants and moles that keep the head informed about the world and the movements of other factions in it. Herbert's Mentat masters of assassins are too tempting to not mention as examples. In Mieville's *Perdido Street Station*, the antennae are all over New Corbuzon, waiting to be activated and made into the stingers. Moles and spies who suddenly turn on former allies and reveal true allegiances remain memorable throughout a story or series.

FACTIONS HAVE JAWS AND STINGERS: soldiers that openly engage the enemy be it in politics, rumor, assassination (character or corporeal) or the back alleys. (In the halls of government, a cunning, charismatic lawyer is every bit as dangerous as a skilled duelist.) These agents tend to keep their weapons hidden until they mean to use them, but remember—sometimes just showing the weapon is use enough. The faction's muscle tends to be featured more prominently in stories as they are in the open, often being the antagonists in climactic fights or tense dramatic scenes. Some stingers are entrenched in their factions, such as (again with the Herbert) Fayde Ruatha. Some, like Ellen Kushner's Richard St. Vier, owe no particular allegiance; they just end up being involved from the outside. Stingers are defined by reputations, quirks and list of enemies destroyed.

**FACTIONS HAVE LEGS AND WINGS THAT GET THEM FROM PLACE TO PLACE, MOUTHS THAT LET THEM FEED AND HARD SHELLS THAT PROTECT THEM FROM HARM.** These people in the faction are usually not so important or interesting, but you should have some idea of where and how many they are, if not who. They are often the same sorts as those who make up the stingers and jaws, but where the stinger is an assassin, the shell is the bodyguard. Where the jaws are a noble with poison on his lips and a wile in his heart, the shell is another noble set to thwart that wile.

**FACTIONS ALSO HAVE COLORS, SOUNDS AND MARKINGS** that show the world what they want to see. Maybe they have rumor mongers who give them warning coloration by planting tales of a secret army the faction does not have (yet), or maybe it's a bard who makes sweet chirping noises or a pretty light to attract prey and mates. Perhaps the faction, like a viceroy butterfly, tries to resemble another faction, one that has a history and renown. It is in this area that the factions become most distinct; and while it isn't absolutely necessary to dwell on this aspect of the faction, it's a rewarding task since it makes for far more memorable factions. Each faction will have its own set of behaviors, some offensive and some defensive. Some will feed off the legitimate proceeds of their labor. Others will feed off other factions, while some will scavenge the remains of those fallen by the wayside. Factions can camouflage themselves to appear as something entirely contrary to their agenda, or merely for seclusion. Some will spin webs of deceit and some will dig political traps. Some will stand motionless until no one remembers they are there, and then strike from surprise. Once you have your factions outlined, their objectives clear, and their behaviors anticipated, you can let them go and play within your world. Pay attention to other factors in the setting and story that will affect what they do and how successful their stratagems turn out to be. If you need a blind spot, make sure it is built in at the beginning. If divinatory magic is common in your setting, make sure that your factions use it and any countermeasures they know. The heads of the factions did not get to be where they are by being foolish or unobservant, so don't you be either.

It may help to outline the political maneuvering that takes place during the run of your story independent of the main thrust of the narrative. It will help you keep track of what everyone is doing within the context. Intrigues are framed by surprise and surprises are some of the trickiest things to pull off in writing. To paraphrase an old dramatic saying: make sure that the gun that goes off in Act Three was on the mantelpiece in Act One. Readers like surprises, but only the ones they could have guessed; and they only know what you tell them. Pulling some completely unforeseeable reversal late in the game will make it harder for the reader to trust you. That trust is essential to the suspension of disbelief that prevents the reader from putting down your story.

## Cast Your Vote: Fantasy Governments,
### When and How to Use them

You have a land and its people, you have a wicked young king, both shrewd and foolish, and you have a number of awful and insidious advisors circling his throne like vultures. You have as much knowledge on how the nation got to its current sad state, and what the hero must do to redeem it. At this point, it may seem like you've got everything you need to make your story everything it can be, but there is still more to consider. Do some of those advisors represent a large, organized religion? Do priests in that religion have supernatural powers and do they get those from a supernatural patron or from study? Is there a criminal underworld that operates in the kingdom, how much power do they have, and what do they think of the king? From the foundation you've built so far, there are a lot of directions you can go.

Now let's take a look at the different types of nations you could use in a story. This section contains a lot of elements you can use to make your story something unusual or unique, and may even remind you of some favorite fantasy works that followed these archetypes.

### The Golden Rule: Rise of the Merchants

A nation might be in place for quite some time with its landed nobility ruling out of their manor houses. In that time, the merchants and skilled tradesmen in the lower class are likely to be at work, improving the infrastructure, communication and trade lines as a consequence of making money. Their money is going to become more and more important to the nobility as the raw materials and crops that the nobles' lands produce become less and less valuable in relation to finished items. Fritz Leiber's Lankhmar setting is a great, highly mercantile society. You can also see some of the same in an earlier form in Howard's *Conan* stories. Merchants start to get nicer houses, organize in guilds and send caravans out to other lands. Suddenly, the people that the nobility thought could be safely ignored are just as well-fed, well-dressed and almost as powerful as they are. It starts to become more expensive to be noble since they now have to differentiate themselves from their moneyed but still low-class subjects. The cost of appearances will grow and possibly eclipse the income of their lands. Suddenly, the merchants become even more powerful, since only they can provide the specialized goods and services to the nobles (at high, *high* prices) who want to make sure that no one mistakes them for a merchant. You see very little of this in most fantasy; Greogry Maguire's *Confessions of an Ugly Stepsister* shows the workaday side of the Cinderella fairy tale and Titus's aunts in Peake's *Gormenghast* are memorable noblewomen gone to seed, but the rising cost of looking rich and the consequences of falling behind are still more the province of Austin than Tolkein. (That, in itself, may be reason enough for you to try your hand at it. Merchants are often interesting folk and their guildhalls can hold as much intrigue as the palace.)

The merchants begin to emerge with economic strength equal to or greater than that of the government, and from there they start exercising influence. At some point, economic power tends to split from military power. In some societies, the economic power structures may gain ascendancy and the Social Contract is modified. In exchange for obedience and resources, the economic powers provide access to goods and services. Military and law enforcement become commodities that the people purchase. When the economic powers rise, your job as chronicler of your nation and heroes is to create an economic system for the power structure to use. It sounds like an awful lot of work, and not a lot of fun. If you can do it, you've already broken from the pack in terms of the originality of your story and your setting. At some point, the power of the nobles and the middle class are likely to shift in balance to the point where society's upper crust is little more than a stumbling block for the merchants who want to run the show. The nobility might find themselves quietly put to pasture, serving as figureheads to legitimize the new regime or lining up in the city's central square to provide the executioner work and the angry townspeople entertainment. The new government replacing the old will likely be representational, with prominent businessmen pursuing agendas eventually running the show. From here begins the circus of modern governance where certain factions, hoping to claim some of the grandeur of the old nobility, struggle for ascendancy. The king may be gone; but as long as there is a kingdom, there is a throne and someone with aspirations to occupy it.

A rising middle class is good to use when you want to show a historical change in your setting. The merchants and moneymakers are going to be at the forefront of anything new or different in your setting, since that is where the money will be. Merchants are good if the setting involves a lot of travel. The hero can hire on to a caravan across the desert where intrigue can be settled by knife fights just outside the circle of the campfires. If your nobility is slowly losing their grip on the power, the middle class is the most historically accurate and expedient group to pick that power up again.

### IMPERIOUS REX: EMPIRES

The major difference between an empire and a centralized kingdom is a matter of scale. Empires are larger in population, area and diverse cultures. This is why they are so much harder to run. The advantage of an empire is that it can devour lesser countries, incorporate them and move on to the next realm. Empires do a lot of building, and serve as really good reasons why there is a giant wall, a tomb complex full of pyramids, or a set of hanging gardens. Once centralized, the country will need to consolidate and decide what its borders are. By establishing its boundaries, the country begins development of their infrastructure. Roads, water and sanitation, based on topography and established cities and shires, become priorities for the newly founded domain. As the population grows, so must the infrastructure. Many rulers are remembered fondly in history as road and bridge builders, and while it is not as exciting as wars of conquest and defense of sovereignty, infrastructure development is one of the most important parts of the development of a nation. It is worth a page or two of notes, if only for reference. All of this is absolutely key to the transformation of a single nation into a continent-spanning empire. (That, and a fight scene in a suspended aqueduct.)

Continent spanning is one of the main reasons to use an empire in your story. Empires are big and grand, and if you're hero is from a small kingdom or an independent tribe, a great source of conflict. Remember that one of the most exciting war stories in history centers on three hundred warriors from the rather small (at that time) kingdom of Sparta holding off the entire Persian Empire at Thermopolis. Empires give that extra layer of grandeur to your setting, allow you to use characters and items from far away lands, or bring your heroes to said far away lands themselves. Empires are also good if you need to pull a governmental shell game on your readers. It gives you plenty of places to hide intrigue, if you cannot introduce it right away. Empires are best regarded as really big sandcastles and that much more fun to kick in. Remember, there are practical limits to what people can govern; eventually, the empire is likely to fracture or collapse. This tends to happen within about a hundred years of someone making a famous speech about how this empire is destined to last for a thousand.

### GOD SAVE THE QUEEN:
### RELATIONSHIP BETWEEN CHURCH AND STATE

Spiritual power and influence is something that shouldn't be underestimated, even in a materialistic society where the supernatural aspects of the world have been largely debunked or incorporated into somewhat more organized systems of thought. The figure of the shaman has always been a part of tribal hierarchies, sometimes at peace with the tribe and sometimes at odds with the chieftain and warriors. Spiritual authority grows both in scope and complexity with the secular society, sometimes as a part of its authority, sometimes independent from it, and sometimes at war with it. Spiritual power structures work similarly to secular ones, more similar than spiritual leaders like to believe. There are a few important differences that stand out though. The first is the differences in the Social Contract. (Remember that contract?) Secular governments provide for the need for safety. Economic power provides goods and services. Spiritual power is far different, a little more ephemeral and based on collected faith rather than tangible materials. The Social Contract of the spiritual world is such that for your resources and obedience, the authorities provide for the safety of your spirit and protect you from the fear of whatever happens to you after you die. Katherine Kurtz and her series based on Camber of Culdi explores a lot of how spiritual power works in a material world, and, indeed, the Church has the power of excommunication (and the attending torment of eternal damnation) to hold over the head of the secular ruler. In our world, spiritual authority has not provided irrefutable, measurable proof that they actually provide what they say, but that does not seem to make them less popular or powerful. In a fantasy setting, it is quite easy to provide that proof and cement the position of your shamans and priests with supernatural powers and widespread, public, divine revelation.

Supernatural power and magic define fantasy, and those means work for you. In order to understand how the secular and spiritual power structures interact, you need to build a spiritual power structure, and do it pretty much the same way you built the secular government. One may be more powerful or more important to the story, and therefore get more development. In Lackey's *Last Herald-Mage of Valdemar* series, the religious authorities in Valdemar only really show up in a brief meeting between the king and the head of the church of the Sun God. Conversely, in her *Bardic Voices* series, the church gets a lot of the development and the secular government much less. You'll need to determine how many different spiritual powers exist in a nation, how separate each one is from the secular government, and who has more power to control the destiny of the nation.

Using organized religion as a power structure is rewarding because the powers that the church and state hold are somewhat separate, bound to cross purposes, and have very different flavors. Contrasting the worldly, well-heeled noble to the learned, ascetic priest is the tip of the iceberg in terms of possible conflicts. Churches may have different hierarchies and different governmental processes, and these can be every bit as interesting to explore as those of the secular rulers. David Eddings does a brilliant job with the Elene church in *The Sapphire Rose*, where the fate of the heroes, as well as the kingdoms of the west, rest on a room full of church elders casting ballots for their next leader.

When dealing with a spiritual authority in your world, you will need to actually design and understand what the people in your country believe. Once you have that, you ought to look into how much supernatural power they have, its scope and its applications. It could be that your spiritual leaders gain all the power they need or want from supernatural sources. If this is the case, they won't have a direct effect on the power structure, but they will still have an effect. Various factions of the secular government are bound to court the spiritual leaders for support, especially if they have supernatural powers. Your spiritual leaders can either give or withhold support as their needs and beliefs dictate or try to hold themselves aloof from government. In this last case, the spiritual power structure is going to have to walk a fine line to avoid persecution. A time-honored trope of fantasy is the destruction of a sect of monks, priests or magicians by a secular ruler infuriated by their lack of commitment to the national cause. In Joe Dever's novels about Lone Wolf (not the samurai with the cub), the Kai Lords were pretty much left high and dry by the country of Sommerlund, which they normally defended, when the villains came calling. If your spiritual leaders have ambition, you're going to have to decide how that plays out. Supernatural powers lend a great advantage, whatever they are, to anyone seeking power, and secular rulers are going to know that.

### GOD IS THE QUEEN: CHURCH IS THE STATE

One of the most important things to consider when writing up a spiritual government is if there is an active, intervening superhuman being in charge of it. Human power structures tend to go out the window when the gods start rumbling around. Very few people, however powerful, are going to go up against a god, and those two or three in all of history who tried tend to serve as very illustrative examples for future generations. In the event where a transcendent being is in charge, be it a deity, spirit, dragon or ascended magician, secular government is going to be smaller and quieter. That doesn't mean it won't be there in some form, but it is more likely to be local and implicit. In these cases, you'll have two power structures: the being and its servants, and the local power structures that sprout like mushrooms in dark places. The gods of Lankhmar sit around in their tombs for years, letting the secular government think they run the show. Eventually, though, they come out; and when they do, they make sure everyone remembers who's boss. The alien adversaries in the movie *Stargate* and the series it spawned rule their subjects as gods, and take names and personae that either inspired or were inspired by the gods of the ancient world. Some very mortal and fallible people with the right blend of power, charisma and guile might set themselves up as gods or godlike rulers, like L. Frank Baum's *Wizard of Oz*.

Putting God on the throne of your country is a good idea if you either want to emphasize the fact that the government is not within mortal's power to change or to emphasize how cataclysmic the changes taking place in your story happen to be. Gods are fun characters to write, and they have the powers needed to run a country no matter how unreliable their personalities would be in mortal form, as we found when Jim Carrey stepped in for God in the fantasy-comedy *Bruce Almighty*. Finally, having a god in charge of the country magnifies the mystery of the setting and, when done right, creates a sense of wonder that upon which fantasy thrives.

### THE AFFAIRS OF WIZARDS: MAGIC AND THE GOVERNMENT

So far, we've been dealing with the supernatural in government as a feature of spiritual and religious authority, but it does not have to be that way. Government becomes a lot trickier when magic is thrown into the mix. J.K. Rowling lends some thought to the interaction between the supernatural and the material in the *Harry Potter* series, if only by neatly sidestepping it, making wizard society and "Muggle" society separate and largely unaware of one another. She does supply a few tidbits, mostly in her history lessons, that the interaction on a large scale was pretty disastrous for the mundane. Supernatural powers can express themselves in different parts of the power structure of a nation. Perhaps, supernatural aptitude is an inherited trait that moves from generation to generation. In this case, large, old families are going to have the powers. They may be the nobles, old merchant clans or backwoods hermits out of sight of most movements of the government. In any case, you'll have questions to answer regarding the families and what their place is in the power structure. If they aren't the nobility, why not? What safeguards do the mundane nobles have to protect themselves from the supernatural families? If they are nobles, how are they different from the mundane nobility? How do they treat offspring born without powers? Inversely, how would they treat an offspring with especially strong powers? What happens to a member of the family who breaks with tradition? Another possibility is that supernatural powers in your world are the product of study, experimentation and knowledge. If so, this raises a whole other set of questions. How much time, talent and study does it take? What purposes do these professional magicians have in the government and society? Are they organized? Where do they base their studies? Are there schools or is it master and student? It's possible for a non-spiritual, possibly university-based or scientific power structure to come into being, in competition and cooperation with the others in the country. Looking through the histories of 17th and 18th century Europe and the early modern scientists might be helpful, as would histories of secret societies and the occult. If that's too dry, look to Rowling's Ministry of Magic, and how Harry Potter's Wizard society is set up.

### THE QUEEN'S A THIEF: CRIMINAL AUTHORITY

Not all power structures have to be legitimate. The Thieves' Guild is an old convention of fantasy, and can generate a whole lot of intrigue if you let it. Viewed in terms of the Social Contract, the criminal power structure is often identical to that of the early warlords: your obedience and resources for protection from other criminals and from reprisal by those that wield the authority. Thieves' Guilds can also provide goods and services proscribed by the legitimate government. Criminal authority is a wonderful place for intrigue. After all, they are already breaking the law. Since criminal organizations do not follow the laws of the land, they are formed around a core of their own values, sometimes (but more often, not) codified into "laws" themselves. Interpretation of these values tends to vary, and enforcement tends to put a lot of hats on the ground. The most common values in a criminal power structure are loyalty and silence. Loyalty, in this case, means you stick with your faction and its leader, help where you can, and strive for a common goal. Silence is golden. You don't talk about the who, what, where or how of your faction to anyone, not other factions, not the legitimate authorities, not gods. (The first rule of Thieves' Guild is you don't talk about Thieves' Guild. The second rule: You do NOT TALK about Thieves' Guild!) Double-crossing your faction is punishable by death. Lieber's Fafhrd and Grey Mouser live this sort of world, and following them around is a good way to see what's there.

As always, it's important to determine how the criminal authorities interact with the other authorities. Chances are there are overlapping, coinciding purposes which allow the criminal power structure to persist. Only in very rare cases do criminal power structures have greater physical resources than the legitimate leaders. In those cases, the criminals become legitimate very quickly through force of arms. Usually, it only takes a reasonable effort on the part of the legitimate rulers to root out and destroy the current crop of criminals. Your job in this case is to find out why they haven't.

A good place to watch criminal authority bloom is that semi-autonomous trade port and city-state full of the best intrigue and nigh anarchy that the renaissance and age of sail have to offer. If Lucas' Obi-Wan were here, he'd be able to tell you all about those "wretched hives of scum and villainy." There might be a legitimate authority here, but you would not know it from the street. Vice, crime and lawlessness are parading openly on the street. The people who live here are hard and crafty, and only honest when they benefit from it. This area is the best place in all worlds to explore the intricacies of the criminal power structure. Gangs, thugs, pimps and pirates all call this place home. It's a dangerous place and takes quite a while to get boring. Howard wrote all years worth of seedy locales for Conan to explore; Moorcock and Leiber spent a lot of time with the scum in the villainous corners of their favorite wretched hives. You can't even keep Disney out of an establishment like the Tortuga of their *Pirates of the Caribbean.* Of all the different styles of government, this one is, arguably, the most fun to write. You can put in colorful characters, really nasty double crosses and dirty dealings, and since nothing is written down, per se, the people who run the underworld don't have to be as consistent as their legitimate counterparts (though many successful crime lords will tell you that it helps). If you have a lot of bad guys who are good guys, good guys who are bad guys and a flair for writing people sneaking out the back door, criminal governments are a riot to write.

Often, that riot is literal.

### KINGDOM COME-AND-GONE: THE OLD WORLD KINGDOMS

Another is the ancient society, full of supernaturally powerful people, gone to seed. Moorcock's Melniborne is lovely in the spring. A cavalcade of dissipated, magic wielding nobles party through the end of the world, the only commoners left being the servants (though they may be dead, look closely at their gray faces). The land itself has either gone dry or gone wild with thorns and kudzu. Intrigues are played out through either bitterness or habit; it scarcely matters who wins or loses. The government, in this case, becomes a character play: A few dozen vie for meaningless power while the world moves on. Like in Peake's *Gormenghast* or the Skeksis' kingdom in the film *The Dark Crystal,* ritual has replaced action, and the rulers endlessly repeat actions that no longer have any meaning. This nation is great to use if you want to tell the sort of story that focuses on the decadent and jaded and gives it the weight of centuries, of dust on gold leaf, wine aged into vinegar. Magic and deceit are grand pastimes. Costumes, masquerades and treachery are all they have left. There are also lands where only the memory of rule exists, such as Mid-World and End-World in Stephen

King's *Dark Tower* Series, where the world has "moved on" and the few stragglers of whatever society existed before eke out their existences at the end of the world. If you're aiming for an oppressive atmosphere and dark, distressed characters, the old kingdoms are where you want to go. Decadence and forbidden magic fit right in, as do jaded characters with rarified and nasty vices. Anything good and wholesome is either going to last as long as a little lamb among skinny wolves, or kick what's left of the castle ruins down. It's worth noting that anything done in the "gothic" tradition has elements of this type of government. Countless Draculas have looked from countless castle balconies over countless Transylvanias with all the elements of the kingdom gone to seed. These governments are showcases for ennui-wracked, sensitive heroes and nuanced, tormented and depraved antagonists.

### This Land was Green and Good
### Until *He* Touched It: The Dark Land

The most beloved and cherished of these, ironically enough, is the dark land, full of monstrous creatures ruled by a supernatural dark lord. It's Tolkien's Mordor and Lovecraft's R'yleh. These nations get run by whim and fiat of their semi-divine masters, who seem to control an endless supply of misshapen, fearsome and wicked subjects. The land itself is blasted and stunted, and the dark lord alone knows how all those endless legions get fed, clothed and equipped with their iron swords and crow-fletched arrows. There is usually a volcano and some deep cracks in the earth, and all sorts of supernaturally-affected areas to confound our heroes as they travel. Alternately, they are at the bottom of deep chasms or under the sea in places that are too dangerous to go near. The nature of the nation takes a lot of the work out of the hands of the writer. The trains, as they were, run on time because the dark lord *makes* them run on time. His subjects are twisted expressions of his hateful will and turn to dust or sand the moment he gets thrown down. This nation is unambiguously evil in every manner and respect, and serves to show the outward signs of its master's inner corruption.

### Conclusion
### (and a Short List of Things Not to Do)

With the exception of grammar, I'm not a big fan of writer's commandments; genuinely good work can be done when the writer ignores all the rules and simply writes. That said, I want to leave you with a list of things to keep in mind in building your government. Although many published and popular authors have disregarded some of this advice, know that keeping these issues in mind will make your writing a lot easier to accept.

FIRST, REMEMBER TO KEEP YOUR GOVERNMENT, LIKE ALL OTHER ASPECTS OF THE BACK-STORY, IN BACK OF THE STORY. If, like Robert Jordan, you have a multi-volume contract to fulfill and your reader base, as I said, is very patient and understanding, then you can go wild. Even then, I'd suggest reading a couple of James Mitchner's novels for pointers on how to lever hundreds of years into a book someone might read. If you only have a single book, or a standard trilogy to fill, and you find yourself dumping the history and culture of your kingdom wholesale into the book, you can safely assume any one of three things:

- You are padding your story and need to go back to the outline and start over
- You are going to bore a portion of your readership to tears, and are going to inflate the number of copies of your book you see on the remainder tables in your local bookstore
- You have a much better career ahead of you writing pretentious literary fiction that the Oprah Book Club will embrace.

SECOND, KEEP YOUR GOVERNMENT CONSISTENT TO THE STORY. Fantasy, as a genre, has one of the widest latitudes in writing style, from fairy tale simplicity to labyrinthine complexity. If your story goes along at a fairy tale pace right up to the point where the hero is infiltrating the court in order to see the princess, and you start in with factions and intrigue and complexity, it's going to be jarring. "Driving down the highway into a pond" kind of jarring. Conversely, if you have everything else well-developed, the pace is very deliberate, and the setting complex, skimping on the government is going to show. Eventually, you are going to have your readers wondering if there was something they missed.

FINALLY *(and this one is really important)*, REMEMBER YOU ARE DEALING WITH A NATION FULL OF PEOPLE, AND THAT WHAT HAPPENS TO THEM IS GOING TO CARRY REAL CONSEQUENCES. If your heroes are also rulers of the country, you need to have them rule the country or lose it. Stories where the heads of state pack their things, slip out the back window of their castles and go off questing to save the world are common in the sequel series that David Eddings writes, and what Richard and Khalan do every time Terry Goodkind publishes something new, and it begs the question, who's ruling the kingdom? If you use this as an element in your story, as Mark Oakley does at the beginning of *Thieves and Kings* (the good Princess has run off into the forest to live under a bridge with a troll, the King is in a coma and the Prince's power is rising, though not yet at its zenith), that is all well and good, but just leaving it while your hero-kings and queens run around the countryside doesn't really fly.

It's said that people who love politics and sausage should never see either being made. Governments are products of the culture, which is a product of the people, and essential to your story. In order to create a convincing government, you need to know your people and know their culture. You need to know what power structures are in place in the government and how they interact. You need to understand what role, if any, the supernatural plays in the culture. None of this work may be more than a dozen words in print; but, in a genre where you are already stretching the average suspension of disbelief with dragons and magic elves, every bit of realism and deliberate thought you put into your story is going to pay off. When working with factions, think of them both in terms of their parts and their whole. Try not to make your government any more complex than it needs to be. By exploring the various institutions cited in this chapter, one explores the points where all life is the same. Remember that most of all, your characters are people (whatever species they happen to be) and the things they create are the works of people, intelligent and stupid, benevolent and cruel. Mostly, like your characters, your fantasy governing body should be alive.

# Thinking Outside the Crystal Ball:
## DEVELOPING ALTERNATIVE MAGIC SYSTEMS

### BY VALERIE GRISWOLD-FORD

*"Umm, Dad?" Kerri asked nervously. "Is the program running yet?"*

*"I'm getting there." Her father's voice was testy. "Why?"*

*"Because one of the others has a Palm, and it's glowing."*

*Her father's dark head popped up from behind the laptop's screen. "What?"*

*Kerri pointed. He followed her finger to the pulsing purple glow around the boy standing above them. He held one of the new Palm Wizards, the source of the glow. Gus bit back the curse that swarmed up from his throat and ducked back down, tapping quickly on the Mac's keyboard. "Come on, baby," he whispered. "Come on!"*

*His beloved Mac responded, as always. The green glow that suddenly bathed his face was as welcome as the relief in his daughter's eyes when he looked. "Ready, Kerri?"*

*"Let's do it, Dad."*

It is one of the great rules of our genre: If you are writing a Fantasy novel, there will be an element of magic woven somewhere into the story. It can be small or large, a major plot point or a minor oddity, but it must be in there somewhere. However, nothing says you have to have the exact same magic that every other fantasy writer has, and this is the part that many writers forget. Even the most mundane can be magical, given the right circumstances and in the right hands.

Case in point—I had written approximately one quarter of this chapter and saved it to the hard drive of my laptop before shutting the laptop down and going to bed. Now, I didn't save it to an external disc (I know. Bad writer! Bad writer!), and I have an older laptop, one that tends to be cranky. I left it plugged in, and didn't get a chance to get back to it until two days later.

Did I mention my laptop was cranky? One of the things that sets it off is leaving it plugged in, which causes it to overheat. Well, after leaving said cranky laptop plugged in for two days, I went to turn it on and got only a black screen with a single, ominous line: "Operating System not found."

Not found? *Not found????*

I was frantic. I was also cursing the fact that not only was my chapter on the hard drive, so was the rewrite for my debut novel, *Not Your Father's Horseman*. After an hour of trying to get it to work (all the time picturing the look of horror on my publisher's face when I told her what was lost), I closed it down, unplugged it and said a quick prayer to St. Vidicon, the patron saint of electrical systems (according to Christopher Stasheff and his *Warlock In Spite of Himself* world) and went to bed.

The next night, after work, I cautiously plugged in the laptop, and booted it up, hoping against hope that St. Vidicon had done his work. The laptop booted up, and there was my chapter, in all its glory. St. Vidicon had come through again.

Yes, perhaps all my laptop needed was time to rest. But for me, someone who knows very little about computers, its revival was nothing short of miraculous. Or magical, for that matter. And in the right author's hands, it can breed an entirely new type of magic for a story.

I come from a family of gourmet chefs, and maybe that's why I look at writing a story the same way as my little sister looks at baking a cake. (Of course, it could also be my addiction to Food Network, but we'll get into that later.) The characters, the plotline, the theme—they are all crucial ingredients. But the spices, the final touch that truly makes MY world different from yours, or Heinlein's, or Prachett's? That's the magic. And just like no two dishes need exactly the same amount of spices, or even the same mixture, so no two worlds should need the same "flavor" of magic. How spicy is your world? If you're now thinking that you need to spice it up a bit, let me give you a tour of my magical spice box. Take what you need and then go out and look around. Odds are, you'll find spices I haven't yet. And they may be just what your world needs.

Ready? Let's go.

## RULE ONE: DEVELOPING A NOSE FOR SPICE

Earlier, I mentioned my addiction to Food Network. One of the shows I'm most addicted to at the moment is a program called "Good Eats," hosted by Alton Brown. I'm not addicted to the recipes (although most look pretty yummy). What I love about the show is his scientific method of dissecting a recipe and deducing how and why it works. Once I took his method and transferred it to my writing, a lot of what I had been doing made sense. Not only that, but I found a lot of potential problems that I managed to clean up, especially in the realms of world building and magic.

As we go through this tour of my spice box, I'm going to be handing out what I call my Golden Rules of Magic. These are rules that I've found incredibly useful, especially when creating a new thaumaturgic system. I'm the type of person that gets bored, especially when I see numerous writers using the same types of magic in their stories. It seems that many writers today are subscribing to the axiom of "If it ain't broke, don't fix it." This translates, in the writing world, as "If it worked for *(insert famous author here)*, I'll be able to sell my book with it too."

No, no, no!!!! Put your hands out so I can smack your knuckles with my ruler. And while you're shaking the sting off, consider this—one of the reasons it worked for that famous author is because it *WASN'T* the same as everyone else's. Editors and publishers don't want to read the same thing in every manuscript they read. If that was all they wanted, it would be a lot easier to get published. What you need (besides a great story, good characters, and at the very least, decent writing) is a spark of something different.

"But how do I know what's different?" you cry.

Here is my first Rule for you: *Read.*

"What? Just read?" you protest. "That's not a Rule!"

Yes, it is. Because in order to do things different, you have to know what is already out there. And the only way to do that is to read what is out there already.

So read. Read everything you can get your hands on. I have heard some writers, some *very successful* writers, say that they never read within their genre because it will "dilute" their unique voice.

And from this one humble author—that's crap.

If it works for them, great. But I don't see how you can write a genre if you don't read anything in it. As Stephen King said in his acceptance speech for the 2003 National Book Award, "What do you think, you get social academic brownie points for deliberately staying out of touch with your own culture?"

Chefs enlarge their knowledge of spices, flavors and combinations by trying a huge number of recipes and dishes. A writer must do the same—increasing his or her "nose" for the spice of magic by reading how other successful authors have used it in their novels. My personal favorites at the moment are the aforementioned Stasheff: both his *Warlock* series and his *Wizard in Rhyme* series; Mercedes Lackey and her *Serrated Edge* series; and Holly Lisle's *World Gates* series. All three have very different takes on magic, and we're going to take a closer look at these takes here in this chapter. Think on your favorite fantasy authors and how they utilize magic in their worlds. What can you learn from them?

## RULE TWO: RESEARCH YOUR TOPIC

Okay, so you've been doing your reading. You've realized that you need to make some changes to your magical system, or perhaps you've had one of those epiphanous moments where you saw a magical effect in your head—now you just have to figure out how your characters can actually do it. We come to Golden Rule #2: *Research*.

As I write this, my eyes drift up to my bookshelf. I have inherited both my parents' love of books and the near-uncontrollable urge to collect them in massive quantities. However, this is a good urge to have for a writer—you never know what direction your story may go, and what you may need to look up. And while the Internet is an invaluable resource, I can't help but enjoy the feel of paper in my hands, especially while researching magic.

There are many, *many* books on magic and it is impossible to list them all and the "magic category" they fall into. However, there are a few types that your bookshelf should definitely contain:

1) AN ENCYCLOPEDIA OF MAGIC. I have two that I tend to get quite a bit of use out of: *The Encyclopedia of Witchcraft and Demonology,* by Russell Hope Robbins, published in 1959, and *An Encyclopedia of Occultism,* by Lewis Spence, originally published in 1920 (my version is the 1960 publication). Notice the dates—I have found that a lot of my older magical books (gotten from used bookstores or my father) have given me some of the best information. I keep my eyes open, but haven't seen a recent one that I like. When looking for a magical encyclopedia, look for one that explains things in clear, concise terms—this may sound like common sense, but you'd be surprised at the lengths some "experts" will go to make their works not only esoteric, but almost unreadable. Research that you don't understand won't help you.

2) MAGICAL SPECIALTY BOOKS. These range from books on incense and herbal magic to divination and shamanism. There are untold books by untold "experts"—be sure to take most everything you read with at least one grain of salt. Authors I can recommend: Scott Cunningham, Wylundt and Sybil Leek. These books take you from the general facts you will get in the encyclopedia to specifics for what you are looking for. Again, you want clear, concise books—even today, there are authors who write simply to show how much they know and you don't. Use what you need, and file the rest in the garbage can.

3) BOOKS IN YOUR INTERESTS. I have interests that range from quantum physics to cooking to bead embroidery, so my bookshelves are stuffed with everything under the sun. My husband likes to joke that I never met a how-to book I didn't like, and he's

probably right. However, these books have provided the basis for several of my magical systems. In one of my worlds, for example, I have a major character who doesn't believe in magic. Period. For Clea, it doesn't exist, and this was giving me a major headache, as she happens to wield a major magical talent that I'm going to need her to use effectively. I was actually flipping through the TV channels when I stumbled across the scene in *Jurassic Park* where Jeff Goldblum is explaining chaos theory. Bingo! It was off to the computer to look up chaos theory and there was the answer to my dilemma. Clea doesn't believe in magic, so to her, her gifts work along the lines of what is called "the butterfly effect"—the theory that if a butterfly flaps its wings in India, the Antarctic ice caps grow thicker, because everything is interconnected.

I'm still working the specifics out, but I think applying "the butterfly effect" will solve this dilemma of mine.

Your bookshelf should be customized to your interests, and so should your magical systems. Are you a chef? Perhaps your characters bake spells into the bread they sell. Interested in needlework? Your lead character could have a faery godmother who embroiders her a magical cloak that lets her speak to trees. Your tastes run to computers? Maybe your characters have some of the computers illustrated in the example at the beginning of this chapter.

### RULE THREE: DON'T BE AFRAID TO BE UNIQUE, BUT DO IT RIGHT.

All right, so you have done your reading, you've decided what to use and you've done some research. Now comes the hardest part of all: actually writing the magical system down.

Yes, you need to write it down. *Now.* Getting the idea on paper helps you see if the system works logically. Then, once you make it work, you can come up with foils for it. Remember, for every magical power, there is something that cancels it or is not affected by it. Newton's law works in writing as well as physics: for every action, magical or otherwise, there is an equal and opposite reaction. You must have those in order to make your magic believable.

And that is Rule Three—*Make sure it's logical.*

"Logic, smogic," you say. "It's magic, that's all. What do I need logic for?"

Well, because if you just expect to wave your hand and dismiss everything as "magic," be prepared for your readers to say, "I don't think so." This remark, by the way, is usually followed (in my household, and many around the world) by said book being thrown against the wall in disgust and being left to die in the dust.

Is that where you want your book to be? I didn't think so.

So take the time to make it logical. If your faery godmother sews her magic into your skirts, what happens if the thread breaks? Or the magical embroidery gets stained? Or torn? How do you wash it? And what happens if someone else wears it? All things that you need to consider. For example:

> Sarta lifted the dancing veil out of the box and gasped at the sparkling embroidery. "Grandmother, how can you part with such a gift?" she whispered, running a reverent finger over the silver threads.
>
> The ancient woman chuckled and then coughed as the amusement caught in her sickly lungs. "It has lain unused for too long, child. It needs youth to revitalize the magic. Where I am going, I will not need it."
>
> Tying the veil delicately around her waist, Sarta closed her eyes and her hips began to sway. As she moved through the first motions of the ancient dance, the embroidery began to glow.
>
> Her grandmother nodded wisely. "I was right," she murmured, watching her granddaughter dancing the gate open. "You will be the one to lead our people along their path."
>
> Sarta floated over the earthen floor, her bare feet inscribing mystic circles in the dust. As she continued the dance, the seemingly random swirls of light coalesced into columns that rose up around her.
>
> She ended her dance in the midst of light. From a distance, she could hear the faint echo of her grandmother's caution, "Remember, child—if the veil should be used too often or taken from you in force, the magic will die. I cannot guarantee that the magic will not claim your life as well. Be careful."

I'm not saying that you can't go over the top, but remember—if you make a magical effect or power that is invincible, you'd best use it sparingly, or it will make your story boring. Yes, BORE-RING. Who wants to read a book about someone who can stop anything thrown at them without breaking a sweat? In the example above, Sarta's risking not only the destruction of the veil, but possibly her own death as well, if she overuses the veil. We're not sure how much use is over-use, and

I'll bet she isn't sure what it is either. This adds a new magical effect and tension at the same time.

*Now* you have a story.

## FLAVORS OF SPICE: EXAMPLES OF ALTERNATIVE MAGIC

Now that I've given you the rules I use when creating alternative magical systems, let me open the spice box I have beside my computer and share with you some of the different kinds of magic that I have run across in my years as a fantasy reader and writer. Feel free to use them, in any combinations that you can come up with, in your stories.

### COMPUTER MAGIC

One of the best examples of computer magic that I have run across is in Diane Duane's series, *So You Want to Be a Wizard*. In one of the books, one of the characters has a laptop that is part familiar, part book of shadows. It is her spell book, but it seems to take on a character of its own, up to and including, in one of the scenes, growing legs and following her out of the room. It was very well done, and I was fascinated.

Everyone, it seems, has at least one computer nowadays. I can personally attest that my husband and I have two, and we don't even have any children to excuse the multiple machines. Most of our major machines (cars, phones, televisions) have some sort of computer within them, and *cyberpunk* (a sub-genre usually set in the future where the Internet is revered as a religion and its followers can literally "plug in" to the network. Some examples of this are *The Matrix, Neuromancer* and *Johnny Nmeumonic*.) is a growing field of both role-playing games and books. Our culture is in love with our techie-toys, and that gives the clever author reams to work with in formulating a new magical system. A good example of this addiction is my co-editor, Tee Morris, who travels with two suitcases—one for his clothing and one for his toys. On a recent tour, I sat and watched as he pulled out (ready for the list?):

- *iPod*
- *Assorted gadgets that go with his iPod*
- *his laptop*
- *a cell phone*
- *PDA*

The occasion? We were working on some writing during a rare quiet period on tour. Yes, Tee is an extreme case (and that is *before* he enjoys his quad-espresso), but look in your own bag or purse. How many electronic gadgets are you convinced you can't live without?

Be creative. Don't limit yourself to what's already out there. There is a world of computer-generated holograms, sentient Artificial Intelligences, and other robots that can be played with. In the role-playing game I'm currently involved in, my character is a half-elven hacker with a computer implant in her head. Well, she *used* to have an implant. Due to her unique magical ability, she's sort of absorbed the functions of the implant directly into her. This is only one example. Duane's magical laptop is another. What can you come up with?

## HERBAL MAGIC

Most medieval fantasy has at least one character that can work herbal magic. In many cases, it's the prototypical healer or that faery godmother again, but don't let the stereotypes box you in. Two books, *Sorcery and Cecilia* by Patricia C. Wrede and Caroline Stevermer, and *Song of Sorcery* by Elizabeth Scarborough, take different approaches to herbal magic.

In *Cecilia*, the herbal magic is practiced by the two heroines, Cecilia and her cousin Kate. The book is set in an alternative Regency England, and their herbal magic is mostly what is called "folk magic"—charm bags, healing teas and things like that. Very small magics, but very effective, especially in this context.

Never underestimate small magics—often, they can be far more creative and successful than the large "Hollywood" magics that the special-effects wizards at Industrial Light and Magic seem infatuated with. The reason? The leap from "reality" to the smaller magics is, well, smaller, and easier for many readers.

The heroine in *Song* is also the herbalist, but Maggie's a self-proclaimed hearth-witch. She uses her herbs and magic to turn the prosaic tasks of housekeeping, especially cooking, from chores to no sweat. My favorite scene in this book is when she's repairing her aunt's house, her aunt who happens to live in your archetypical Gingerbread House. (Grandma had a taste for small children.) Maggie spends the afternoon reshingling and casting preservation spells in the same breath. The end result—a cottage that's no longer edible, but still looks good enough to eat. I kept reading this wonderfully fun novel (based on the folk song "The Gypsy Rover," by the way) and wishing for Maggie's gifts.

How can you take a staple of fantasy like herbal magic and make it fresh? For more ideas, check out Evo Terra's chapter in this book on herbalism.

### PSIONICS

Mind over matter. ESP. Telekinesis. Once found only in Science Fiction, *psionics*, or mind magic, has become the spice du jour in a myriad of Fantasy series. Some of the best, in my opinion: Christopher Stasheff's *The Warlock In Spite of Himself* series, Mercedes Lackey's *Valdemar* series, and of course, Anne McCaffrey's *Pegasus In Flight* series. Each of these takes the idea of powers hidden deep in the mind and moves off in their own direction.

Stasheff's reasoning behind the large (relatively speaking) population of psis in *Warlock* is solid and engaging. The people are colonists who fled from Earth and immersed themselves in their ideal version of a medieval culture. His Gramarye "witches" and "warlocks" are actually psis: the female witches are telekinetics and the male warlocks are levitators. This world actually combines several different takes on fantasy and magic, as science and "modern" culture is safeguarded in the monasteries (how's *that* for a twist on the normal?) and, in the later books, Stasheff actually brings in some meshing of computers and psi powers.

Lackey's Heralds run the spectrum of psionics—from pyrokinesis (fire starting) to empathy (the sending and receiving of emotions). In her world, these gifts are used instead of magic, which hasn't existed in the kingdom of Valdemar for centuries due to the fact that every traditional mage that comes into the kingdom goes slowly mad. I'm not going to ruin the story, but trust me, she's on solid ground with this one. Outside their kingdom, there is an interesting juxtaposition of traditional magic and mind magic. Lackey does a good job of balancing between the two.

McCaffrey's psis are another example of melding two types of magic: mental and mechanical. Psionics and computers, combined with electrical generators supplying additional energy, fill the roles of interstellar "postmen" as they transfer packages and ships across the galaxy.

Three different series, with very different uses of the same gifts. The mind is a mysterious organ, and there are depths that still have yet to be mined by authors. It is an area ripe for exploration.

### RITUAL/RELIGIOUS MAGIC

The traditional image of magic is one where the ancient wizard, with his long, flowing white beard curling down over either stained robes or gorgeously embroidered ones, stands in the center of a chalked circle, chanting in some dead language as he conjures spirits to do the bidding of his monarch. This image of magic is the one that generally springs to mind when someone says, "I write fantasy." There's nothing wrong with it, and used correctly, it can be a very effective system.

Katherine Kurtz's *Deryni* series is a great example of this. So is J.K. Rowling's *Harry Potter*, and, lest I forget (and be reamed by readers later) J.R.R. Tolkien's *Lord of the Rings*. Mary Stewart's *Crystal Cave* series (talked about more in Kim Headlee's "Writing Arthurian Legends" chapter) is yet another well-written example of more traditional ritual magic.

Kurtz takes her mages in the direction of Roman Catholic High Magick (yes, with a K) in the *Deryni* series. All the spells are cast with the same air of reverence as a High Mass—many are actually cast in Latin, all with the blessings of St. Camber, the Patron Saint of Deryni magic. Kurtz has actually written an entire book on the magic system she created for this series: *Deryni Magic*. It's well worth the read for anyone interested in creating this kind of magical system. While I enjoy reading novels with High Magick, the system itself is a little too structured for my taste. However, when done well, it can add depth and resonance not just to traditional fantasy novels, but those set in the modern day as well.

Some people might be surprised that I would include the *Harry Potter* novels in my section on religious and ritual magic. However, my definition of ritual magic is "a magical system that relies on the structure of the magical ritual to define the magical power." Rowling's characters learn rituals of spells as they go through their schooling. This is a very traditional way to teach magic, and they use their spell books, wands and the magical incantations they learn the same way wizards and witches of their world have been using them for millennia. Harry and Ron might not be your typical view of a traditional wizard, but give them a few years to grow those beards and you might be surprised.

As for Tolkien—well, no chapter on magic would be complete with a nod to "The Master." However, what intrigued me so much about the way he built his magical system was not how traditional it was (and there are many nods to the ceremonial magicians of his time in these books), but how the magical system was secondary to the language in the conception of this world. Tolkien was a professor of language—he wrote the books to showcase the language of the elves that he dreamed up. As such, his magical system was approached with the same consistent care that his language system was, which is why it is so believable and logical.

## CONCLUSION

This chapter is your starting point for an incredible journey—a fire, if you will, that creates a spark in your own mind, a hunger for even more information that you can use.

Take these spices, place them in your own box and let your imagination go. As long as you remember these three rules—read, research and make it logical—don't be afraid to try exciting and original combinations. Your stories will be all the richer for the unique magic you create.

Let me end with one more nod to my favorite network and assume the robes (and lord, where *DOES* he get them?) of Chairman Kaga from "Iron Chef." I invite you into the fantasy world's version of Kitchen Stadium. The spices you found today are your secret ingredients. In Kaga's immortal words, "Allez cuisine!"

Or rather, start cooking!

# Fun with Flowers, Ferns and Philodendrons:
## HERBALISM IN FANTASY

### BY EVO TERRA

Here's the funny thing about herbal medicine, or medicine of any kind, really. It's not some highly guarded super secret, and it isn't as difficult or complicated as you might imagine. Yes, modern physicians of our western world are highly trained and quite skilled at their tasks. True, when we go to the drug store, we see a dizzying array of pills, liquids and other concoctions that are completely foreign to us, each producing almost magical effects on our bodies. And how many of us could really handle an emergency first aid situation where an inebriated friend has nearly chopped his leg off with a chainsaw...again? These facts mean only that we as a people have become less familiar with the ways of medicine. The medicine, at its most basic form, hasn't become more complicated.

The fact is, we've become far removed from our medicines, leaving healthcare and all medical matters up to a select segment of our population. Doctors and nurses collectively consume and dispense the bulk of this knowledge, and the common person is more than happy with this arrangement. It wasn't always this way. Only a few generations ago, the ability to keep ourselves and our loved ones healthy was as ingrained in each of us as the ability to prepare our own meals. While serious life-threatening conditions might still have required the attentions of shamans, medicine men or some other specially trained healer, first aid and day-to-day afflictions were treatable by the masses. Considering your fantasy tale is likely to be set against a backdrop where technology is limited, your cast of characters would arguably come equipped with similar knowledge of how to heal.

So don't have some lackey running off to fetch a healer when your protagonist gets himself pinchushioned by a unicorn with a bad attitude. Your characters can handle this, assuming said beast didn't etch his lineage upon the offender's internal organs. In the immortal words of Monty Python's Black Knight, *"It's only a flesh wound."* Welcome to Herbal Medicine 101, where I will show you how to deal with flesh wounds, as well as other afflictions and ailments, in a convincing and plausible manner, thereby adding new layers of depth and dimension to your storytelling.

## Why Herbs?

You have probably been working on your world for a long time now, and there are likely many fantastical elements which require suspension of disbelief. Herbalism, however, is *not* one of them. Plant-based medicine works. It worked thousands of years ago, and it continues to work today. A century of amazing developments in scientific medicine does nothing to negate the effectiveness of herbs. If you are unable to accept that simple fact, I can guarantee you'll be unable to convince your readers of the "reality" of your fantasy medicine.

Botanical remedies are the primary choice of medicine in most of the world. In second and third world countries (perhaps more like your conceived world than the one we live in), plant-based medicine accounts for nearly 80% of all medicinal treatments. That's not too surprising, as pharmaceutical companies can make a lot more selling drugs to middle-class Westerners than they can from selling to poor Chilean llama herders. Even in the US, where modern medicine is widespread, around 25% of all prescribed pharmaceuticals are derived from plants. One out of every ten of the most popular prescriptions today continues to be manufactured from plant extractions.

Your characters are going to use plant-based medicine in your world—just like we use plant-based medicine in ours. For them, however, it's not a matter of taking a trip to the drug store or rushing to the emergency room. That's a good thing for you as a writer. I mean, who wants to read a story where the hero spends hours agonizing over which is the right antihistamine? Botanical remedies allow for you, the writer, to be a bit more creative with how you deal with medical situations.

## CHOOSING COOL AND REAL-SOUNDING NAMES FOR YOUR PLANTS.

Selecting a name for a plant to be used in your story should not be taken lightly. You agonize for days over just the right name for your characters, do you not? Some authors even go so far as to keep a list of all the names they dream up which "sound cool," saving them for future stories yet to be written. Extending the process to weapons, beasts, countries and even plants seems a logical choice.

Traditionally, several factors were influential in how a plant received its common name:

- *How it looked*
- *Where it grew*
- *When it bloomed*
- *Who it is named after*
- *What it did*
- *Why it was useful*

### PHYSICAL CHARACTERISTICS

*Shepard's Purse* is a common urban weed. Medicinally, it's used to staunch bleeding externally or internally, but you wouldn't guess it from the name. When the plant begins to seed (the right time to collect it, by the way), it forms small heart-shaped seedpods, similar to how a shepard's purse would appear with straps lifting the flimsy cloth on either side and drooping in the middle. You'll find many "emergency" herbs with names based on their appearance for easy identification by those who need it immediately. No description is necessary.

This takes a fair degree of creativity on your part, as you'll need a name that is unique to the physical characteristics of your plant. Naming a plant *Dagger's Blade* brings to mind every broad-leafed plant imaginable, but calling one *Scribe's Quill* leaves little to be misconstrued. One approach is to pick something or someone fairly common in your land. Picture this in your mind and select an interesting item or element to focus on which you are unlikely to find on anyone or anything else. Maybe it's an interesting animal *(Stork's Bill)* or a nasty-looking object *(Devil's Club)*. Once you've got it, play around with the words until something sounds interesting and flows right.

### HABITAT AND DISTRIBUTION

Names can also help people remember where to find a useful herb. No one would look for *Marsh Marigold* on a flat, treeless plain. Instead, when someone was suffering from lung congestion (perhaps a human slave irritated by the dust working in a dwarven mine), a companion would seek out some boggy seep or other area with standing water to find this beneficial plant ally. Was the plant named before its medicinal properties were known? It's hard to say, but *"Cough-helper Marigold"* doesn't sound quite as elegant.

This method gives you, the writer, nearly unlimited possibilities for your plant names. *Mountain Cherry, Stonefast, River Poppy, Desert Ivy...* pick your landscape and take it from there. This might also inspire whole new sections of your book, or perhaps even a new novel. Quest-driven fantasy epics are quite popular, but rather than questing for the magic talisman, why not the illusive *Crag Spruce*, which grows at the top of Mt. Desolation and is the only thing which will save the princess from a nasty case of flatulence threatening the peace negotiations between her warring factions?

## Seasonal Changes

Plants that receive their names based on their blooming times are by definition unusual. It makes no sense to call something *Spring Bloom*, as thousands of species are putting out flowers during the spring. The plant needs to do something a bit more unusual than its neighbors to be named for the blossom. *Evening Primrose* is a good example. The flowers (present in early summer) stay tightly bound during the daylight hours, only opening their brightly-colored yellow or white petals to attract nighttime insects and other pollinators. As a medicine, Evening Primrose is useful to assist with skeletal and muscular cramps particularly in the area of the reproductive system. If you know someone in need of this remedy and you happen to pass by a primrose plant (common enough) in the daytime with its flowers retracted, you know what you've found.

Don't limit yourself just to blooming. Plants go through a series of physical changes throughout the year; all you have to do is pick one that seems out of place with the rest of the plant community. Maybe your plant does something really unusual, like dropping its leaves during the rainy season. I don't know why it would do such a thing, but let's run with it. Choose a name that highlights this action. Perhaps *Rain Bane* or *Storm Shy* does the trick.

## Honoring a Person

Probably the least helpful of all naming conventions is the practice of naming a plant after an individual. *King's Foil* in *Lord of the Rings* comes to mind. *Fuller's Herb* is a real-life example of this utter lunacy. This name is of absolutely no use to anyone other than the now-forgotten Fuller and his band of idiots. As you might imagine, plants named in this fashion quite often have alternate names. Many others (except Fuller) know Fuller's Herb as *Soapwort*. It doesn't take a rocket scientist (or an herbalist) to derive the property of the plant by its alternate name.

## Other Uses

Many medicinal plants are useful for things other than healing. Plants still contribute greatly to our way of living, from the wood to make the studs that hold your house up, to the cotton used to make the clean underwear your mother wants you to wear just in case you are in an accident. Some medicinal plants still bear the names given to them for less-than-noble purposes. Take *Desert Broom*, for example.

Its closely thatched stems and thin but sturdy leaves can be tightly lashed together to form a quick and efficient tool to sweep out the dust. Many traditional peoples continue to utilize the plant for this purpose today. It's also quite helpful for stomach ulcers. "Oh, your tummy hurts? Grab some of that Desert Broom and make a tea. And while you're out there, grab an extra branch and sweep the porch while you're waiting for your water to boil."

### How or What It Heals

*Self Heal, Yerba Buena* ("good herb"), *Locoweed* and *Scurvy Grass* are all names of real plants that do exactly what is indicated by their respective name. This common practice speaks to the pervasiveness of medicinal plants and how they are recognized the world over. It is also an extremely effective way to pass on the knowledge to future generations. A neophyte might forget what conditions *Butcher's Broom* is helpful for, but that'll likely never happen with Scurvy Grass. There is a drawback to this nomenclature, however, but only to botanists and anal-retentive herbalists. Many cultures are likely to use the same name for entirely different herbs. This causes a problem for such broadly named plants as Yerba Buena, which is likely good for many ailments but not necessarily the same as your characters are used to treating with their own native Yerba Buena. Even more specific names can still cause problems. Take *Sore Eye*, a common weed found in the desert southwest for example. Is it good for sore eyes...or does it cause sore eyes? Before making a wash with *Globe Mallow* (another name for the same plant), it would be a good idea to check with the local population. It's the latter, by the way...

### Healing Properties of Plants

Medicinal plants affect the human (and sub-human) body in a myriad of ways. Some are cooling and others hot, some tighten tissues where others relax, and some stem the flow of blood as others stimulate circulation. Understanding some of these basic actions and how they affect the body is a great tool to add to your writing arsenal. While there are at least fifty individual actions on the body caused or initiated by plants, we'll touch on only a few of the more common properties which are most likely to wind up in a fantasy tale.

### Pain Relief

Geeky modern herbalists refer to this action as *anodyne*. Aspirin is an anodyne you're probably familiar with. The active ingredient in aspirin, acetylsalicylic acid, was isolated from a plant called *Meadowsweet* over 100 years ago. For thousands of years before the Bayer® company patented aspirin, people were using Meadowsweet, *Willow* and a host of other plants to alleviate mild pain. (Some of us rebels still do.)

The power of an anodyne should not be underestimated, much like the power of cheese. (Sorry. I hope someone gets that reference...) Modern people run to the pill bottle at the first sign of minor pain and discomfort, lest they be bothered by the slightest little twinge. We expect to be pain-free all the time, and the faster we can get to that state the better. That's not the case in non-industrialized societies. In those cultures, anodynes of a similar strength to aspirin and acetaminophen were used (and often still are used) to treat serious pain, like the loss of a limb. Of course, we scoff at the thought of over-the-counter (OTC) medicines for something this major, especially when a whole host of Rush Limbaugh-style opiates are just a phone call away. But we're pansies. Your creatures and characters likely are not. They'll turn to an anodyne herb when necessary, but not for a splinter.

Anodyne herbs can be used both internally and externally. In fact, some herbs only work when applied directly to the skin, where others only provide their medicine when ingested. Others work better by both combining direct application and internal consumption.

### WOUND CARE

Cuts, bumps and bruises are as common in fantasy tales as sexually transmitted diseases (STDs) are strangely absent in sappy romance pulp. Characters fall off dragons, are bashed in the head by a flail, or get a nasty gouge by the oh-so-friendly-looking puppy-looking thing with three heads and a poor disposition. Untreated wounds in a less-than-sterile environment (or from less-than-sterile instruments of destruction) will quickly fester, causing a host of unpleasant symptoms and larger problems.

Some herbs are *antiseptic*, inhibiting the putrification of wounds and delaying gangrenous conditions. These are usually applied directly to the wound itself, usually in the form of a *poultice* (see *Preparations*), though others are helpful internally. It's a good idea to follow treatment with an *antimicrobial* herb to help the body destroy the nasties that most likely accompanied the axe blade on its journey through the thigh. Herbs that have an *emollient* action sooth inflamed tissues when applied topically. Very handy for abrasions and scrapes after a scuffle. The next time Biff gets into a knife fight with a lighting quick Halfling, have him chew up the appropriate leaf, spitting some into the wound(s) and swallowing the rest. His cuts will knit nicely in a few days while he contemplates the shame of getting his butt kicked by someone too short to ride the Ferris Wheel.

### WORM EXPULSION

*Anthelmintic* plants have a singular job—to expel worms. *Eeewww!* But think about it: You're living in a world without refrigeration (most likely) and less than USDA-level standards of food preparation. In our world, it's estimated that 10–20% of modern civilized Americans live with some sort of parasite in the body. (See my earlier *"Eeewww!"*) Your hero could be walking around right now with a whole civilization living in her gut, wreaking havoc on nearly all of her body systems. A nasty rash, headache, asthma, severe abdominal pain—all are signs of a parasitic GI infestation. Luckily for you, Mother Nature (or whomever your benevolent planet deity might be) has instilled fast and reliable cures for these critters in plants.

All meat eaters are susceptible to getting worms. And since dung makes a nice patch of fertilizer for plants to grow and be nibbled upon, herbivores get their fair share of exposure as well. It's a natural and instinctive behavior for animals to seek out anthelmintic plants and ingest them. How do they know? We can only speculate, and I don't have the time (nor word count) to tackle that question here. Suffice to say that they do know. We know too, either from observations of other animals, or the same instinctive knowledge blessed upon the other inhabitants of this planet. They know on your world as well.

### NAUSEA RELIEF

A friend of mine writes pirate stories and must contend, one would assume, with seasick passengers from time to time. *Antiemetic* herbs help block the vomiting reflex. Sometimes puking is good for you (as we'll get to later in *Vomit Instigation*), but when it's brought on by external influences like a ship rocking back and forth, up and down, side to side...*mmmphfffff!* (Sorry. Took some *Ginger*. All better now. Where was I? Oh yes, stopping the Technicolor yawn...) It's never good to have the Prime Minister lose his lunch on his first diplomatic mission, or to subject an initiate to a turning tummy as she is embalming a fallen warrior. In situations where you're likely to encounter nausea, someone should be prepared to delve out some antiemetic herbs. And be quick about it!

### Vomit Instigation

Mother always warned you about putting things in your mouth, but she wasn't there when you and your sage companion discovered the green glowing vial which he could have *SWORN* said "invisibility." So there you are, opaque as ever but turning an ever-increasing intensity of green, contemplating the best way to dispatch your partner in crime—assuming you don't drop dead first. You need to barf, and you need to do it *now*. *Emetic* herbs work really well and really quickly, so hopefully you brought some along for this journey under the dark, dank tower. No, they don't taste good and yes, you often times have to drink a lot to reach a therapeutic dose. Don't blame me. You're the mental midget that drank the stuff in the first place.

### Sedatives and Hypnotics

Ah yes, the recreational aspects of botanical remedies. Many of you have likely been exposed to the powerful aspects of plants on the brain and nervous system. Historically, these plants served purposes more noble than making those around you at the company party more interesting. *Sedatives* help calm down a nervous, anxious or otherwise excited individual. Quite handy when you have to again deal with the same guy who cheated you and your crew out of your fair share of the booty five years ago, and all you can picture is how nice his head would look on your mantle. *Hypnotics* have a much stronger action and help bring about sleep. Large doses can knock someone out completely, and excessively large doses can make them never wake up again. For some plants, there exists a fine line between the therapeutic and lethal dosage.

There are legions of other actions which plants cause upon a body. Herbs help with all aspects of digestion (from start to finish, if you know what I mean), are valuable allies during childbirth, arrest cancerous growth, alleviate the symptoms of venereal disease and even enhance the sex drive. If the bodies of your characters are under stress or just not acting up to snuff, there's a plant out there that will them help get back to normal. Or take them far from normal. Whatever you think they need.

### PREPARING HERBAL REMEDIES

As important as it is to understand the actions of plants, so too should you have an understanding of the many ways in which botanical remedies are prepared. Simply ingesting a plant may be sufficient to pass along the medical properties to the body. This is fine for green leafy plant parts, but less of an option for roots and bark. *(Mmmm... bark.)* Making an *herbal preparation* presents nature's medicine in a more consumable form, concentrates the active ingredients and increases the chance of patient compliance. Most herbal preps taste like... well, medicine. But most folks would rather swallow some foul-tasting brew than emulate a cow chewing their cud. *(Mmmm...cud.)*

Preparing plant-based medicines also greatly increases the number of remedies in your apothecary. Remember our blood-staunching friend Shepard's Purse from earlier in the chapter? Your characters are just as likely to cut themselves in October when the plant is dormant as in March when it is widely available. And since the medicine in Shepard's Purse only works when the plant is fresh, you need to somehow extract the medicine now, as the dried-out specimens you collected six months ago are today only useful as a snack for your horse. Plus, it's a lot easier to carry around small vials of liquid or pouches of powder than bales of hay and bundles of sticks, right? Increased portability is a great benefit.

In reality, there is no "one right way" to make an herbal preparation. Each culture around the globe has its own methods for extracting the beneficial components from plants. It's not like plants come equipped with a recipe book. It has always been a trial and error way of exploring the world, ditching what doesn't work and refining what does. Western herbalists think the Chinese herbalists apply too much heat for far too long to the plant, where the Chinese cry foul as we in the West discard the "good stuff" once our extracts are finished. Variations on a theme are fine, and here's one place where you can exercise a significant amount of creative license in your world. There are, however, some basic preparation methods of which you should be aware.

### POWDERS

The simplest and easiest way to make a *powder* is the way you would make any powder: *grind it up.* A mortar and pestle is the classic way to do this, but other contraptions, from grinding stones to mills, are all options which can be employed in getting the whole plant down to a fine consistency. Remember, the plant needs to be completely dry before attempting to create powder. One would not anticipate good results from yanking up a fresh root and tossing it on the grinding stone. Think of the last time you grated cheese. (Told you...powerful stuff, that cheese!) Yep, it's a lot like that.

Powders are also made from the dried-out remnants of liquid preparations. (We'll get to liquids in a moment.) This is a much more time-consuming method, as you're really making two preparations in the process. The *extracting agent* (water, alcohol, vinegar, etc.) of a pre-made liquid preparation is either allowed to evaporate or boiled away, leaving a fine residue in the bottom of the vessel. There will not be much left, further compounding the issue. It takes an incredible amount of raw plant material to come up with a decent supply of powder processed in this manner. And since the medicine was already in the liquid itself, this seems like a wasteful proposition. Unless, of course, you can come up with a good reason in your story. *Hint, hint.*

Once the powder is prepared, storing it is a simple enough matter. A nice waterproof skin perhaps, or a glass or ceramic vial are excellent methods of keeping the powder contained, yet isolated from moisture. Moisture and powder are a bad combination for storage. (See Flour and Water in your own pantry for more details.) *Avoid leather pouches,* as they tend to soak up moisture from the outside world, transmitting it to the contents and ruining all of your hard work.

Powders can be utilized in a variety of ways. They can be added to liquids, snuffed up the sinuses, sprinkled across a wound or abrasion, or dusted lightly on the skin. They can even be smoked. They are versatile, simple to make and arguably the easiest to transport of all the preparations you're likely to see.

### TEAS OR TISANES

Medicinal *teas* (also known by the more archaic term, *tisanes)* require no great skill other than the ability to boil water and chop up plant matter. Hot water is a very good extracting agent for many plant-based compounds that have medicinal value to other living organisms. Teas can be made from either dried or fresh materials, usually in the ratio of one to two teaspoons per ounce of water. Teas should be allowed to steep for 15 – 30 minutes to reach full potency. If you've been taking your *Chamomile* tea bag out of your cup after five minutes, you've been drinking flavored water and sleeping better from the psychosomatic effects more than anything else. Once the plant matter has steeped, separate the liquid (the *menstruum*) from the spent plant matter (the *marc*). Drink the menstruum and discard the marc as you see fit. For a nice touch, add a bit of ceremony and ritual to your actions as you return the marc to the earth. Don't just toss it on the ground or in the closest garbage pile. Have some fun with this sacred process of returning the spent remnants of this important gift from nature to the earth spirits. You might create a special ritual, or have your character chant softly while burying the spent plant material in a sacred spot. By doing so, you add more depth and dimension to your world.

For as simple as they are, teas present a problem for travelers in a fantasy realm: they cannot be pre-made. Teas have a very short shelf life, even with modern refrigeration. Water, though an excellent extracting agent, sucks as a *preservative*. Teas should be made in the quantity necessary for the job at hand and then utilized. Now. Tomorrow will be too late, as the preparation will already be spoiled.

Plants, or their parts, which are very herbaceous (as opposed to woody) usually make for the best teas. If your plant has a strong scent, pleasant or otherwise, be sure and cover the tea during the steeping process. That smell likely comes from *aromatic compounds* that will float away with the steam given the chance, and nearly all aromatic compounds have medicinal value. Some plants high in *mucilaginous compounds* (like okra) make a thick gooey tea, quite soothing to inflamed mucous membranes of the throat and mouth or other digestive systems if taken internally.

### DECOCTIONS

Another type of aqueous extract, *decoctions* are much stronger preparations than teas and tisanes. Decoctions are made by adding the plant matter to the water and bringing the mixture to a boil, usually for 20–30 minutes. The intense heat constantly added to the plant matter allows the water to penetrate further, extracting difficult to reach compounds. This is not always a good thing, as some delicate elements of a plant (like the aromatic compounds above) are actually damaged by too much heat, ruining your preparation. As such, decoctions are usually reserved for roots and bark, or other stiff, fibrous portions of plants.

Decoctions share the same drawbacks as teas in that they cannot be stored for any length of time. They are, however, quite nice as the finishing touch to a long day of campaigning, when a nice cup of willow bark tea is just what your characters need to soothe away their muscle aches and pains.

### LUNAR AND SOLAR INFUSIONS

Teas and decoctions are both *infusions*, and the basic idea is to allow the water to extract the materials. Heat is added as the catalyst, but other energy sources are available as well. Many of you have enjoyed a cup of sun tea, and a *solar infusion* is no different. Plant matter (usually dried) is added to a vessel (usually glass) and allowed to sit in the full sunlight for several hours. The infrared radiation put out by the sun will cause the temperature in the vessel to rise slightly, gently extracting the beneficial compounds from the plant and adding them to the water. Yes, I realize your characters probably don't have a firm grip on scientific concepts such as "infrared radiation." I'm explaining this to you, the writer, not Grandix the Magnificent. Use this method with delicate plants and their parts, as the slower extraction process makes for a better taste, as well as better medicine.

*Lunar infusions* harness the power of the moon and are almost always accompanied by ceremony and ritual. A crystal bowl is set out during a full moon and filled with fresh spring water. The crystal focuses the light from the moon and transfers the energy in to the fresh and pure spring water. Plant material (usually flowers and leaves, often fresh) is gently laid across the top of the water, disturbing the still liquid as little as possible. The lunar-charged water slowly penetrates the leaves and flowers, allowing some to settle to the bottom, while others remain suspended. A few may remain on top, which is nothing to worry about. As the morning sun warms the horizon, the contents are strained and the liquid enjoyed by the weary-eyed participants, who likely stayed awake all night chanting and singing, further intensifying the power of the infusion.

### EXTRACTS AND TINCTURES

*Tinctures*, also known as *extractions*, are concentrated and preserved forms of liquid preparations. Unlike infusions, they can be made in large batches and saved for future need. Due to the concentrated nature of tinctures, they are also much easier to transport than cups of hot tea. The drawback (everything is give and take, even in herbalism) is the amount of time necessary to create the tincture. When you need it, you better have already made it.

Tinctures start with plant matter, either dried or fresh, and a quantity of a liquid extracting agent, usually alcohol or vinegar. If you're using dried plant matter, you'll likely need to add some water to the mix, as some of the elements will be water-soluble. A 50/50 ratio is the most common form of folk medicine, often referred to as a *dilute* mixture. If you're using fresh plants, don't use any additional water and go with straight alcohol. The plant brings its own water to the party, as most plants are at least 70% water; some as high as 90%.

A quick note on alcohol: not all booze is made of the same strength. You might call that bottle of Smirnoff® in the cupboard "alcohol," but it's really 60% water. The closest thing you'll find to 100% pure alcohol is Everclear® or some other sort of grain spirit. It's made in a lengthy, difficult and expensive distillation process. Unless there is a significant medicine-making industry in your world, the alcohol available to you will be most likely only slightly stronger than vodka, right around 50% alcohol. This doesn't mean you can't use fresh plants; it's just that they are not likely to be as strong as dried. Though some plants require tincturing when they are fresh—what a dilemma. Glad it's your book and not mine.

To start the tincturing process, add some herbs to a jar or other vessel which will accept a tight lid, then pour the liquid over the plant until completely covered. Tightly close the lid and set it in a dark and cool place. The next day, give the jar a healthy shake to help the extraction process along. Repeat for 14 days. Yes, fourteen. On the 15th day, strain the liquid into a new vessel using a fine cloth, squeezing out every last drop of liquid you can get. You can use your hands or a press to accomplish this goal. The latter is more effective, assuming you brought one in your bag.

Traditionally, tinctures are started on the eve of the full moon and then *decanted* (the process of separating the marc from the menstruum) on the eve of the new moon. The lunar cycle (at least on this planet) is roughly 28 days, a great way to remember when your 14 days are up. For those plants requiring a higher alcohol content than your civilization is able to provide, the *maceration process* (soaking in the liquid) should last longer. Leaving the marc in the menstuuum in for extra time isn't really harmful to the medicine, as the alcohol can't extract any more after a certain time and is preserving what was extracted along the way. But you shouldn't leave things in maceration any longer than six months. That way lies madness and jars full of sticky black goo which more resembles orc snot than botanical medicine.

Since tinctures are more concentrated than infusions, the dosage is much less. Tinctures are usually taken in *drop-dosages* ranging from five drops for the most powerful to one hundred for the more regularly consumed preparations. Add a few drops (or a splash) to a small amount of water and toss it back. While they are rarely tasty, the smaller quantity required usually increases the chance for patient compliance. And since liquid gel caps haven't been invented yet—what are you gonna do?

Some tinctures are amazingly fast-acting. A few drops of *Lobelia* applied under the tongue of someone in the throws of a *grand mal* seizure can calm the misfiring nervous system in under a minute. Others take months to affect a change in the individual, requiring a commitment and constant nagging to "take your medicine" by those around the patient.

### INFUSED OILS AND SALVES

*Oils* can effectively transmute the healing properties of certain plants. Much like the aqueous infusions described above, heated oil is added to plant matter (usually dried) and allowed to sit. If the heat is constantly applied (but not to the boiling point), the oil can be decanted in as little as an hour. If it requires a good soaking, you're back the to the 14-day range of a tincture. Oils are useful as topical agents or can be added to some form of wax (usually beeswax) to make a salve.

*Salves* combine oils, teas and tinctures together. Adding melted beeswax provides the thick consistency, allowing the medicine to be applied to a large area for extended periods of time. Salves are quite helpful when treating burns or other abrasions, softening the skin while constantly bathing the afflicted area in the healing power of the plants.

### POULTICES AND COMPRESSES

By using a *poultice* or a *compress*, the medicine of the plant is constantly in contact with the ailment or injury, much like a salve minus the oil and waxy mess. To make a poultice, simply bruise, mash or chew up some fresh and appropriate plant matter, and apply it directly to the area needing attention. Wrap the area in a thin, breathable cloth to keep the medicine in place, and change the dressing as necessary. This is an excellent way to stimulate the healing of deep wounds or to extract toxins from wounds that have been allowed to fester.

A compress is similar in application, but uses the aqueous extract of a plant by way of infusion or decoction. Soak a clean cloth in the medicinal liquid and apply directly to the skin. Wrap again in a clean, dry cloth and change as needed. Sprains and bruises respond quite well to the power of a compress, especially if it is kept warm by frequent changes of the wet cloth. Make a big batch of your infusion only if you can keep it warm throughout the treatment. If you're on the move, you'll have to make a fresh infusion each time you stop to rest.

## REAL MAGIC: SHAMANS AND MEDICINE MEN

Here's another place for you to have lots of fun as a writer: creating your own healing modality. *Western medicine* is the brand of healing most widely used in the US, encompassing medical doctors, chiropractors and even the quirky herbalist. It, like all other medical systems, makes some basic assumptions on how things work in the body. Western practitioners, like myself, see the human body as made up from a variety of organs and tissue types, all working together in healthy harmony. When one organ is not functioning up to par, other related organs may be affected and a state of disease sets in. Western medicine also recognizes the role pathogens, such as viruses and bacteria, play when introduced into the body and how they in turn stimulate the immune system response.

Other healing modalities operate in this world as well and have for centuries; no less valid than the one your medical doctor was taught twenty years ago. *Traditional Chinese Medicine (TCM)* practitioners see the body as made up of *body systems* rather than individual organs, placing more emphasis on the body as a whole than any one malfunctioning part. TCM relies on the principals of Yin and Yang, as well as a life energy called *Qi* (Chi, Gi...hey, you say tomato, and I say...) that the human body both ingests and produces internally. It's the disruption of the flow of Qi through the body which causes the state of disease, and TCM treatments are focused on reestablishing this balance.

*Ayurvedic* medicine practiced in India is similar to TCM, with heavy emphasis on life energy and balance. Ayurvedic practitioners look to achieve not only balance within the body, but with the entire universe. Understanding a person's constitution, or *dosha*, is crucial to Ayurveda, as different constitutions exhibit different types of diseases, therefore requiring specific approaches to heal each. A heavy emphasis is placed on spirituality and ritual as well.

Sir Arthur C. Clarke once said, "Any sufficiently advanced technology is indistinguishable from magic." The same holds true for advanced medicine. It doesn't take a radiology lab to qualify as advanced medicine. It does, however, require a systematic observation of the human, or non-human, body and the world in which it lives, a bit of trial and error, and lots and lots of time to develop. If a poor beggar is cured of his blindness, does that constitute a miracle? Maybe. Should we call it magic, or intervention by the gods? Why not? It doesn't matter if a shaman understood the problem to be a lack of blood supply to the optic nerve or an issue of stagnant Blood of the Liver (a TCM diagnosis quite different from how we Westerners define "blood" and "liver"). What matters is the result. A Western practitioner might suggest circulatory stimulating botanical remedies as well as tonics with an affinity for the eye. TCM doctors might recommend herbs to break up the congested Blood of the Liver as well as smooth and regulate the Qi. Both are likely to be successful, as they have been observed to be successful for hundreds or thousands of years. Which is right and which is wrong? Neither! While each modality would describe the actions and the condition differently, the overall affect on the body is the same. It is all a matter of perception.

This is one aspect of your book that need not be believable to most of your readers. What is important is that it be both believable and consistent for the characters in your story. Don't agonize over anatomy, symptom profiles or biochemistry. Make some assumptions about the way your world works and write them down. Create a special sect to deal with the really complicated cases, like extreme battle wounds, a plague or the extension of life for elder statesmen. Some have labeled them *medicine men, shamans, healers* or *green witches*. Pick a name that seems right for your world. By any name, they will have devoted their life to the study, practice and rituals far beyond the common knowledge of plant-based medicine used by the everyday person.

I've said it before and I'll say it again: you don't need to be a rocket scientist to use and understand botanical medicine. That's a good thing for you, as rocket science probably doesn't play too great a role in the fantasy worlds you have created. But just like any other avocation, discipline or area of study, there are some aspects of herbal medicine that are reserved for a special sect of learned individuals. Some are called to it by a higher power. Others are born into a particular caste system. A few are recognized by elder sages for their raw or latent talents. Whatever the method by which a neophyte healer was chosen, a long and arduous path lies ahead of him or her. If the initiate has shown proficiency with the healing arts prior to his indoctrination to the sect, the journey might be less mystical, but no less of a challenge.

There is an incredible wealth of knowledge beyond the simple remedies encountered and called for in a normal life. Your shamans will need to be well-versed not only in the healing modality you have created, but the plant life around them. Commoners know the handful of plants necessary to help them out in day-to-day situations. But shamans, and even their apprentices, must have an intimate and deep understanding of their local botany that encompasses so many more situations. To illustrate this point, take a look at this Indian legend (the sub-continent India, not the indigenous tribes of the Americas):

> A student of medicine many years in the training approached his master one day and asked when his studies would be over. The apprentice had learned much from his master, but was eager to go amongst the people and share his knowledge of healing with his community. It was, after all, the reason he devoted the last ten years of his life to his studies.
>
> As a final test for the student, the master told his student to search the hillsides far and wide and to return with as many plants as he could find which were of absolutely no value to mankind. The student quickly set about his task, convinced of his abilities and eager to prove his proficiency to his master. But as the minutes turned in to hours, and the hours into days, the student fell into despair. This task was proving harder than he imagined.
>
> Days later, and with his proverbial tail tucked between his legs, he returned to his master and admitted his failure. He had not been able to find a single plant which did not have at least

*one use to the people of his village, and was therefore resolved to spend much more time with his master, for surely there must be so much more yet for him to learn. "You are ready," said his master. "You have learned all you can from me when you can see the healing powers and proper usage in every plant you encounter. You are now ready to teach others what you have learned so completely."*

Your healers should be the closest things to gods your other characters are likely to encounter, at least on the "mortal" level. As such, don't be afraid to imbue your shamans with a certain amount of mysticism. Perhaps they speak an arcane language amongst themselves and have ancient tomes of cryptic writing known only to those practicing the arts. I would, however, advise caution when combining healing and theocracies. It's fine to seek out a priest who has the ability to heal, but if that priest also has governmental duties then the suspension of disbelief becomes less easy, in my opinion, especially if the theocracy is really an autocracy, and the priest/healer has power-hungry obsessions like any politician. Thucydides wrote *"Absolute power corrupts absolutely,"* and is that really a direction you want to take with your healers? Dark wizards and evil clerics are plausible enough, if not a bit cliché, when you consider the single mindedness it takes to master the powers of the underworld in a mad rush to dominate the entire population. But healers by nature are helpful to the people around them. I find it hard to believe that decades of dedication and the devotion required to master the healing arts would lead someone down a darker path. Not that there isn't room for dark arts in fantasy tales. Maybe your evil wizard started on the path to be a healer and was mesmerized by the narcotic principals of a few local plants, figuring out how to knock off his rivals and leaving him in a position of power, with just enough information and knowledge about a few sacred and powerful plants to be dangerous, but not a healer.

## SPEAKING OF THOSE SACRED AND POWERFUL PLANTS...

Life on earth, according to modern scientific thinking, assumes two basic forms: *animal* or *plant*. Some biologists recognize two additional forms, but *bacteria* are really more or less mini-animals, and *fungi* are quite plant-like. Let's lump *viruses* in with other mini-animal forms to keep us all sane, shall we? Plants and animals, while varying widely in function and form both in-kingdom and out, are all made up of the same "stuff," albeit in different quantities, proportions and molecular arrangement. An alien scientist analyzing and comparing any two given life forms on this planet at the chemical level would be drawn to a single conclusion: they are different manifestations of the same thing. There is no question that we are all Earthlings. From oxygen-breathing human to carbon dioxide-consuming elm tree, we are all cousins on this rock hurtling through space.

It is not a huge leap of faith to extend this commonality beyond the physical plane. Plants provide the base of the food chain from which we all derive nourishment. Plants provide us with invaluable compounds to heal us when we are sick. Might not our fellow companion plants also interact with our species on a less-tangible level? This almost laughable assertion was, and remains today in places, a well-accepted statement of fact for the majority of human existence. Many species, including but not limited to our own, have been drawn to these sacred plants on seemingly a primal level.

*Sacred plants* exude a powerful presence about themselves. Even in modern times, where our intuitive sense of perception has been dulled by centuries of humanism and technological advance, the power of certain plants is nearly palpable to those who make the effort to truly "see." You will have to decide on the level of perception carried about by the inhabitants of your world, and how tuned-in they are to the power plants around them. The plants themselves, however, require no modification—their power is constant.

It is a common misconception that all sacred plants are *psychotropic*, or that all psychotropic plants are sacred. Take the case of *Osha*, for example, a strongly scented plant growing in the higher elevations of the Western US. Called *bear medicine* by the native tribes of the area, it will not get you high upon ingesting. Nor is it highly toxic. However, it is of the highest order of sacred plants among the people who lived alongside Osha. Rather than opening a doorway to the spirit world, Osha *is* the spirit world, in a physical manifestation. Not only is it useful for physical ailments, particularly of the respiratory system, Osha is used with ailments of the spirit, providing protection and shelter from malevolent incorporeal forces wreaking havoc on the physical plane. Seen in that light, it is no wonder that much ceremony and ritual accompany the harvesting, preparation and consumption of Osha and the medicine it provides.

Sacred plants that are psychotropic usually offer their trip with a hefty price. In most cases, toxic compounds accompany those that facilitate the hallucinations. *Sacred Datura* is another plant native to the western desert portions of North America. Used for centuries to assist local shamans in accessing the sprit world, Datura is not a benign plant. All parts of the plant are highly toxic, to the point where the plant is rarely used today in ceremony, and then only by elders who have been taught the complex preparation and rituals necessary to reduce the possibility of poisoning. Sadly, many youngsters ignorant of the dangers but seeking a cheap escape wind up blind or worse each year after experimenting with the plant. Similar stories of accidental death or injury are recounted from inexperienced individuals ingesting *peyote*, another desert southwest plant, or *"death cap" mushrooms* that grow in more moist climes. Yes, these sacred plants will likely give you a glimpse of the spirit world...one way or another.

Most sacred plants, at least those used ceremoniously or as a powerful medicine, are uncommon. They often grow in difficult-to-access areas, or inhospitable environments, further adding to their mystique. By and large they are not rare, as rarity suggests little chance for observation of the effects of ingesting the plant, even over a great span of time. Sacred plants are, however, traded far and wide, allowing high latitude cultures access to species that will only grow in the tropical zone. The trade in sacred plants has been big business throughout time, among merchants as well as those trained in the healing arts. Most large population centers would house a brisk trade in medicinal, cooking and ceremonial plants, showcasing specimens from around the globe.

The *ceremonies* surrounding the use of sacred plants are as varied and as complex as the preparations to make the plant ready to release its power. Just as with medicinal preparations, sacred plants are used either dried or fresh, though drying the plants first is more common in ceremonies. Sacred plants are almost always harvested according to the teachings of arcane texts or during precise astrological conditions, such as the summer solstice, a solar eclipse or under the light of a full moon. Specialized tools are used to harvest the plant, often crafted exclusively for this single purpose. Even the attire of the harvester is distinctive during this time, reflecting again the true magic of this venture and instilling as much power into the situation as possible.

Sacred plants are smoked, drunk, worn, smoldered, buried, waved about, eaten, smelled, rolled around in, sung to, sprinkled on, fed to animals before slaughter and even tucked under a pillow at night. It all depends on the need and the cultural aspects of your story, of which you have full range of control. But in all cases, sacred plants are used sparingly and only by those who have the necessary training, knowledge and wisdom to harness and channel the power from within them.

## BEYOND HEALING

As mentioned earlier, plants truly are our companion species on this planet. Before this chapter, you had intimate knowledge of how plants are useful to our species for food and shelter. I'm assuming you all have partaken of at least some type of fruit in your life and are familiar with the two-by-four concept of House Building 101. Now you have added to that knowledge a glimpse of how plants are also useful as allies of health, providing people medicine for thousands of years. But plants are more than just tools, food or medicine, and there are many other uses for plants that can add depth and richness to your worlds.

### COLOR

Anyone who has walked outdoors in the spring can attest to the fact that flowers are the rainbow of the world. Throughout the ages, mankind has learned to harness the vibrant colors of flowers by creating dyes and paints, allowing the brilliant hues to be passed along to hides, fabrics, walls and other objects. Fruits also make an excellent base for a dye, as do roots and other plant parts. Dye and paint making is more an industry than an art, requiring a good chunk of resources, time and physical labor to produce. Getting into the mechanics of making paint is about as much fun as watching it dry. Plants, water, fire, lots of sweaty bodies and voila!

### SCENTS

Many plants have distinctive aromas, many of which are quite pleasant to the human olfactory sensors. Wearing a wreath of flowers imparts the smell on to the wearer, though the effect is often only as good as long as the flowers are fresh. Many processes exist for isolating the aromatic compounds of plants, though *distillation* is the most common. It is also quite expensive, as the equipment necessary is quite intricate. Roughly described, the condensation from boiling plant matter is collected and concentrated over a long period of time to create distilled scented oils. There is a lot more to it than that simple description, and many books have been published which do the process a much better service than I would be capable of achieving here.

## FLAVORING AGENTS

That is actually a misnomer. Perhaps "flavor masking agents" would be more indicative for how plants were originally used to "season" foods. One of my personal favorite dishes to make and enjoy is rosemary pork chops. Combine a finely chopped sprig of fresh *Rosemary* with a bit of olive oil and rub briskly into a few pork chops. Allow the chops to marinate for at least an hour, grill and serve. Delicious. And practical. Rosemary is a powerful antioxidant, which keeps meat fresh for longer periods of time. The volatile oils of Rosemary also can mask the flavor of meat which is a little (or a lot) past its prime. This dual nature of many plants, acting as a preservative and mitigater of bad taste, has resulted in the flavorful nature of our cuisine today.

## A FROND FAREWELL

Man's relationship with plants predates writing, agriculture, religion and civilization itself. This relationship has been built slowly over time, piece by piece, by observation as well as trial and error. Every society on this planet has their own stories, fables and mythologies describing in great detail the plants growing alongside those who created the tales. Even in our modern times, where technological advances push our species further and further away from the natural world, people continue this love affair with the plant kingdom by planting gardens and buying fresh-cut flowers at the market. Still others are intimately involved in growing food and producing medicine, continuing a cycle of symbiosis between plant and animal with origins at the very beginning of our species.

If you choose to introduce plant medicine into your fantasy world, take the time to make it right, yet unique to your world. Do not make it an offhand comment, relegated to a single line of text when your hero is gravely wounded. Hopefully this chapter has inspired you to seek out the depths of what you have created. Who knows? There might be a story idea or two in here for you.

Namaste.

## Evo's Suggested Reading List

Herbal books, called *herbals* oddly enough, tend to be dry reads for everyone other than herbalists. There are, however, a few books with excellent narrative that also convey both traditional and contemporary herb wisdom. Your local city library may not have copies on hand, as these appeal to a small niche of people. If you have a major university library near you, you're likely to fare better. Those lucky enough to live near naturopathic medical schools will be striking gold. Here are my recommendations in no particular order:

*The Lost Language of Plants* by Stephen Harold Buhner—By far the most eloquent dissertation on the state of the planet, medicine, our bodies and our souls. Read it again and again.

*Green Pharmacy* by Barbara Griggs—A journey through the history and evolution of Western herbal medicine. Great info on the shift from natural to pharmaceutical medicines.

*Ayurveda – The Science of Self-Healing* by Dr. Vasant Lad—An excellent introduction to the principles and practical applications of Indian Ayurvedic medicine.

*The Web That Has No Weaver* – Ted J. Kaptchuck, O.M.D.—Understanding Tradtional Chinese Medicine is hard for us westerners. Ted makes it easier than most.

*Healing Wise* by Susun Weed—Susun brings the plants to life in her books, with entertaining characters and points of view.

*Medicinal Plants of the Desert and Canyon West* by Michael Moore—Michael is a personal hero of mine, having a great wit and biting sarcasm as he describes the plants or their uses. If you want to "know" plants of the southwest, he's the guy to teach you.

*Gathering the Desert* by Gary Paul Nabhan—Understanding the history and legends of plants is just as important as knowing how they heal.

*The Mysterious Lands* by Ann Haymond Zwinger—Further information on the southwest desert from a naturalist who should be a poet.

# Getting in Touch with Your Inner Fan:
## WRITING FOR RPG AND MEDIA TIE-INS

### BY WILL MCDERMOTT

Novels based on movies and television shows such as *Star Wars, Star Trek, Buffy the Vampire Slayer* and *Angel*, as well as such fantasy-oriented games as *Dungeons & Dragons* and *Magic: The Gathering*, now make up a significant portion of the science fiction and fantasy (SFF) market. Just go into your local bookstore and head to the science fiction section (which is where fantasy novels still get shelved). At least one-quarter—and perhaps as much as one-half—of the shelves dedicated to science fiction and fantasy will be filled with role-playing game (RPG) and media tie-in novels.

These books are often discussed under the umbrella term of "shared world" novels because many different authors are all writing stories in a single world using shared settings and shared characters. As such, this large market requires a large number of authors. The *Magic: The Gathering* series alone currently numbers over thirty novels. Most of these shared world novels are printed as series, so the books get shelved together under the series title. This makes it easy for readers interested in that series to find your book. And, as most novelists will tell you, this is at least ninety percent of the battle for making sales—especially for a new or up-and-coming writer. You might not have name recognition yet, but if a series is popular, even a first-time novelist can get decent sales and instant fame with a shared world novel.

But don't expect that name recognition to automatically transfer to more work and higher royalties down the line. In the minds of most SFF writers and publishers, shared world novels are still very much the Harlequin Romances of the genre. These novels are often seen as little more than pulp fiction by other SFF authors. This is ironic considering that the entire SFF genre has struggled against that label for half a century from mainstream and literary writers and publishers.

However, many well-known SFF authors got their start writing shared world novels. One of the best-known success stories in this section of the genre is R. A. Salvatore. As the story goes, Salvatore was found in the "slush" pile at TSR, then the publishers of the *Dungeons & Dragons* games and novels. He was asked to write the initial novel in a new series—*The Forgotten Realms*. Salvatore's style and characters hit a nerve in the gaming community, propelling his work to the *New York Times* bestsellers list. Salvatore has now published over thirty novels, including more than a dozen written in worlds of his own creation for such "mainstream" SFF publishers as Ace and Del Rey.

R. A. Salvatore's story is a shining light to aspiring writers who want to break into the publishing business. It is possible for an unknown writer to get a foot in the door and jumpstart a career in the RPG and media tie-in subgenre of SFF. However, there are many pitfalls to avoid along the way, and contrary to popular belief, it's not really easier to write shared world novels—or to get published in this subgenre—than it is in the general SFF field. It's just different.

This chapter will take you through the steps to getting that first shared world novel published and discuss the unique problems you will encounter along the way. We'll talk about how to get work in the field and what to expect once you're offered a contract. We'll discuss doing research (which is just as important as when writing your own stories), and then talk about writing the story and doing the re-write.

## What We Aren't: Shared World v. FanFic

First, though, let's talk about the differences between shared world fiction and *fanfic* (or fan-written fiction). The basic difference is that shared world fiction is authorized by the *licensor* (the company that owns and controls the story), while fanfic is unauthorized. This may seem like a small difference to those fans who just want to write a *Star Trek* or *Buffy* story, but there are some consequences resulting from this distinction you should consider before writing fanfic.

First of all, fanfic does not become *canon* (official storyline history), so a fanfic author can never truly affect the destiny of any characters in the world. Of course, most fanfic writers don't care whether their story is canon. They just want to have some fun with the characters and see what might happen if Buffy and Xander ever got together (or Kirk and Spock, but that's a completely different type of fanfic altogether). However, if you want to write authorized stories that have a real impact on the storyline of your favorite show, fanfic is not the venue for you.

Plus, some licensors like to control their properties (the stories and worlds they have created) very closely. You can face legal action if you publish a story in someone else's world without permission, even if you only publish it on the Internet. Now, most licensors will simply ask you to cease publication or force you to remove the story from the website. But if you have been profiting from the sale of fiction written in a licensed world without permission, that is considered stealing and you could face serious punishments.

Of course, most fan fiction is not written to make money, so the chances of getting sued are minimal. Fanfic authors write for the simple joy of playing with their favorite characters or favorite world. The stories are posted free on fan sites or printed on copy machines and given out to friends. Realistically (and legally) you can't make any money from writing fanfic, as you can from writing authorized, shared world fiction. In addition, fanfic rarely advances your professional career. Most fanfic is written by amateurs and lacks the polish of novels that are written by professionals. Thus, most publishers regard fanfic with a certain amount of disdain.

If you are looking to cross over to the professional, shared world market where you can actually get paid for your work, you would be wise to keep your fanfic career under wraps. Even though fanfic can be a way to practice your craft and get feedback from readers on your abilities, if you do publish some fanfic, do so anonymously or write under a pseudonym. Publishers won't count fanfic as publishing credits on your resume anyway because of its amateur status, and those publishers who do control their licenses very closely will never hire a fanfic writer for an authorized, shared world fiction project.

## Paying Your Dues: Getting Work

Now that you know what we aren't, let's look at what shared world fiction really is, and how to get work in the field. Probably the main difference between shared world fiction and the rest of SFF (at least from the perspective of a potential author) is how you get published. Most, if not all, shared world novels are "works-for-hire." This means that the publisher contracts you to write the novel instead of signing a contract with you to publish a novel you've already written. Thus, while you may have some input into character creation and development, story setting, and maybe even the plot of the novel, you are still writing the publisher's story in *their* world. Therefore, you will be writing under certain constraints that authors writing in worlds of their own design generally don't have to worry about.

What this also means, though, is that the publisher owns all of the rights to the work after you deliver the final draft. As I mentioned earlier, you are writing in *their* world. You will still get paid for writing the novel and may even receive royalties after it is published, but you cannot re-sell the work later once it's out of print and you won't cash in on movie rights or other spin-off's of your work, unless compensation for those extra rights are specifically spelled out in the contract (but only established authors have the clout to pull that off). The novel belongs to the publisher once you're finished with it, and not all authors are comfortable with that type of arrangement.

Work-for-hire has its perks, though. For one thing, you know you will get paid for your work. In fact, you generally get part of your *advance* upon signing the contract. An advance is a financial sum paid in installments, usually one at the beginning and the remainder payable upon completion of the rough draft and/or the final draft. Most first-time authors spend months or years writing their novel and then spend many more months or years trying to attract a publisher before they get a single dime for all their work.

Plus, while you still have do your homework on the world and characters to avoid making mistakes in dialogue, characterization, or setting descriptions, writing in a shared world allows you to concentrate more on plot development and writing and less on world building and research. Much of that work is already done for you. Everything you really need to know is in previous books, on the screen, or comes from the original creators of the world.

But that doesn't mean you can necessarily go from one shared world project to another with no downtime for research and no breaks between work-for-hire paychecks. Consider this kind of project as freelance work, which means that not only do you have do the work, you have to go out and find the work. You're going to need more than the ability to write good dialogue and a love for a particular fictional world to get a job writing shared world fiction. You need both of these as well as talent, some luck, a lot of perseverance and (nowadays) an agent.

Contrary to popular belief, it's not all that easy to get your start in shared world fiction; at least, not anymore. Remember, shared world publishers are almost never going to publish *your* story. They generally have a continuing storyline and each novel has to fit into it. That means you will be writing *their* story. So how do you get their attention? Some publishers, such as Wizards of the Coast, still accept unsolicited manuscripts. Wizards has several shared world lines tied to the games they publish. These include the popular *Dragonlance* and *Forgotten Realms* novels, a series of novels tied to the *Magic: The Gathering* trading card game, and two new young adult lines—*Dragonlance: The New Adventures* and *Knights of the Silver Dragon*.

But Wizards isn't going to print *your* novel. They look through the pile of *unsolicited manuscripts* they receive looking for potential authors. Unsolicited manuscripts are any stories or novels that the publisher did not ask to see. These go into what is called the *slush pile*, which is a stack (or many stacks) of unsolicited manuscripts that only gets read when the editor has no other work to do. Not many writers make it out of the slush pile, even though that is supposedly how Salvatore's career got started. But even Salvatore had done a lot of work refining his style, *and* he got lucky that the right editor saw his manuscript at the right time—when TSR needed an author to jumpstart a new line of novels.

But many publishers don't accept unsolicited material anymore. For example, Simon Pulse publishing—the imprint of Simon and Schuster that publishes all of their media tie-in novels—only accepts *agented* submissions. These are submissions presented to the publisher by an agent working for the author. The agent makes the contacts and sends your work to the publisher. So you need an agent to get noticed by Simon and Schuster, which makes it especially tough on authors interested in breaking into shared world fiction. Simon Pulse publishes novels for all of the following shows: *Buffy the Vampire Slayer*, *Angel*, *Charmed*, *Star Trek*, *Warcraft*, *Terminator*, *Transformers*, *Blade*, *Battlestar Galactica*, *Resident Evil*, *Ghostbusters*, *Law and Order*, *Everwood*, *CSI*, *The Wire*, *SpongeBob SquarePants* and others.

In addition, neither Del Rey, the publishers of adult *Star Wars* novels, nor Scholastic, publishers of the *Jedi Apprentice* and *Jedi Quest* young adult novels as well as such children's media tie-in novels as *PowerPuff Girls* and *Jimmy Neutron*, accepts unsolicited submissions. This leaves the shared world field looking much like the rest of the publishing business—a tough place to break into for novice writers.

So what can you do to get noticed? As with any other fiction field in this day and age, you have to make your own breaks. Generally, you need to know someone on the inside, find an agent to represent you, or have enough name recognition in the industry that you can cut through some of the red tape. All of these require you to pay your dues. Good agents (the kind that will actually get you noticed by one of the top publishers of shared world fiction) only represent authors they believe have the stuff to make it (and make them money). Name recognition comes from getting published in other paying markets, or through strong ties to the actual RPG or media tied to the novels. And, having a contact on the inside either comes from dumb luck or—more likely—from actually working in the industry for a decent period of time (anywhere from two to twenty years, depending on your drive).

If you are serious about writing shared world fiction, there are some options. Short fiction is a great way to hone your craft and get published in respectable outlets. Most SFF magazines still accept unsolicited manuscripts, so you can get published without an agent and then use those credentials to either get an agent or make a name for yourself that might open doors down the road.

There are many magazines out there looking for fiction. The top magazines like *Isaac Asimov's Science Fiction* magazine, *Fantasy and Science Fiction* magazine and *Realms of Fantasy* will pay for your work, but they may be tougher to break into at first. Luckily, there are hundreds of smaller publications (many of which only pay in *author copies*—copies of the issue in which your story appears). The best way to find markets for your work is to buy or borrow a copy of the *Writers' Market*, which lists book and magazine editors, as well as agents, with complete details of what they are looking for, how much they pay, and how long it will take for them to respond. Here are some websites to jumpstart your search for short fiction markets.

- www.writersmarket.com (the online version of the Writer's Market guide)
- gilaqueen.us (Gila Queen's Guide to Markets, which lists numerous markets)
- www.ralan.com (Ralan's Webstravaganza, which lists SF and humor book, magazine, and anthology markets)
- www.burryman.com/scifi.html (The Burry Man Writers Center, which lists SF and horror markets)

Look for magazines or anthologies that are publishing the type of stories you like to write. You don't want to send a sword and sorcery story to *Isaac Asimov's Science Fiction Magazine*. They just don't publish that type of story. The best way to find out what a magazine wants is to buy a copy and read the stories inside.

You can also look for other opportunities outside the major publishing houses. Wizards of the Coast still accepts unsolicited manuscripts, so that's one place to start. Many of the fiction writers for Wizards got their start by working on RPG products. And while you may not be able to get an RPG freelance job through Wizards, there are magazines such as *Dragon* and *Dungeon*, and many small companies that produce d20 (D&D compatible) products out there. These magazines and small companies are always looking for capable writers to work on new products.

Some of the d20 companies are even beginning to publish fiction in their own worlds, which is another place to get your start. In addition, small press publishers often gain access to the rights for smaller or newer media properties. These small press publishers are usually less strict about submission guidelines and can be a great place to get your start. And, if that property takes off, you can rise with it as one of the original authors.

The best way to keep on top of these kinds of opportunities is to track the industry. Find some properties that interest you and watch the Internet for information about publishing opportunities for that show or game. If you're a fan of the show, you may already know where to find the information you need, and that interest will help you throughout the process. The company that produces the property is a good starting point, but often the most up to date information will be found on fan sites. It may take some digging to find the right sites, but here are a few URLs to get you started:

- www.aicn.com (Ain't-It-Cool-News—a great source for info about SFF movies and T.V. shows)
- www.enworld.org (EN World—*the* spot for information about D&D and d20 publishing companies)
- www.gamingreport.com (Gaming Report—news about the gaming industry)

## GAME ON: WHAT TO EXPECT
## ONCE YOU GET THE JOB

So, you've done your homework. You've made some contacts or worked your way up through the ranks from editor to game designer to short story writer. Now you're getting your first shot at writing a novel set in the shared world you love so much. What happens next? Well, first the publisher will give you a contract to sign. Most publishing contracts for first-time authors are pretty standard, so if you understand publishing contracts, there shouldn't be too many surprises inside.

Still, you should read the contract *carefully*. You might even want to get an agent or a contract lawyer at this point to make sure you get the best deal possible. But don't fool yourself. As a first-time author you won't have a lot of clout. There probably won't be much room for negotiation. If you're unfamiliar with publishing contracts, find someone you trust to help explain the fine print. The SFWA (Science Fiction Writers of America) website at www.sfwa.org has advice on contracts that can be invaluable.

Probably the most important parts of the contract are: assignment of rights (including subsidiary rights), advance and royalty amounts (or payment structure if there are no royalties), word count and deadlines. Let's take a look at what you can expect from each of these sections.

### RIGHTS

As was mentioned earlier, most shared world fiction is owned by the publisher. If this is the case, the contract will state that the publisher owns all rights to the work. In other genres, the author owns the rights to his or her own work and gives only a limited amount of rights to the publisher—usually first North American rights. This gives the publisher the right to publish the work before anyone else in the geographical location specified in the contract. But after that, the rights revert back to the author. So, you could possibly sell it again. For example, many authors make a great deal of money from foreign editions of earlier novels.

If the publisher owns all rights (as in most shared world fiction), the author won't get any additional income from foreign language editions or if the work is adapted to other media such as movies or video games. This may not be a problem if you don't think there is much of a chance that the other rights will ever bear fruit. But there might be some wiggle room here. Some shared world publishers will put foreign language or subsidiary publication clauses into their contracts, providing the author some compensation for adaptations or reprints in other forms. It can't hurt to ask.

### ADVANCES, ROYALTIES, PAYMENTS

Of course, the first thing you will probably want to check in the contract is what you will get paid. Work-for-hire is often paid as a flat fee (or lump sum payment). This can actually be a good thing for a first-time author as the lump sum may well be more than you would ever earn from royalties. You may even be able to negotiate a higher payment if you decide you'd rather take a lump sum than an advance on royalties. It depends on the publisher.

But don't expect an exorbitant amount of money on your first few books. Five cents per word is probably about all you can expect for the lump sum or the advance. And for a small press, that amount might drop to as low as one cent per word. Of course, the advantage of writing in a shared world is that you will get at least part of your advance upon signing the contract—even before you start writing the book! The rest of the advance will then be paid in installments based on completing certain milestones, such as the outline, rough draft and final draft.

If you get royalties on the book, you won't see any of that money until a month after the end of the quarter when the book is published (for example, not until February 1 for a book released in October, November or December). Even then, you have to *earn out* your advance before you get any royalties. This means that if you were paid a $5,000 advance, the book has to sell enough copies that your royalties (usually one to four percent of retail sales) exceed $5,000 before you get any royalty payments at all. Now you see why it may be better in some instances to just take a lump sum.

### DEADLINES AND WORD COUNT

Deadlines and word count are pretty straight-forward, but it's important that you are aware of what you are getting into before you sign the contract. Many authors in other genres spend years writing their first novel. You won't get anywhere near that much time to write a shared world novel. These novels are all linked to a continuing storyline and are probably planned a year at a time on the publisher's schedule. Much of that year is already eaten up in editing, typesetting, printing and distributing, and those dates will often be locked in on the schedule.

You could get as little as four to six months to write the novel, which can be anywhere from 50,000 to 120,000 words. This includes the time it takes for you to create an outline, which some shared world publishers require before you begin writing. They want to make sure you understand where the story is going. They may also need to know how your story starts and ends so they can pass that information on to the author of the next novel to maintain continuity between stories. A chapter-by-chapter outline describing the major events of each chapter in a few sentences or a couple paragraphs should be sufficient and can help you organize your thoughts before writing.

After you make the first draft deadline, you will probably only get another month (or less, depending on the demand for the title) for re-writes. As you can see, you have to work very quickly in shared world publishing, so check the dates in the contract carefully. They should all be spelled out there for you.

And, above all, don't miss your deadlines. That's a sure sign to the publisher that you can't be trusted with more novels in the future. Of course, emergencies do crop up that can affect your delivery of the novel, and most editors will be sympathetic. But unless you are in a coma for a few months, your editor will still expect the first draft within a reasonable amount of time. It's vitally important to keep your editor up-to-date on your progress. If it looks like you're going to need a few extra weeks to finish, let your editor know as early as possible (at least a month before your original deadline). Remember, editors and publishers have deadlines as well, and the publishing schedule for your book is based on your delivery of the novel by the deadline in the contract. If you mess up that schedule without warning, your publisher will not be happy, and you may never get another chance to prove yourself.

## SWEATING THE DETAILS:
### CONTINUITY AND RESEARCH

Even after you sign the contract, though, you're not ready to write. Now it's time to do your research. Of course, research for a shared world novel is a little different from the research you would do for a regular SFF novel. Instead of worrying about world building, setting up your magic system, and studying various social mores and religious iconology, you have to spend some time catching up on *continuity*.

Basically, continuity means creating a continuous storyline with no unexplained breaks or plot holes. However, in shared worlds, continuity takes on a much larger and more important meaning. With different authors writing about a single set of characters all living in one coherent world, continuity encompasses a number of elements that need to be monitored to make sure the stories flow smoothly. These elements include: *backstory, characterization* and *setting.* Here are some definitions to help you understand what we're talking about in this section.

**BACKSTORY:** The story behind the story. Backstory includes all of the previous adventures the characters have had, as well as any behind-the-scenes information relevant to the current story, the history of the world and its characters and any past relationships that might have an impact on the current plot.

**CHARACTERIZATION:** How the characters act, talk and behave. Characterization includes mannerisms, speech patterns, personal views and biases about the world, other characters, society and religion; and how each character reacts to such things as stress, fear, sadness and confrontation.

**SETTING:** The world within which the story is set. Setting includes physical descriptions of the places the characters will frequent in the story as well as the history of those places. But setting also includes the rules that govern how the world works and the history of that world (which may or may not be independent of the characters' backstory).

Maintaining continuity in a shared world is one of the most difficult tasks for the writer, editor and the owners of the license because if the line is successful, there could be literally hundreds of stories written about the characters that need to be tracked. Just take a look at *Buffy the Vampire Slayer.* In addition to all of the novels that have been written in the "buffyverse," the show was on the air for seven seasons, so there are over 140 episodes. The backstory encompasses information from all of these episodes, plus all of the novels, plus information from the *Angel* series and books, plus any additional information still inside the head of *Buffy* creator Joss Whedon.

So, if you thought you were going to get off easy when it comes to research, you were wrong. You may not have to create the world and make it internally consistent, but you do need a firm grounding in the entire backstory (or at least enough of it to keep your story consistent within the time frame of your novel's plotline).

For example, in the case of setting, if the story is set in a realistic setting that also includes vampires and demons, then you need to know the rules that govern those supernatural elements. Or if the story takes place in a fantasy world with magic and monsters, then you need to know how the magic system works and which monsters are likely to show up in a given locale.

For characterization, you want to make sure that the characters "ring true" for the readers. You wouldn't have Buffy dating Xander in a *Buffy the Vampire Slayer* novel because the history of their relationship rules out that possibility. Or if you were writing a *Farscape* novel, you wouldn't have D'Argo sell out the crew because that's inconsistent with his character. Remember, these characters may have shown up in many dozens of books and episodes, so readers will have an intimate knowledge of each character's personal history, as well as all of their mannerisms, speech patterns, allegiances and prejudices—not to mention any supernatural powers (and any limits) they may have.

Backstory is a little trickier. This basically encompasses setting and characterization as well as the history of the world and the storyline. You can often get away with only a rudimentary knowledge of the backstory except for those aspects you need for setting and characterization. But the more you know about the history of the world, the richer your story will become. Sprinkling references to earlier stories, using quotes that characters have said in similar circumstances and including familiar places and characters from old storylines can help embed your story within the rich tapestry of the backstory and provides observant readers with little gems of insight into your story.

Luckily, you don't have to go far to get the information you need. Most of the backstory can be found in the episodes of the show or movie and its previous books. Of course with a very popular series, catching up on the entire storyline can be a daunting task. It helps if you're already a fan of the *property* (the show or game world). Most writers of shared world fiction were fans before they began writing in that world. If you are new to the story, you will want to get your hands on as much source material as possible. That means reading the books, renting or borrowing the episodes or movies or, in the case of a game, going through the rules of the game and catching up on the major events in the world of the game through source books or by talking with players.

If you need help, the Internet may come to the rescue for you again. Most properties have a very strong fan presence on the World Wide

Web. These sites often contain character bios, episode synopses and even favorite character quotes. The most popular properties will have official guides to the show, which you can read through to get a head start on your research. Your best bet is to google (www.google.com) the title of the show or world and find fan sites with episode guides or storyline spoilers. The TV Tome website (www.tvtome.com) is a great place to start as well. They have episode guides for many popular shows.

Even then, just watching the show, reading all its previous novels or educating yourself through a printed guide or fan sites won't tell you everything you need to know. There will always be new backstory information that you may need to know for your book. This is where *style guides*, sometimes called *bibles* or *godbooks*, come in.

Godbooks are the writer's guide to the backstory. These are maintained by the licensor (the owners of the media or game property). A godbook will have character profiles (perhaps with favorite catch-phrases), a brief history of the world and the story, and information about the setting and how the world works. Pretty much *everything* (and then some!) an author needs to know to write in that world.

Not every licensor will have a godbook. Sometimes that wealth of information is all contained in the very big brains of one or two people. Some might have multiple style guides keyed to different seasons of the show or editions of the game. But it doesn't hurt to ask your publisher if you can get hold of the style guide, bible, godbook or whatever your particular licensor calls this document. It can be invaluable not only for research before writing, but as a resource for descriptions and dialogue during the writing process.

## ROLL THE BONES: WRITING THE STORY

Once you're comfortable that you've read everything you need to know about the shared world or can find answers through available materials, you're ready to work on the story. Now, writing a shared world novel is not all that different from writing any other genre novel. You follow a plot wherein your protagonists are faced with some sort of crisis they must find a way to resolve. This crisis is most likely precipitated through the ministrations of an antagonist whom the heroes must locate and stop. There will be rising and falling action throughout the novel until you finally reach the climax wherein the heroes meet and defeat the villain or villains.

There are plenty of books out there that will tell you how to write a novel, so I won't spend any more time on that here. Instead, let's take a look at how this process is affected by writing in a shared world. The first task you will probably be asked to complete will be an outline. Outlines are mostly to insure that you are writing the story the licensor wants written. However, they can be a great tool for a beginning writer to help organize the novel and make sure the action flows well throughout the entire story.

How much input you have into the plot of the story will vary from licensor to licensor. Some take a very collaborative stance, providing new information about the setting and characters and some general guidelines on where the story is going, and then work with the author to come up with the plot. Author Terry Brooks, who wrote novelizations for both *Star Wars: The Phantom Menace* and *Hook*, shows both the good and the bad sides of licensor relationships in his memoirs, *Sometimes the Magic Works*.

Other publishers even accept proposals for new stories. A proposal is a short description (no more than a single typed page in length) that describes the plot, themes and characters for a story idea. Unlike an outline, you don't have to detail all of the major action in a proposal. All you need is a simple overview of the story. If the proposed story works within the continuity and doesn't violate the timeline of the backstory, the author may be given a lot of leeway and allowed to run with it. This is more likely for episodic stories where each novel can stand alone and doesn't lead directly into the next book.

In a shared world series where the story follows a specific arc that has been laid out by the licensor, you will probably have very little input into the main plot elements of your own novel. A *story arc* is a smaller story within the larger backstory or history of the world. For example, each season of *Buffy the Vampire Slayer* follows a specific story arc that culminates in a fight against the "big bad." Many shared world novels are written within such story arcs that have specific beginnings and endings dictated by the licensor, so you are basically writing the story the publisher wants written. You may even be given an outline to follow.

Whatever the case, you will definitely be constrained by certain factors as you write. For example, you cannot kill off major characters without express permission. These characters must be around for future novels, so you can't simply kill them off. Conversely, you may be asked by the licensor to kill off a major character, which can alienate fans of the series and cause you a lot of grief. But generally, you cannot do anything that will permanently change the setting or the characters unless that is part of the approved plot. Remember, you are sharing this world with other authors and basically playing in someone else's sandbox.

For example, while writing *Apocalypse*, the world-destroying finale to a four-year, 14-book cycle in the *Magic: The Gathering* universe, author Rob King wanted to kill off the big bad guy—Yawgmoth (think Sauron or Voldemort). Wizards of the Coast, the owners of the *Magic* brand and storyline, wanted Yawgmoth to survive. It wasn't until the editor stepped up and pleaded Rob's case to the powers that be that he was allowed to take out the big bad in a conclusive (if costly) battle.

The basic problem is that your novel will be considered canon for the world in which you are writing. This means that the information within your novel will become part of the continuity for future books. That's why you will be asked to write an outline and/or write from an outline. Failure to follow the outline will mean bigger re-writes down the line, so stick to your outline as closely as possible and make sure you get *written* permission for any major deviations. And keep that memo close—you may be asked for proof of that permission at a later date!

Now, this may sound like you going to be put into a straitjacket as you write. That's not really the case. Remember, a 300-page novel is about 90,000 words. An outline—even a detailed, chapter-by-chapter outline—might run ten pages (no more than 5,000 words). If you were to copy all of the information from the outline, word-for-word, into the appropriate spots of the novel, you will still have to come up with 85,000 words on your own. That's a lot of room for creativity and for making your mark on that story...and on that universe.

For instance, you will invariably need some extra minor (and possibly even major) characters for your story. If an appropriate character does not already exist in the backstory, you should be able to create new characters as needed for your plot. Again, this may need to be approved by the licensor, especially for new major characters that aren't killed off by the end of the book. But this is one area where you can be very creative within the context of a shared world setting.

You may even make an impact on future stories. If your new character becomes popular with the fans, that character might show up in other novels (even ones you don't write). Remember, once it's published, your story and characters—*your* creations—becomes canon.

Here is an example drawn from my experiences in the *Magic: The Gathering* universe. I created a character named Slobad for *The Moons of Mirrodin*. I felt the main character needed a goblin sidekick to act as foil, guide and comic relief; and I couldn't help but find inspiration from my "Mr. Fixit" brother-in-law who helped us out of a jam with my car. Slobad was supposed to be a minor character who could move the plot along when needed and make readers laugh at other times. But by the end of the third book (*The Fifth Dawn*, which I did not write), not only had Slobad survived, but he was taken to the brink of virtual godhood and sacrificed that power for the greater good. This minor character I created as an homage to my brother-in-law became much more than I had ever envisioned. But it can go the other way just as easily in a shared world. A fire god I created for a *Magic* short story titled "The Lady of The Mountain" showed up in a later novel as no more than a powerful mage with a messiah complex.

## DRAWING FROM THE DECK AGAIN: THE RE-WRITE

Okay. You're in the home stretch now. After putting 90,000 words together in as little as four months, how hard can it be to go through and make the changes requested by your editor? The answer to that question depends partly on your abilities as a writer, but also on the needs of the licensor. The main difference between doing re-writes for your own novel and doing re-writes for a shared world novel is (once again) that this story doesn't *really* belong to you.

When you write your own novel, you are the expert on the story, characters and plot. Your editor can give you suggestions, but it's easy enough to override those objections when you know you are right about how a passage should read or how a character behaves. A good author/editor relationship is a partnership. Your editor makes suggestions that he or she believes will make the novel better. You, as the author, are free to make suggested changes that make sense to you and explain to your editor why you believe you are right on other points.

However, in a shared world novel, there is another layer above you and the editor. The licensor normally gets *final approval* on the novel.

So some or all of the edits that come back on your first draft may well be set in stone. You may be asked to change the name of a character because the name you chose doesn't fit into the naming scheme the licensor had in mind. You may be asked to re-write dialogue in a scene or throughout the book because it doesn't match with the guidelines established for that character.

If you disagree with the editorial comments, you first need to find out if they came from the licensor or from the editor. If they came from the licensor, then you probably have to make the changes. I've said it before and I'll say it again (and again…and again…): the world and everything in it belongs to the licensor. They created it and have a vested interest in making sure that every product that comes out meets their standards. You can still make your arguments for why you think it works better your way, but be prepared for an uphill battle. You are not the final word on your novel. They are.

However, if you have done your research and followed your outline, any problems you encounter at this point should be relatively small. The publisher should be getting approvals every step of the way on the project. So the story idea has already been approved. The outline has been approved. Even hiring you to write the story had to be approved. With any luck, getting approval on the first draft should only require minor changes. And, while you may be obligated to make those changes, how you re-write the affected sections is entirely your business.

## THE ENDS JUSTIFY THE TROUBLES

In the end, writing a shared world novel is really no easier or harder than writing a novel of your own. You still have to put words down on the page. You still have to do your research to make sure your novel is internally consistent and consistent within the continuity of the ongoing story arc. You still have to deal with editorial comments and re-writes. You still have to sell the merits of your work to a publisher.

Some things are simpler. You don't have to do your own worldbuilding or as much character creation. You don't have to write the entire book before you see some money from your efforts. But there are also problems that creep up in tie-in novels that you will never have when writing your own stories, such as bowing to licensor pressure on re-writes or plotlines and giving up all your rights to the story.

But in the end, when you see that novel with your name on it sitting on a shelf in your local bookstore, you will realize that all of the problems, all of the grief and all of the long days of staring at the computer screen were worth it. And for those authors who are true fans of the world in which their novel is set, there's nothing better than seeing your name printed below the logo of your favorite show, movie or game in an authorized publication. You've made it! You have become a part of that world. You're on the inside now.

# Beyond Swords, Stones and Grails:
## WRITING AND PUBLISHING
## THE ARTHURIAN LEGENDS

### BY KIM HEADLEE

The timeless magic of the Arthurian Legends has inspired authors for a millennium and a half to produce their own versions of the tales. From "dark age" brutality to high chivalry, Victorian veneer to futuristic flair, some twenty-five thousand renditions of the Legends exist.

And you wish to increase the corpus, the size of which comes in second only to the number of works inspired by *The Bible*, to twenty-five thousand-*and-one*.

Well, as the saying goes, "There's always room for one more good book." Before you fit fingers to keyboard and plunge into the task of translating the ancient romance into modern fiction, however, there are a few issues related to writing in general and the Arthurian Legends specifically that you may wish to consider.

## UNDERSTANDING THE "ARTHIVERSE"

Face it: stories centering upon the Arthurian Legends are a form of fan fiction. The writer inherits an established universe in which to play, and the discerning audience judges an Arthurian work's merit based upon how it contributes to the understanding of that universe and its players, minor as well as major.

I may have the soul of a writer, but a three-decade career in the computer industry has bequeathed me with the head of a scientist, so let me define exactly what a story centered upon the Arthurian Legends is, and perhaps more importantly, what it is not.

A story featuring a kid named Arthur who separates a sword from a stone (with or without involving an implement typically employed by blacksmiths) thus earning an exalted position of leadership is Arthurian Legend. A story about a kid named Arturo who pries a crowbar from a log and wields it to become head of his neighborhood gang is not Arthurian Legend.

Why? On a basic level, the elements are the same, are they not?

The late mythologist Joseph Campbell in *Hero With A Thousand Faces* described the Hero's Journey (a pattern of quest, achievement, death and resurrection) as being common not only to all myth systems but to events that happen in everyday life. This is the very reason myths appeal to human beings. Subconsciously, we are programmed to resonate strongly with them.

According to Campbell, King Arthur was just one hero among billions. In the course of pursuing his personal Hero's Journey, Arthur happened to achieve an extraordinary goal: a twenty-year respite from the Anglo-Saxon invasion of Britain, which cemented his memory in the minds of subsequent generations worldwide. The Arturo in my example might perform similar feats, perhaps even with the "altruistic" motive of, say, uniting all the gangs in his city, which unquestionably makes Arturo the hero of his story. But it doesn't cause his Hero's Journey to qualify as being "Arthurian."

Think of it in terms of the chicken and the egg, with the chicken being the Hero's Journey motif, and stories about King Arthur and Arturo as being just a few of many, many eggs.

Don't misunderstand me when I refer to "myths" and "King Arthur" in the same literary breath. I firmly believe that a warlord named Arthur must have existed at some point in Britain's history, because the odds of such a vast body of literature springing up around an invented character, no matter how virtuous or successful that character might be portrayed, are ridiculously remote. *Tarzan* might have assured Edgar Rice Burroughs literary immortality, but I sincerely doubt that the number of derivative works will ever approach even a tenth the number ascribed to the Arthurian Legends.

Could you write a science fiction novel about a planet named Camelot, people it with characters whose names read like a "Who's Who" from *Le Morte d'Arthur*, and give them the same sorts of relationships and a medieval environment? Sure you could, although Arthur Landis beat you to it with *A World Called Camelot*. But I wouldn't label the end result "Arthurian."

However, stealthily spirit Earth's King Arthur from Camlann's bloody battlefield in a space ship, piloted by his sister and her cronies, so that he can be healed of his mortal wound on a planet named Avalon and return to Earth in its hour of greatest need, and not even the pickiest scholar could deny that tale's classification as "Arthurian."

In short, any fiction that deals specifically with the King Arthur of this world, his family, courtiers, advisers, friends, allies or enemies is "Arthurian." This includes stories in which the major Arthurian characters play only a minor role, to give lesser known or an author's invented characters time in the limelight.

I don't believe there is ever a "bad" Arthurian idea, for what doesn't appeal to me may very well be your favorite treatment of the Legends, and vice versa. Every version, popular or otherwise, contributes to the continual expansion of the "Arthiverse."

Consider the following envelope-pushing ideas, all of which have been showcased in one public forum or another, and see how many you can identify.

- Guinevere proves that "opposites attract" when she, the most beautiful woman in the world, falls in love with a Lancelot who happens to be the world's ugliest and most self-esteem-challenged man.
- Merlin serves as an invaluable mentor to Arthur, not in the guise of a bumbling sorcerer or canny Druid, but as a wealthy Christian bishop.
- Sir Gawain beheads a knight, only to find himself invited to the knight's castle in a year's time so that the victim can return the favor.
- A two-headed dragon that excels only at arguing with itself helps a young woman and her blind male companion to recover Excalibur and earn their places at the Round Table.
- Arthur is summoned from Avalon to the late 20th Century, where he finds that some of his staunchest allies exist as monsters by night and as statues by day.

I could cite more examples, but I think you get the idea. Now it is time for you to go forth and devise wonderful Arthurian ideas of your own!

Just how, exactly, does one go about doing that, you ask?

Read on, intrepid Author-Errant, read on.

## BE KIND TO YOUR MUSE

Being enslaved to the writers' muse is a lot like being married. Unless you actively "court" your muse, she will, at best, mutate into a haranguing shrew and, at worst, desert you altogether.

Most writers admit to engaging in a ritual to put themselves into a proper frame of mind, anything from the elaborate lighting of candles and incense to the more mundane performing of a household chore to prevent a guilty spirit from gagging the creative one. Never having held too great an interest in the former, I tend to employ the latter, especially when my subconscious is still percolating a scene that isn't yet ready for the page.

Regardless of how I prepare to write, I fill my environment with dozens of writing-related reminders, mostly Arthurian, so that whether I am actively writing or not, my muse is constantly nudged. Books and movies form the backbone of my collection, which also encompasses artwork, tapestries, recorded and sheet music, knick-knacks, clothing, PC wallpaper and screensavers, even useful pottery pieces I have brought home from renaissance faires over the years.

My muse wallows in hog heaven.

There are times when this level of "care and feeding" isn't sufficient, grief being the most difficult to work through. Painful experience has taught me to be patient with myself during those periods, to feed my muse extra treats in the form of watching my favorite Arthurian and medieval movies, while at the same time not expecting anything from her until she is ready to deliver.

If you and your muse are suffering similar difficulties, I offer you my sincerest condolences, but take heart. Your muse will heal in her own good time, and the depth of your writing will benefit as a result.

Looking for some muse-friendly recommendations? Here are a few of my favorites. All are, to the best of my knowledge, readily available, as are most of the movies' soundtracks.

*Camelot*, starring Richard Harris (Arthur), Vanessa Redgrave (Guinevere) and Franco Nero (Lancelot). Two scenes from this movie, when I saw it on the silver screen as a little girl, I credit with jump-starting my interest in the Arthurian Legends: Guinevere in her fabulous fur coat, and the knights fighting on horseback across the top of the cracking Round Table.

*First Knight*, starring Sean Connery (Arthur), Julia Ormond (Guinevere), and Richard Gere (Lancelot). I may be the only Arthurian scholar on the planet who actually liked this movie, and I commend it to your attention for its superbly crafted story, even though it deviated significantly from Arthurian norms.

*Excalibur*, starring Nigel Terry (Arthur), Cheri Lunghi (Guenevere), Nicholas Clay (Lancelot), Patrick Stewart (Leondegrance), Helen Mirren (Morgana), Nicol Williamson (Merlin), and featuring the screen debuts of Liam Neeson (Gawain) and Gabriel Byrne (Uther). This is a cinematically impressive rendition, complete with music from Richard Wagner's *Neiberlungenlied, Tristan und Isolde, Parzifal,* and *Lohengrin*—though please be mindful of watching it in the presence of young children. The DVD version features a voiced-over commentary by director John Boorman, which is quite fascinating.

*A Knight's Tale,* a movie starring Heath Ledger. Not strictly Arthurian, although one of its musical interludes is titled "Guinevere Comes to Lancelot." Regardless, it's another well-told tale, and the soundtrack, available on two different CDs, is nothing short of terrific. My favorite line is uttered by Paul Bettany, playing the part of Geoffrey Chaucer: "I am a writer. I give the truth scope." May it be true of us, too.

*Ever After,* starring Drew Barrymore; again, not Arthurian, but the Cinderella tale with a medieval setting. "The point, gentlemen, is they lived." Indeed.

"A Late Delivery From Avalon" is an episode from the excellent science fiction television show *Babylon 5* that features Michael York as "Arthur." The haunting music, by Christopher Franke, is available on CD.

I've seen Disney's *A Kid in King Arthur's Court* only once, but the soundtrack CD is a lovely compilation of medieval-themed music, and I play it often.

Another CD soundtrack I enjoy, although the television series has not aired since the early-1990s, is Hearst Corporation's *Prince Valiant* cartoon. If some network ever digs the show out of mothballs, I do commend it to your attention.

Whenever my muse demands whimsy, I watch Warner Brothers' *Quest For Camelot,* starring the voices of Pierce Brosnan (Arthur) and the late Sir John Gielgud (Merlin). That soundtrack CD is another favorite of mine, especially Celine Dion's performance of "The Prayer."

Maddy Prior, a British folk artist to whose music I was introduced in the late 1970s, released a CD of haunting Arthurian songs in 2001 titled *Arthur the King.*

Unique for its depiction of a Saxon King Arthur, Henry Purcell's opera titled *King Arthur,* composed in the late 17th Century, is a valuable addition to the collection of anyone who's a fan of both the Arthurian Legends and classical baroque music.

For more Arthurian-themed material, I highly recommend obtaining a copy of Bert Olton's reference, *Arthurian Legends on Film and Television.*

Having achieved a contented muse, the next step in the process of writing about the Arthurian Legends is to...

## Be Knowledgeable

It's extremely easy to slam shut an Arthurian novel that makes you want to spew in your boots, and, knowing in your heart-of-hearts that you can do a far better job, march to your computer and start pounding away.

If you're a beginning writer and have flipped to this chapter, skipping everything else in between, chances are good that you know exactly the emotion I'm talking about. (Just please be kind and don't tell me if it was *my book* that made you spew!) Such high emotion is not a bad thing, for it means that you feel passionately enough about the subject to want to "get it right" for the rest of the world, and that passion will drive you to see your project through to completion.

But I heartily recommend you resist the temptation to dive right in. Otherwise, you run the risk of creating a two-dimensional, derivative story that may satisfy your gut-level reaction but doesn't stand a snowball's chance of ever seeing another reader's bookshelf.

I present three words of advice for combating this literary sin: *read, read, read.*

For the Arthurian Legends, the list is legion. Even after studying the Legends for more than thirty years, I've hardly made a dent. But the end result is well worth the effort.

Regardless of which "flavor" of Arthurian Legends you favor—historical, medieval, high fantasy, romance or something else—the following fiction titles will give you a solid foundation.

*The Mabinogion*, a 14th Century compilation of ancient Welsh stories, including the earliest Arthurian story ever written, "Culhwch and Olwen." Different English translations are available from Penguin Classics and Everyman Paperback Classics.

*History of the Kings of Britain* by Geoffrey of Monmouth, the 12th Century book responsible for igniting "King Arthur Mania" in Europe nearly a millennium ago. Available from Penguin Classics.

*Sir Gawain and the Green Knight*, anonymous 14th Century epic poem. Many modern English renditions abound, including a particularly good one rendered by J.R.R. Tolkien, a top-flight scholar before he invented hobbits.

*Knight of the Cart, Erec and Enid, Cligés, Perceval* (the first written Grail story), and *Yvain* by 13th Century French author Chrétien de

Troyes. Various English-translation editions exist, and the complete collection is offered by Penguin Classics.

*Le Morte d'Arthur* by Sir Thomas Malory. If you enjoy Arthurian artwork, I highly recommend obtaining copies of *A Boy's King Arthur*, illustrated by N.C. Wyeth, *The Romance of King Arthur and His Knights of the Round Table*, illustrated by Arthur Rackham, and *The Story of King Arthur and His Knights*, written and illustrated by Howard Pyle.

*Idylls of the King* is a Victorian epic poem by Sir Alfred Lord Tennyson that contains memorable imagry.

*A Connecticut Yankee in King Arthur's Court* by Mark Twain is probably the first, and arguably still the best, Arthurian paranormal-fantasy.

*The Once and Future King* by T.H. White is a pre-World War II treatise on the evils of war, if you read it closely enough.

*The Crystal Cave, The Hollow Hills* and *The Last Enchantment* by Mary Stewart, collectively an outstanding fictional foray into "dark age" Arthurian Britain. Again, if you enjoy fine cover artwork, try finding the three-in-one edition of this series, titled the *Merlin Trilogy*, which features a lovely representation of Arthur pulling the sword from the stone by the Brothers Hildebrandt.

*Dawnflight* by Kim Headlee (well, what did you expect?!). In my defense, I am honored to report that the novel garnered more than thirty excellent print and electronic magazine reviews, including a positive treatment in *Arthuriana*, the academic journal for Arthurian studies published by the North American Branch of the International Arthurian Society. Not many other contemporary Arthurian novels can claim that distinction.

If you feel inclined to chase after "the real Arthur," these nonfiction titles are a good place to begin the hunt.

*The Quest for Arthur's Britain* by Geoffrey Ashe, which constituted my first exposure to the "historical King Arthur," lo those many moons ago, and is still a good general-purpose reference, even if the archaeology is dated. Mr. Ashe has written dozens of other Arthurian treatises, including an excellent guidebook to public-accessible Arthurian sites in Britain, but this remains my favorite.

*Arthur's Britain* by archaeologist Leslie Alcock, also is an "oldie but goodie," as my well-worn copy attests.

*Warriors of Arthur* by John Matthews and Bob Stewart gives good insight into 5th-6th Century Britain, and is invaluable for such details as its list of Welsh knights' names gleaned from the Triads, the type of warfare Arthur might have conducted, how his knights probably were armed, etc.

*King Arthur* and *Merlin* by Norma Lorre Goodrich. Most Arthurian scholars scorn her work as being scrawny on fact and overweight on speculation, but as a novelist I found those books to be a veritable gold mine of ideas.

*New Arthurian Encyclopedia*, edited by Norris J. Lacy, et al. In a word—*indispensable*.

*The Arthurian Companion* by Phyllis Ann Karr, author of the innovative Arthurian murder-mystery *Idylls of the Queen*. This reference discusses, encyclopedia-style, every character in Malory's *Le Morte d'Arthur* and is particularly handy if you wish to craft your story around some of the lesser-known characters.

Your personal tastes and the needs of your story will, of course, dictate the direction in which you expand your knowledge base. And no author worth his salt can even begin to contemplate his story's needs until he determines the nature of his target audience. For that you must first decide which genre your story will best fit. Arthurian tales tend to be classified as "fantasy," but in truth they run the gamut: action-adventure, high fantasy, historical fiction, romance, spiritual, mystery/suspense and even science fiction.

Each of these audiences approaches their favorite genre with an immutable set of expectations. For example, readers of modern romance (not to be confused with Arthurian Romance) expect a happily-ever-after ending, which presents a stiff challenge to the author when everyone knows that Arthur will suffer betrayal and death at the hands of those he loves and trusts the most.

Once you identify your audience, you can make intelligent decisions about the direction in which to pursue further research.

Of course no discussion of Arthurian resources is complete without pointing the 21st Century reader toward the Internet. Even though the Web changes faster than Sahara sand dunes, these sites have proven faithful—in content if not necessarily in URL address—since at least 1998, when I created my Arthurian site, and are still online at the printing of this title.

**ANGLO-SAXON AGE** (*http://www.lauraloft.com/saxon/a-saxon. htm*) offers a good collection of information relating to the Anglo-Saxons.

**ARTHURIAN RESOURCES** (*http://www.arthuriana.co.uk*), compiled by Tom Green, is a good general-purpose list.

You must be a member of the North American Branch of the International Arthurian Society to surf the archives of its publication, **ARTHURIANA** (*http://www.arthuriana.org/*), but it is well worth the modest annual cost if you wish to keep abreast of published Arthurian research and reviews.

**ARTHURNET** (*http://lists.mun.ca/archives/arthurnet*), managed by the Memorial University of Newfoundland, is the premier Arthurian email list for discussions of scholarly research. Professors and amateurs alike from all over the world contribute to the often quite lively discussion threads. The site mentioned here gives subscription information as well as access to the keyword-searchable archives.

If Arthurnet seems a bit too intimidating, another good list of Arthurian references can be found at **THE CAER** (*http://home. earthlink.net/~neatoguy/caer.htm*).

The **CAMELOT PROJECT AT THE UNIVERSITY OF ROCHESTER** (*http://www.ub.rug.nl/camelot/cphome.stm*) is a tremendous collection of information, pictures, bibliographies, essays, and online texts.

**CAMLANN MEDIEVAL VILLAGE** (*http://www.camlann.org*) refers to an annual Arthurian-themed renaissance faire held in Carnation, WA, with an on-site medieval research library, seminars and medieval dining experiences offered year-round. I was privileged to visit the faire in the mid-1980s and can vouch for its authenticity.

**CELTIC STUDIES** (*http://www.geocities.com/~dubricius/*), presented by Toby Griffen, is a good site for general Celtic research.

**CELTIC TWILIGHT** (*http://www.celtic-twilight.com/*) While somewhat commercialized, this site still presents an excellent collection of online Arthurian texts, book reviews, general information and a bulletin board.

Professor David Nash Ford's **EARLY BRITISH KINGDOMS** web site (*http://www.earlybritishkingdoms.com*) is a must-bookmark, especially for writers interested in the historical approach the Arthurian Legends. It contains hundreds of articles describing the

Celtic kingdoms, their rulers, genealogies, contemporary saints and adversaries, archaeology and a section devoted to King Arthur.

**EARLY MEDIEVAL RESOURCES FOR THE BRITISH ISLES AND BRITTANY** (*http://members.aol.com/michellezi/resources-index. html*) offers timelines, bibliographies, more links, etc.

**THE HEROIC AGE** online journal, edited by Michelle Ziegler (*http://members.aol.com/heroicage1/homepage.html*), presents many fine articles and book reviews relating to "dark age" and medieval history.

If you're interested in researching the Scottish Arthur, you will surely benefit from visiting **HISTORIC SCOTLAND** (*http://www.historic-scotland.gov.uk*), the official government-run site that contains a wealth of information regarding places and events in Scotland.

**KING ARTHUR** (*http://britannia.com/history/arthur.html*), a site sponsored by *Britannia Magazine*, is a great starting point for basic research about the Arthurian Legends. Its articles are well written and attractively presented, owing to History Editor David Nash Ford's expert guidance.

**THE LABYRINTH** (*http://labyrinth.georgetown.edu*), sponsored by Georgetown University, will get you virtually any place you wish within the realm of medieval studies.

A site deserving special mention is **PICTISH NATION** (*http://members.tripod.com/~Halfmoon/*). Online since 1994, it bills itself as "the oldest Pictish site on the Internet," and it is a source of great information and Pict-related links, such as a recipe for heather beer.

Sponsored by the University of Idaho, **THE QUEST** (*http://www.uidaho.edu/student_orgs/arthurian_legend/welcome.html*) has not been updated since 1998, but it's still worth a visit for its superb art gallery and essays.

**THREE GEESE IN FLIGHT BOOKSTORE** (*http://www.threegeeseinflight.com/*) is a brick-and-mortar shop run by Sam Wenger, specializing in Arthurian works, especially rare and out-of-print editions. Mr. Wenger's online catalog is hosted by Advanced Book Exchange (*http://www.abebooks.com*).

For a more comprehensive list of sites I've found useful over the past several years, pay a visit to my own Arthurian page (*http://home.usaa.net/~kimheadlee/arthur.htm#Sites*). With most of these sites, including mine, you may email the webmaster once your book is in print, and he or she usually will be delighted to include a reference on the appropriate web page.

God—or the devil, depending upon your frustration level—is in the details. Although I love conducting research (and the farther afield, the better), I realize not everyone possesses the same level of enthusiasm for ferreting out historical detail.

However, even if you plan to craft a purely fantastical slant on the Legends, in the tradition of Michael Greatrex Coney's *Fang the Gnome* and its sequels, your story will become richer by the judicious addition of key details, whether geographical, political, anthropological, historical, military, economic or even religious in nature, depending upon what you wish to accomplish.

Another way in which to demonstrate knowledge of the target audience is in the crafting of characters' dialogue, and the overall tone of the story itself.

Narrative style and dialogue are always a tightrope-walk, and this is especially true with the Arthurian Legends. Fans of Arthurian stories with a high fantasy or historical slant may tolerate a greater degree of formality in narration and dialogue, while romance readers usually prefer a writing style that's more contemporary and easier to relate to.

I try to strike such a balance by avoiding anachronistic words and phrases, while striving to make my characters sound as natural as possible.

Whichever genre you're targeting for your story, you need to remember that maintaining a connection with your readership is of primary importance. Once you lose your readers, you may have a difficult time wooing them back. And if that lost reader happens to be an editor...well, I think you can fill in the blank.

Your best defense against dooming your story to your desk drawer lies, again, in reading. If you're writing a short story, read several issues of the magazines to which you plan to submit to get a feel for the overall tone. Stories published in *Realms of Fantasy*, for example, differ significantly from those published in *Fantasy and Science Fiction*.

With novels, that level of market analysis becomes more difficult to conduct because book editors working for a given imprint acquire manuscripts featuring a wider variety of styles and tones. But you can still apply a basic level of analysis. For example, if you showcase

Lancelot and Guinevere in explicitly described love scenes, you probably won't want to send that manuscript to a Christian publisher. Don't discount the Christian market segment, by the way; that's where Stephen Lawhead's Arthurian series got its start.

If you want to land a sale, and you've identified a publisher that might be more likely to buy your work if you did something a little differently, don't be afraid to rework your story to improve its chances of acceptance. In these days of multi-gigabyte storage, it's no big deal to keep multiple versions on your hard drive.

And if you're someone who perceives that suggestion as a crass way of subverting "art" for the sake of commercialism, you are of course entitled to that viewpoint. I leave you with one question, though: If you have created something that no one else has the opportunity to admire, is it still "art?"

## Be Unique

One of the reasons the Arthurian Legends have endured well into their second millennium is the timeless thematic elements the stories encompass. Authors down the march of centuries have tapped into this fount of ambition and valor, honor and horror, cravenness and self-sacrifice, loathing and laughter to express their own era's foremost issues in Arthurian terms.

Sir Thomas Malory, considered by many to be the "father" of Arthurian literature, probably saw all manner of ills from the tiny window of his 15th Century jail cell while writing his epic work, *Le Morte d'Arthur*. Malory's approach to the legend of King Arthur attempted to inspire his contemporaries to return to the chivalric ideal. While this goal was perfectly fine for Sir Tom and his times, a 21st Century author will serve the public far better with a unique rendition rather than retreading Malory's medieval journey.

Some writers consider anything that's not a derivative of a favorite Arthurian author's work to be "inferior." I once heard a prospective author express a desire to stay "true" to Malory's storyline while offering a unique perspective, writing style and presentation of Malory's characters.

However, writing quality and character development don't sell manuscripts to editors. The story concept is the key element. By "concept" I mean such phrases, ideally in seven words or fewer, as "pagan women who manipulate Arthur's kingdom" (*Mists of Avalon*),

"Atlantis meets Camelot" (Stephen Lawhead's *Taliessin*, et al.), and "female *Braveheart*" (*Dawnflight*).

The seven-word guideline is lifted from Hollywood practices, by the way. If you can boil your story down to seven words that ignite an editor's interest, you are well on your way to clearing that first hurdle toward getting your work published.

If the only concept to emerge from your literary crucible is "Mary Stewart revisited," then you may have major work in front of you. Submitting a manuscript that amounts to little more than Malory with the serial numbers filed off may very well earn it a one-way trip from the slush pile to the recycle bin.

Exceptions always exist, of course, such as Thomas Berger's *Arthur Rex*. One could even argue that Mary Stewart's Arthurian collection is a Malory derivative updated with a "dark age" flair. But those books stand out by virtue of their original elements, such as humor and realistic setting.

People thinking to retread Malory (or White, or Bradley, or [hah] Headlee) by simply presenting a similar story line with a different writing style and perhaps a differently envisioned character or two are welcome to write their hearts out. In fact, emulation of the masters is how all artists—painters, sculptors, composers and even writers—begin to learn their craft. But that technique should result in the blossoming of the apprentice's unique talents.

Witness the scene in *Finding Forrester*, where Sean Connery, playing a crotchety and reclusive author, sits his unlikely but promising disciple Jamal (played by Rob Brown) down in front of an antique Smith-Corona. Forrester pulls one of his published articles out of a file drawer and tells Jamal to start copying the article until he felt his muse take over. After just half a page, Jamal's own style and thoughts emerge.

Imitating Malory was how I started developing my version of the Arthurian Legends as a 9-year-old kid. In the ensuing decade, I wrote a short story, an illustrated novella, the first novel of a planned trilogy, and I even began work on a play. The play had the highest degree of originality, but even that project I eventually abandoned, unfinished, because I realized it was too derivative of Mary Stewart, and I wanted to display something far more creative to the world.

One of your primary tasks as an author is to ensure that your work stands out from the rest of the Arthurian crowd. The form that uniqueness takes may involve humor, meticulous research, exploiting an under-utilized theme, focusing on characters traditionally relegated to a minor role in the Legends or just spinning an impossible-to-put-down yarn, depending upon your skills, ambitions and inclinations.

But you cannot possibly achieve all your Arthurian writing goals unless you can...

## Be Thorough

This next snippet of advice may seem like it should go without saying, but I will state it anyway: *Finish your manuscript.*

No excuses, no cheating by writing the last chapter first, just get all the way from Chapter 1 to "The End" of that first draft. Then go back and polish, polish, polish.

With the publishing industry imploding upon itself as bigger publishers buy up smaller ones, a writer's chances of selling a book on proposal (usually defined as the story's synopsis and first three chapters) are next to nil, especially manuscripts submitted by first-time authors. Even published authors can't seem to catch a break these days, unless his or her name happens to be "Jordan" or "Rowling."

The best favor you can do for yourself is to finish your story. Then get yourself a good critique partner or five. Showing your manuscript to Mom may yield some valuable ego-stroking, unless Mom happens to be a published novelist, but usually you need to find fellow authors who are willing to point out your work's flaws as well as its strong points. I prefer the approach of cultivating two or three people whose judgment I trust implicitly.

Some authors are brave enough to post their work for open critique among strangers. While that approach may yield some fine discussion, care must be taken that you do not compromise your work's ability to become published in standard print form. Some publishers will flatly refuse to publish a story that first saw exposure on the Internet, on the grounds that its "First Publication" right no longer exists.

To survive what can sometimes be a harrowing critique process, you must develop an instinct for gleaning the useful suggestions from the not-so-useful, and heed it. It is your story, after all. A reasonably perceptive person should be able to discern a constructive comment from a destructive one.

James Mitchner once revealed how he functioned as his own critique partner: he typically shelved a work-in-progress for up to a year before attempting to edit it. When I read that, while deep in the throes of polishing *Dawnflight*, I thought the man had to be crazy. I couldn't fathom putting my manuscript aside for one day, to say nothing of an entire year! But shortly thereafter events conspired to send my writing into a lengthy hiatus. When I emerged from that particularly dark period of my life, I gained the unforeseen benefit of a fresh perspective on my writing that I never would have possessed otherwise.

Another aspect of thoroughness that many writers fail to exploit is conducting market research. The annual *Writer's Market* and *Literary Marketplace* resources are great places to start, but you can also benefit by subscribing to magazines such as the Fantasy-genre staple, *Locus*, and joining email and bulletin board forums. I would not have obtained my literary agent had it not been for a timely and informative posting on a fantasy writers' email list.

However, if the Internet were governed by "laws" as in physics, its First Law would be: "For every key stroke, there is an equal and opposite time sink." In other words, don't let your surfing and networking interfere with your writing!

## BE COURAGEOUS

Once you have finished your scintillatingly detailed, dazzlingly unique Arthurian manuscript, schlepped it around your critique circle, polished it to within an inch of its life and conducted mind-numbingly thorough market research, only three tasks remain: *submit, submit, submit.*

Okay, I admit that's an oversimplification. In reality the process goes something like this:

1. *Submit to Publisher A*
2. *Take up Zen meditation to curb your impatience.*
3. *Wait a couple of months, during which time you can't resist reading your manuscript one more time. You find four zillion typos and want to crawl under the nearest rock.*
4. *Since disturbing the rock would throw the whole pattern out of cosmic alignment, you make the manuscript changes anyway, and decide to revamp 11 scenes while you're at it.*

5.  You get a hot tip about Publisher B, who will accept simultaneous submissions, although Publisher A does not. You send a polite query to Publisher A, asking about the status of your manuscript, which they've had in house long enough for it to start asexually reproducing itself. You pray that someone in the mailroom doesn't decide to enter your letter in the weekly paper-airplane races.

6.  After you've chewed several millimeters off your knuckles, you learn that Publisher A never bothers to send out rejection letters or answer status queries. (No joke; this is official policy with some publishers.) It's a darn good thing you're a pacifist, although the Zen routine is starting to wear a little thin, and you begin to fantasize about how the rocks in your carefully raked garden might look with a splash of color...such as red.

7.  A year after your initial submission, you write it off as a loss and work up the courage to submit your manuscript to Publisher B, only to learn that Publisher B's lineup is booked solid for the next decade.

8.  Publisher C looks promising, and you even strike up an Internet acquaintance with one of the chief editors, who happens to be highly respected in the fantasy field and adores everything Arthurian. At last, a place to truly pin your hopes! You take another swing through the manuscript, just to be ready for Acceptance Day, and send it off.

9.  However, after another 18 months of finger-gnawing, you read an open letter on alt.writing.forget_it_bub that the aforementioned editor at Publisher C has experienced a major falling-out with her colleagues and refuses to wear the green visor ever again. Not at Publisher C, Q, X, or even M-O-U-S-E.

10.  You master the art of yodeling the therapeutic scream in your first try.

11.  But because you are a writer, and could no sooner stop writing than chop off your right hand, you go back to Step 1 and repeat the entire process over again, as many times as it takes until you finally experience the magic moment when the book sells. The only difference being that you sod over your Zen garden because coloring the boulders represents too great a temptation.

Some of the above scenarios, while deliberately presented in a humorous fashion, represent events that happened to me during my own sacred quest: publication of *Dawnflight*. You are welcome to corner me at a writers' convention for the full story.

One hint: I never have and never will own a Zen garden.

## BE TOUGH

To survive the rigors of the publishing business, a writer must grow a sturdy hide, for the rejections inevitably will roll in. *Dawnflight* garnered more than two dozen, counting agent rejections, before it finally sold.

The rejections I find easiest to swallow are the banal "doesn't meet our needs at this time" variety. With those you can try submitting your piece in another year or two, providing the publication still exists, of course.

It's a shame that *Marion Zimmer Bradley's Fantasy Magazine* folded shortly after her death in 1999, for she was notorious for sending out the most creative form-rejections in the business. The laughter invoked by receiving a comment such as "Suspension of disbelief does not mean hanging by the neck until dead" alleviates the sting but can inspire an author to take a hard look at the story.

My favorite rejection quip to date came from Tor Books. In 1997, Tor was in the midst of cranking out Jack Whyte's Arthurian series. The editor who turned down *Dawnflight* responded with "Our Arthurian cup runneth over." That's hard to argue with, especially since it sounds as if God Himself has spoken.

Given responses of that nature, then, is there ever truly "room for one more good book?"

I say, most emphatically, yes.

Here the trick lies in knowing the works that compete with yours well enough to describe how your book is better. In this phase of the writing process, you are the salesman. Modesty and humility, while fine virtues to possess, have no place here. As in the case of a prospective employer evaluating your résumé, editors expect a high degree of hype. The absence of it can trumpet a lack of confidence on the author's part. And if you're not confident in the quality of your work, chances become vanishingly remote that anyone else will be either.

Even if you are fortunate enough to retain a literary agent, he or she will most likely come to you for specific ideas on how to present your manuscript in the best light. Fair warning about agents, though: your hide had better be thick enough to withstand being bombarded by tenfold the number of rejections in a tenth the time it would have taken for you to manage the submission process yourself!

To craft an enticing yet fundamentally accurate comparison of your work, first review novels or short stories that can be classified in a similar manner to yours. Again this advice may seem obvious, if not unnecessary; but I look at it the same way I do with inane product-warning labels: if I don't state what ought to be intuitively evident to most people, I'll probably get an irate email one day from someone wondering why, when he held up his magic-laden vision of Camelot to Bernard Cornwell's gritty Arthurian tomes, the unpublished writer earned an editor's snigger.

Once you've selected an appropriate array of competing works, here's another obvious tidbit for you: read them. And I don't mean gloss over the Cliff Notes, surf the reviews on Amazon.com or ask someone on Arthurnet to provide a summary. Sit down and carefully, analytically read those books.

While you're analyzing the competition, ask yourself the following questions:

- How is your story similar to the published one?
- What makes your story unique?
- If you notice flaws in the published novel that remind you of issues you didn't address in yours, how can you go back and work them into your story to make it that much better?
- How does your story satisfy the needs and expectations of the target audience in ways the published one doesn't?

## FULFILL YOUR QUEST

While this technique should be applied to all fiction, it becomes essential with Arthurian stories because so many versions abound. And, lest you believe this may be a one-time exercise, it will behoove you to master it, for you can employ the same techniques when hand-selling your published work to prospective buyers. This is one very important element of market research that many authors of all types of fiction, Arthurian or otherwise, fail to tackle as aggressively as they should.

If all of this seems like a whole lot of work to produce a story that falls within otherwise fairly well-established parameters, you're absolutely right. Congratulations—you've paid attention. Welcome to the wooly world of Arthurian writing, and getting published in the Fantasy genre.

Forsooth, ride boldly forth with God's speed, brave Author-Errant. Acquit thyself well with strength of thought and might of pen, and may ye one day sup from the Grail of publication!

# Facing Your Harshest Critic:
## SELF-EDITING

### BY JULIANNE GOODMAN

I'm a firm believer that good editing can make a mediocre book great, while bad editing can reduce a good book to nothing more than kindling. Writers who claim to perfect their writing during the initial writing are either:

- (A) unpublished, and unlikely to *be* published
- (B) so far beyond professional that they are Brooks, Asaro or Jordan
- (C) revising as they write the rough draft

You want to make a decent living at writing? You have the completed story in front of you, yes? Then you have to come to grips with that tough critic inside of you and begin the hardest phase of this creative process: *editing*. Editing is what separates those who write from those who write as a profession. I've been asked to critique or evaluate many unpublished manuscripts over the years, and the following is a compilation of what I call "Big Baddies" of writing fiction.

Let's assume that you've read *The Complete Guide to Writing Fantasy* and that you've risen above standard grammatical errors and typographical errors. Here in *The Fantasy Writer's Companion*, we're going to take a close look at those "Big Baddies" as they relate to plotting, pacing and other important components of telling more than just a good story, but a *damn* good story.

As the title indicates, it isn't enough to type "The End," hit spell check and call a novel complete. Every author has common writing habits—and I don't mean staying up too late, allowing daily responsibilities to slip and forgetting to eat—that weaken their writing, and thus every author must seek to counteract them. For space constraints, I'll hit on the most common.

But before I dive into the bad habits, let's talk about objectivity. An essential component to being an effective editor is the ability to view your writing with an objective eye. It's difficult, true. You've spent months, perhaps years, crafting this masterpiece. But every artist knows you don't slap some paint on a canvas and call it finished. You need time to become objective about your work, to fine tune your focus and to polish and hone your little gem until it sparkles. Then you can send it off for someone else to admire.

## SIX DEGREES OF SEPARATION:
### GETTING OUT OF
### THE "WRITE" FRAME OF MIND

After you have completed your manuscript, this living, breathing essence of your soul, the first thing any smart author will do is put it aside before the editing phase. Preferably for a week or two, but if you're up against a deadline and can't wait, then at least a few days. I once read that Ray Bradbury finishes a first draft and puts it on a shelf in the closet of his office and doesn't touch it again for a year. Not a bad system, but your time constraints may not allow for such a lengthy cooling period. Spend your free time reading something enjoyable and take a break from the demands of the creative process. Every book is a learning process and you need time to digest what you've learned on your last foray. Take time to clear your mind of the words you bled onto the pages, time to become objective, time to separate yourself from your work. This technique will come in handy when you get to the next phase of your journey—revision and submission. You must learn to disconnect yourself from your work so you can utilize the critiques of others and understand that rejections do not pertain to you personally but to your novel. Nothing in this business is personal, it's *business*. It's *work*. When next you pick up your novel for editing, try to pretend it isn't your life in those pages.

When you feel confident that you can objectively evaluate your own writing, find a quiet spot where you can read through the entire book in one sitting. I know authors who revise as they write the first draft and others who go on "retreat" at the end of the completed first draft. They hole up in some remote location and switch to editor mode with more aplomb than the Sorting Hat weeds out the Slytherins from the Griffyndors. I champion the latter approach, as composing words and editing are two distinctly different aspects of writing. Better yet, *do both!* Having a place to edit that is different from your drafting workspace is a great way to divide the two actions of writing and editing. Print off a clean copy, head to a favorite hotel or bookstore (if home is not a viable option) and load up with munchies and plenty of strong coffee. You'll catch more inconsistencies on paper than you will on your computer screen.

Now that you have your editing space defined, let's begin with the "Big Baddies" that will cause any reader to lose faith in your ability to tell a good story. The "Big Baddies" are the gremlins that infiltrate your writing and make it less saleable. They encompass the main flaws inherent in newly-drafted manuscripts, the ones that make editors and agents cringe. This is by no means a comprehensive list, but this will introduce you to the laborious task of self editing.

### BIG BADDIE #1: THE "THROWAWAYS"

Throwaways are any agent or situation that can be effectively cut without changing the overlying story. The first of these are prologues. I've had the good fortune to chat with many editors and agents, and they are of one mind when it comes to prologues. If possible, find a way to tell the story without them. Prologues weaken the immediacy of the reader's immersion into the story by giving us a diluted prelude to what actually happens in the story we wish to tell—sometimes years or centuries prior to the real action or conflict taking place in the novel. No one wants to fall in love with characters only to discover that the real characters the novel focuses on aren't the ones they thought!

Prologues, by and large, are a weaker form of writing. You're establishing that you cannot set up the story mood, character motivation or plot points without resorting to an "easy out" of writing it all up front. I'm not saying that prologues should be banned. There are a few authors that have used them to good effect, but a truly talented storyteller can find a way to insinuate emotion, plot and setting in a story without resorting to prologues. If you have perfected your craft, you should be able to establish setting or mood without resorting to those first few "throwaway" paragraphs or pages of a prologue.

An exception would be to establish a character's motivation or important plot point, but even that can be done without the clumsy approach of laying it all out up front. Think of telling a story as a fishing analogy. You don't want the fish to see the frying pan before you toss in your line. You want to reel him in slowly until you're sure the hook is imbedded. It takes more finesse to write without using a prologue, just like it takes a certain finesse to land that big fish. This holds especially true when the characters you introduce in the prologue don't return to the spotlight for half the book, if ever.

And since we are talking about prologues that feature characters we shouldn't get attached to, let's discuss another "throwaway" in writing: the dreaded *"Character with No Name"* (hence referred to as *CNN*). A CNN is the Captain, the Wizard, the Woman, the Monster, etc. ad nauseum. A CNN is any unnamed character who receives undo attention from the author. Most common is to place CNNs in a prologue, but I've seen them materialize in sagging mid-sections of many a manuscript.

If my lead character walks into a java hut to order a coffee, we don't need to know that the coffee barista had a bad childhood and beats his wife. It's enough to know that the barista gave our POV character a cup of joe just the way she ordered it—hot and sweet. His function is simply to fill her order. He is a throwaway character. No name is necessary. End of his function and his one line of fame in the spotlight.

The problem with a CNN arises when the character is given undue importance. He is a POV character, or has a lot of important dialogue. Say the barista above turns out to be the ultimate evil doer, who is bent on destruction of the realm. Important, yes, but no name? Who will remember him?

Here's a radical thought. If the character is so fascinating and integral to the plot that you cannot tell the story without them, then perhaps that character ought to have a *name*, so the reader can identify and remember them! No one gives a rat's patoot if an old withered King quaked in his tower by the sea, they want to know *who* he is and *why* he's so afraid of unicorns. Otherwise our poor King is the epitome of a throwaway character.

Conversely, it is not acceptable to simply go in and name every character in your book. Names have an important function in fiction. They cue the reader into paying special attention. A name signifies that there may be some greater importance for this character than what is currently depicted. You don't want your reader to be introduced to a character by name, unless you have a specific reason for doing so.

If you can't substantiate why a particular character is in your main POV focus, then perhaps that throwaway character should be tossed into the round file or could be used in another book to better effect. Introducing minor characters who will appear in an overall story arc that stretches across several books is acceptable, but be certain that this character has some degree of importance in *this* book, or your reader will lose faith in your ability to lead them through the world you've created.

We'll discuss this in more depth in my next Big Baddie. There are ways to tighten your writing. One of them is to insure that every character has a purpose for being "onstage" in your story at any given time. Chefs hold to the rule of three in creating a new delicacy. That is, they only use three main "flavors" or the recipe becomes a mishmash of tastes, the original flavor lost and overwhelmed by the sensory stimulation of the palette. The same holds true in writing scenes with characters. More than three to five and you've overdone your scene as in the next Big Baddie—the Cast of Thousands.

### Big Baddie #2: The Cast of Thousands

As authors, we tend to know our plot and characters intimately, as if they were flesh and blood. As Supreme Creator, it's our job. But not every character is necessary. Less can be more, especially in fiction. Part of being a good storyteller is knowing when to cut the fat from the meat of our tale. The empty carbs of writing, to use a popular dietary analogy. A cast of thousands is like a diet of potatoes, pasta and beer. It's heavy, bland and unfulfilling, not to mention Atkins Unfriendly. As you edit your manuscript, ask yourself if you have too many characters for each scene. If you have more than five named characters going about their business onscreen, chances are you've got excess flab. Yes, there are exceptions, but if you can cut or condense characters it will allow for deeper characterization of the remaining individuals and help prevent two-dimensional cutouts from appearing onscreen. Make sure you ask these key questions when creating heavily-populated scenes:

- Can you cut someone out of the spotlight?
- Can you combine two or more characters into one?
- Will they serve the same function?
- Do we really need to know this character's name?
- What is their function in the story?

Too many characters can take the focus away from your lead POV character and lead to head-hopping or cheating your reader out of personal emotional impact. We don't know who to follow, because frankly everyone is fighting for our attention.

Take the following example:

> Sir Rodderick sets off to fight a battle against the evil mage Proscipio. Assisted by his page, a young boy named Tom, Tom helps Rodderick clap on his metal armor and sword. Then the squire, Franklin, assists Rodderick onto his horse, and warns him to be careful of Proscipio's henchmen, who have been sighted nearby. Suddenly, a stable boy, Theodore, runs to Rodderick's side. Still wearing the signs of mucking out the stalls, he is captured by Proscipio's henchmen and forced to tell what he overheard of the knight's plans.

Confusing, eh? Even I had to go back and reread it. And I wrote it! For a single plot point in the story, there are far too many characters on the scene, even though we've only named four, and one, Proscipio, is off-screen at the moment. The reader will quickly become confused.

Who is this knight Rodderick? What about young Tom? Should we heed the words of the squire Franklin? And what of poor Theodore? Will Rodderick even care?

*I sure don't.*

For our purposes, this scene has too many guests coming to dinner. We don't need the stable boy, the squire and the page in the scene where our hero mounts a steed to ride off into glorious battle. Time to find a focus in your scene. Trim to just the squire, a young boy—once a mere stable boy?—who assists our hero onto his mount. And don't give the squire a name, unless he plays an important part in the novel later on. If he's just there to saddle the horse, no need to put a badge on the kid. Depending on how you handle the remainder of the story, determine if it is important to remember who Tom was, and why his acts have created such conflict for our hero.

By trimming down your cast, you can find a better focus for your scene and pacing of the plot. Perhaps you'll discover scenes that can be trimmed away completely. If the main focus of the scene isn't moving the story along, then you can probably cut it without changing the end result of your plot points, which leads us into the next Big Baddie.

### Big Baddie #3: Lazy Writing and Clunky Pacing

Lazy writing is perhaps the number one downfall of writers who haven't yet learned the craft of revising a manuscript into something saleable. Let's start with clichés and redundancies. *Clichés* are when the author resorts to commonly used phrases or concepts—cold as ice, black as coal, running to the neighbor's to borrow a cup of sugar, beer-guzzling construction workers and fat-cat businessmen—that are as tired and stale as the air in the Mines of Moria, unless they are used for humor—but even then, as writers, can we not think of a better way to describe such instances? A writer can "explode" or change an existing cliché to great effect without resorting to the same tired lingo that makes a reader's eyes glaze over.

Use your POV character's unique background to create your own analogies without resorting to lazy clichés. Take a color, for example—red. How would a privateer captain describe it? What about a temple courtesan? A vampire bent on self-destruction? Take into consideration your character's gender, if any. Men tend to be less descriptive than women. A male character might be reminded of something from his past, something with a tangible, physical response...

> *Her lips were red, really red. The color of ripe cherries, like she'd been sucking on one of those cheap drugstore lollipops before entering his office. Cherry red. The same tint as the first car he'd owned in high school—the first place he'd made it with a hot piece of ass he didn't have to pay for. He licked his own lips, an involuntary reaction to the memory, and shuffled the papers on his desk while she settled into the chair.*

While a woman might have a more emotional reaction....

> *He wore a shirt the color of her grandmother's roses. She'd never seen such a color before, on a man. Cerise. The saturation of it made her feel giddy and young, especially on a man like him. He vibrated sensuality like concrete sends off waves of heat on a summer day. She wanted to bury her face into the collar of her shirt, just as she'd inhaled the scent of roses in her grandmother's garden so long ago.*

Now, let's address *redundancies*. These phrases clutter your writing. They make what you say less important. Phrases like "circle around" (is there any other way to circle?), "young baby" (have you ever seen an old one?), "gather together" and "jumped up" are excessive, to name only a few. She didn't "sit down" in the chair, she *sat* in the chair. He didn't need to "stand up," he *stood*. Wherever you can make one word do the work of several, use it. Your writing will be tighter and more evocative, especially if you can avoid repeating yourself. Repeats are when you echo a statement or sentiment within a short space. If you wrote, *"The knight contemplated his next move, the most merciful maneuver that would end the battle"* at the top of the page and then later you add, *"Sir Ralph considered what would be his next strike for victory and what would be the most merciful"* at the bottom, that would be unnecessary repetition.

*Adverb use* is another potential minefield. As above, it uses multiple words to do the work of one powerful verb. Why use *"walked briskly"* when you can use "strode," "sauntered," "stalked" or "sped?" And those are just "s" words! Think of better ways to depict the emotion behind the action. Perform a search on *"-ly"* in your manuscript. How often do you use adverbs? When possible, revise adverbs out of the text.

One very common place authors tend to overuse adverbs is with dialogue tags. These can almost always be dropped, ie: don't tell us she "snapped angrily" at her husband. Show us—even through use of non-verbal tags:

> "I don't know. It might be difficult to get away alone. Maybe you could meet me at the airport? You could do that, right?" His fingers played along the back of her neck. She could feel them curl, as if he was about to grip her tender skin.
> "Stop it!" She slammed the teapot on the stove top. "You're always hounding me."

Non-verbal tags, also called *beats*, are a powerful way to use language to get your point across. We'll go into more detail about this in a later section.

Let your dialogue and your verbiage do your work for you, and cut the adverbs and sloppy dialogue tags. In fact, cut all but the necessary tags that must be maintained for the reader to understand who is speaking. And though I'm stating that you should vary your word choice, people cannot laugh, snort, growl, smile or grimace words. If you plan to use those attributions, make them an action.

*"Quit playing around." She laughed. Her voice was like sunshine in Seattle. "I'm serious."* Not *"Quit playing around," she laughed.* To improve the pacing and tension of your story, say what you can in as few and precise words as possible. It doesn't matter how in love with a phrase or passage or even chapter that you are—if you can condense or cut without changing the story, then do it. Save them somewhere else, for possible reuse.

But don't feel that you need to completely delete sections that you cut. It's a good idea to save chopped bits in a separate file, granting you the freedom to slash away without fear of losing something important. Then later, you can determine if what is removed should remain deleted. When I follow this approach, I review the pages of sentences, paragraphs and phrases deleted to streamline my tale, and discover an odd sense of accomplishment. You will too. It's like dieting successfully. You'll get over the pangs after a while, and stop repeating your flab-grabbing mistakes.

### BIG BADDIE #4: PASSIVITY, REPETITION AND GRAMMATICAL ERRORS

*Passive voice* is when action is not attributed to a subject—things "happen" to a character instead of the character "making" them happen, ie: *"She was being led from the stable with her hands bound"* as opposed to *"They bound her hands and led her from the stable."*

Your reader will lose faith in your ability to tell a compelling story if you overuse passive voice. Use it only when your intention is to disassociate the reader from an act or situation—and even then, use it sparingly. No one wants to read a story about things that just happen to a character. We want the larger-than-life, I-would've-done-that characters who transcend our human failings.

There has been much confusion over the dreaded *-ing* words. Some are *gerunds*, or words that end with -ing that can be used as an adjective or noun, ie: *"We liked her writing."* "Writing" is a gerund. Nothing wrong with that. What can be problematic is when -ing verbs are paired with an auxiliary or "helping verbs" such as *been, being, do, does, did, are, am, is, was, were, have, has* or *had*. It's more concise to use the simple form of the verb instead of the participial form, ie: *"They had"* as opposed to: *"They were having"* or *"It took"* instead of *"It has taken."* There are some instances when that particular verb form is needed, but not as often as it appears in an unrevised manuscript. Use the search function on your word processor to revise.

Also watch for over-reliance on *participial phrases*, particularly ones that begin with present participles—those -ing verbs again. They indicate a weaker writing style because the action in the phrase is less important than the action in the independent clause. The actions can also be impossibly linked: *"Running across the room, I yanked the door open."* Technically, one cannot run across the room and yank the door open at the same time. Also limit use of "ing/as" dependent clauses (typically adverbial because they modify the verb in the sentence) which indicate parallel action, like *"Tugging up her jeans, Kira disappeared into the bathroom."* Again, it's difficult to complete those actions simultaneously.

I'd like to display this on the bumper of my car for those who insist on talking on cell phones whilst navigating rush-hour traffic on a six-lane highway...but I digress...

*Repetition of word choices or phrases* is another common mistake, one that all of us make. An author with a distinct voice will have a defined speech pattern. It's what makes us unique, and is usually a sum of experiences during our formative years. As writers, we must revise those "trigger" phrases from our work—before a reader does it for you.

Who wants to be asked during a book signing, *"Do you know how many times you referred to the ship as 'immense'?"* I'm not referring to an author's voice—but the repetition of words or phrases within a manuscript. If you read a word more than twice in a short space—say three paragraphs—try doing an edit/search and see how often it pops up in your manuscript. It could be a trigger phrase with you.

One good way to curb repetition is to utilize voice-recording software or to read your novel into a tape recorder and play it back. You'll be amazed at how many errors you'll catch. I once counted twenty-six various descriptions of an "upset stomach" in a single chapter of a first draft! Damn, that hero wouldn't have been able to leave the chamber pot, let alone draw a broadsword! Sometimes using a phrase as an action (in this case the upset stomach) can be a trigger for repetition. Don't get so caught up in telling a story that you fail to choose your words carefully. Resist the urge to explain! Give the reader only what is vital to know at that particular moment and move on.

*Watch your use of contractions, possessives, and plurals.* Spell Check will not guide you through grammar. *Nor should it!* Sometimes, Grammar Check is *wrong.* An editor once told me that a manuscript was destined for the bottom of the slush pile if it contained errors of the preceding nature in the first three pages. This is one of the few parts of writing you either get *"right"* or *"wrong,"* so it's also one of the few aspects of writing you can guarantee is saleable if you learn correct grammar and spelling!

And to add to this little rant on *Spell and Grammar Check,* I assume by now that you realize you can't rely on spell check for everything. Know the difference between "heirs" and "hairs" or "reins" and "reigns." Also check for mistakes masquerading as acceptable words. Typing "he" for "hers" is a typo but you won't catch it without a thorough read during the editing phase.

Possessives like *his, hers, ours* and *yours* don't have an apostrophe. *"Its"* is just another possessive. It doesn't require an apostrophe either.

Contractions, however, do. The apostrophe signifies the missing letter/letters when two words are combined. Get into the habit of saying "it is" any time you type an "it's" to make sure you aren't using it as a possessive. It'll save you from the dregs of the slush. Plurals never require an apostrophe.

Finally, remember that ellipses "..." are for gaps in thought or conversation and dashes "—" are for interruptions.

### Big Baddie #5: Talking the Talk

Our next Big Baddie relates to speech in writing. Dialogue is one of the most difficult aspects for some. Cadence, flow, characterization—it all comes down to dialogue. This section will help you address some standard problematic areas regarding dialogue in your own writing.

I have an assignment for you. Go to your local shopping center and eavesdrop. Listen to how people speak. By nature, most humans do not use overly-narrative, preachy, stilted infodumping. Sometimes when we put words on paper, we forget what normal conversations are really like in our urge to create great "art." We forget that we are no longer bound by the conventions of a classroom. Yes, Virginia, there really is a place for fragments in good fiction!

In a mall, you'll get a great feel for how much we imply—both verbally and non-verbally—during normal conversation. Go back to your own writing. Check your dialogue for consistency and flow. Are you overstating your dialogue?

Aside from paying attention to stylistic differences between genders, races or status, a useful technique is to identify certain dialogue patterns with certain characters. Remember our discussion about authorial voice and repeated phrases? Repetition weakens the main body of your writing, but people can and do repeat key phrases and fall into speech patterns. If you create a few idiosyncrasies for your characters, your readers can then associate such language with those individuals. Are you writing aliens or foreign speakers? You can give them speech patterns outside normal conventions for native English. Otherwise it sounds stilted and overly expository as in the following passage:

> "Hello, Vixylert. I'm glad to see you aren't working in the pixie factory in this lovely, but unusual 70 degree weather on Treruse Nine," pontificated Fred.
> "Yes sir, meesa sorry sir," said Vixylert. "Please to forgives mes for the intrusion."

Now let's talk about dialogue tags. Yes, I recommend avoidance of repetition, but most of the time "said" is good enough, especially in dialogue or exposition that is speculative. It's less obtrusive. Hardly noticeable, really, and that's the *point*.

We want our readers to be enthralled with what's being said, not how. Don't give your readers a new "sound" at every speech—she whined, he cried, she sighed, he ejaculated (don't even get me started on that usage!), they whimpered...and as I stated earlier (and will state again, and again...*and again...*), people cannot laugh, snort, growl, smile or grimace words! Descriptive tags such as these should be like sprinkles on a birthday cake. You don't want a whole mouthful all at once. If you simply must use those attributions, make them an action:

> "*Let's move this barge!*" *She grimaced.* "*The evil Overlord approaches.*"

In fact, you can cut all but the necessary tags that must be maintained for the reader to understand who is speaking. Renni Browne and Dave King, authors of *Self Editing for Fiction Writers*, call the non-tags that identify a speaker "*beats.*" In the example above, "she grimaced" is a *beat*, not a dialogue tag. You could also write:

> "*Let's move this barge!*" *She punched him on the arm.* "*The evil Overlord approaches.*"

Be certain that your dialogue serves a purpose. At the same time, don't use it to convey too much. Tell your reader what is absolutely imperative for them to know at that time. And only have your characters say what they'd naturally say in that situation—it might not cover everything you want your readers to know, but that's how human nature is. We aren't all open...er...books. You must be ruthless with this, and remember that emotion can be represented by actions and not simply words.

### THE FOUR-LETTERED BOMBS

Another major component of effective dialogue is knowing when to use profanity. The fiction market is not your high school English comp class—sometimes cursing is the best way to get your point across. Remember to use profanity for a purpose and, unless you're Neil Gaiman and writing the award-winning *American Gods*, use it sparingly. There is still much debate over approval for pushing the proverbial envelope of decency. Your jury, the editors, will look on any profanity-laden novel with some trepidation. When in doubt, don't. But if your character is a street smart thief, maybe a curse is just the distinction you need to bring that character to life. And as we all know, sometimes nothing else will do.

Author Stephen King said in his National Book Award acceptance speech that authors need to be honest with their work. This includes adding an element of realism to stressful situations and possibly using profanity to get your message across. In his words, when faced with an impending death bed scene:

> *"Folks are far more apt to go out with a surprised ejaculation, however, then an expiring abjuration like, 'Marry her, Jake. Bible says it ain't good for a man to be alone.' If I happen to be the writer of such a death bed scene, I'd choose 'Son of a bitch' over 'Marry her, Jake' every time."*

Stand up comedians have a term for this—*working blue*. It's the difference between Bill Cosby's set and anything from Eddie Murphy or Robin Williams. Judy Carter, author of *Stand Up Comedy: The Book* cites a great example of how there are alternatives to working blue:

> *"Comedian Jordan Brady is now legendary for using something other than the dreaded "F-word." When he had to clean up his act for a morning show, Jordan told the following joke THIS way:*
> *"The only thing I like about porno movies is the early seventies jazz theme music -- 'bau-chicka-boom-bau.' When you heard that music, you knew what was going to happen..."*
> *"The housewife is all alone, the gardener comes in for a drink of water...and he could have drank from the hose, but instead he wanted 'bau-chick-aboom-bau.'"*

This substitute for "the F-word" pops up often in everyday conversation as a nice way to talk about "the nasty."

Just as it is with stand-up comedians, there are options available for writers. If you must use profanity, and you don't care for working blue, try making up your own, a la Robert Jordan. *"Aemon's Bones!"* and *"Odain's Eye!"* even *"Great googly moogley!"* are great ways to exercise your right to write profanity whilst keeping your prose out of the dreaded blues.

## You're Not From Around Here, Are You?: Dialects

Now ye scurvy dogs, let's discuss dialects. Again, this can be a dialogue enhancement, but best used sparingly. You don't want to require your readers to use a translator to make sense of your speech. Scottish brogues are nigh impossible to understand, as anyone who has traveled to Scotland can tell you. So is Gaelic. Any non-English speech should be used as a subtle flavoring to your tale, not the meat and potatoes of it.

> *"Och! Willna ye ar ye gwan te take off yer bloos o' shud*
> *I cut if off ye with me pigsticker, missy?"*

Besides being difficult to understand, there is too much "flavoring" for this simple phrase.

You will also want to avoid using faux archaic or Middle English speech patterns. Words like *twas, harken, yore, yon, forsooth, verily,* and *doth* don't add character—they make you sound like an amateurish hack. Such word choice will grab an editor's attention, and not in a good way. If you wish to establish an archaic tone to your text, resort to formal English, like Carol Berg uses in her novel *Son of Avonar* or Jacqueline Carey's *Kushiel* series. Their command of English differs enough from contemporary English that it has the feel of a foreign land without resorting to posturing.

### Call It What It Is

Please refrain from throwing in the odd "foreign" word when doing your worldbuilding. A good rule of thumb is that if it looks, walks, talks, smells, eats and hops like a rabbit—call it a rabbit. However if it talks, walks, eats and looks like a rabbit save for the purple fur, three-inch claws and bat wings for ears, then you are safe calling it a Fidgbet. All goes back to ensuring a purpose for your choices.

## Unleashing Your Inner-Editor

Now that we've covered some of the basics of revision, let me show you a great example of how in-depth self-editing can be. Let's combine what we've learned so far and apply it. There is so much to consider when polishing your draft into a saleable piece.

Take the following passage in desperate need of revision. It has the bones of a good story, but not the refinement to make it great. I'll place my revisions in double parentheses (( )) so you can follow along, and see how bloody editing can be. It's rewarding and kind of fun once you've learned sufficient objectivity to distance yourself from your writing.

It all starts with a red felt tip pen...

> "Leave me alone," Daphne hissed angrily ((hiss is reserved for sibilant ending sounds—think Golum, my precioussss)). She walked to the stove and picked up a pot. She slammed the pot down into the sink, splattering the burnt oatmeal around the kitchen. She went over towards the back door and grabbed the knob. ((started the last three sentences with "She." Telling, not showing. Revise.)) "You're always hounding me!" she yelled.
>
> "Daphne, I'm sorry," he sighed.((sighing is not the same action as speaking)) "Please, will you not come back and discuss this pressing issue with me?" ((stilted conversation))
>
> "Talk?" she moaned. ((moaning is not speaking)) "What is there to talk about?"
>
> "Please?" he wheedled. ((We've used "yelled" "sighed" "moaned" and "wheedled." "Said" is less obtrusive)))
>
> Daphne paused. Daphne's ((repeated word—Daphne)) hand was on the doorknob. He was wheedling again. She hated weaklings, ever since that day long ago when her father had pleaded with her mother not to leave them. ((unnecessary back story? If it's important it should've been mentioned prior to this and it interrupts the rapid fire flow of a tense scene))

There are many ways to complete the editing phase. Some print it out and use a highlighter or red pen to mark in comments. I strongly suggest that you print out your manuscript at some point in the final editing phase. I cannot stress this enough. Others use the Revisions and Comments feature in their word processing document. If you're not super computer savvy, you can use the above format of typing inside parenthesis or using all capitals to draw your eye to editorial passages. Don't forget to give it a final print and read before you call your novel complete.

If all else fails, get a critique from another author you trust. Or several. Be leery of spreading your work on every loop and group you find. Search for authors whose skills are at or slightly above your own for the most benefit. Never, never, never hand your printed manuscript to any published author, unless you have an established prior relationship that can withstand a professional critique. Not only is this bad form, but most published authors will not read another's work, for legal reasons if not for a lack of time and opportunity. If you are mentored by a published author whom you respect, count your blessings!

I would also recommend avoiding editorial services for a fee. Most are nothing more than an attempt to make money off of someone else's dreams. Remember money flows to the author—not the other way around! You do not pay an editor to read your work, they pay you for the privilege of publishing it. Aside from parting with your money, you may get little to no useful feedback or worse, they might completely lead you astray. Your best bet for getting sound editorial advice is to keep writing, keep self-editing and keep submitting. Eventually, editors will recognize your growth as an author and may make more substantial comments on your submissions.

## AN EDITOR'S EPILOGUE

Now that you know the Big Baddies to put on your hit list, I make one last suggestion for what to do after you have completed your edits: *put your novel away*. Maybe only for a week. Then sit back and read it cover to cover. Keep a pile of sticky notes or a highlighter handy. Every time you pause to look up, every time you break to eat or sleep, every time you catch yourself "skimming" as you read—highlight that section. That's a section that may need to be revised to better captivate your audience. I learned this trick from editor Russell Davis of Five Star, and I have to say, it does wonders for your writing. If you're boring yourself (and yes, I am taking into consideration that you've bled and read these pages so many times you could cite them in your sleep) then how do you expect to catch the bleary eyes of an editor after he's waded through mountains of manuscripts?

There are many fantastic books on self-editing that you can use to further enhance your understanding of ways to improve your skill. You might want to pick up the following from your local bookstore:

*How to Write a Damn Good Novel II* by James Frey
*The First Five Pages: A Writer's Guide to*
    *Staying Out of the Rejection Pile* by Noah Lukeman
*Writing the Breakout Novel* by Donald Maass
*Elements of Style* by William Strunk Jr. et al

*Words Fail Me: What Everyone Who Writes*
*Should Know about Writing* by Patricia T. O'Conner

In addition, many authors publish articles or non-fiction books about writing. Try an online search and see who pops up! Remember that not all online information is reliable, so use your best judgment.

There is so much that goes into the preparation of a good novel. Putting words to paper is just the beginning of the journey. Elements of editing like pacing, dialogue, repetition and grammar are what separates the pros from the unpublished. Remind yourself that every novel or short story is a learning experience, and you will improve with time. The more you write, the better you will become.

Good luck and good editing!

# About the Authors

## TINA MORGAN

At the age of four Tina Morgan's mother recorded her telling a story of an unfortunate princess. Since that time, Tina has found great pleasure in creating fantasy worlds and life-like characters.

The Managing Editor for Fiction Factor (http://www.fictionfactor. com), an online magazine for fiction writers, Tina enjoys researching and learning more about the art and business of writing. She's a contributing author to *The Complete Guide to Writing Fantasy* and has articles on more than 36 websites worldwide. Her current project is the Fractured Publisher (http://www.fracturedpublisher.com), "an entertaining way to browse for books."

She's married and the mother of three children; two with special needs. Other than writing, she enjoys riding her horse, working in her rose garden, attending renaissance festivals and sewing costumes. She also admits to being a geek in training.

## BOB NAILOR

Bob Nailor currently resides with his wife, Violet, near Monroe, Michigan. He has been published in different anthologies both nationally and internationally, and was a reporter for the Brunswick newspaper in Maryland when he resided on the East coast outside of Washington, DC. Bob currently works as Poetry Editor and Production Manager of *The Emporium Gazette*, an online ezine for writers which has received many favorable mentions and awards by Writer's Digest. His book *Spirits of Blue and Gray: Ghosts of the Civil War* is available from 23House.com. When he is not writing, he is the Unix Systems Manager for the U. S. Federal District Court of Eastern Michigan.

## LAI ZHAO

Fantasy, with generous servings of other genres, is Lai Zhao's favourite feast, with plenty of maniacal laughter and insane plots added for taste. Known to talk to stuffed bunnies and converse intelligently with cats, Lai has been accused of being "crazy" and "weird." Fortunately, no one has ever labelled her "certifiable." *(Yet.)* When she surfaces from her fiction-writing, Lai lives and works in

Hong Kong. She is immersed in all things Chinese punctuated with healthy doses of Japanese. To date, she has been involved in various commercial non-fiction projects and has had her fiction published online. Currently, Lai is working on two fantasy novels. *The Fantasy Writer's Companion* marks her first non-fiction foray into the world of Fantasy Writing.

## MICHAEL R. MENNENGA (MEN-EN-GAY)

Michael is a published science fiction/fantasy author and host of "The Dragon Page—Sci-Fi/Fantasy Radio Talk Show" (www.dragonpage. com). Along with his co-host Evo Terra, they broadcast worldwide on the Internet, and in syndication across the United States on AM & FM radio stations. The talk show has featured interviews with guests such as Ray Bradbury, Sir Arthur C. Clarke, Piers Anthony, Terry Brooks, Stan Lee, R.A. Salvatore, Tracy Hickman and Boris Vallejo.

To date Michael R. Mennenga has released three books. His first book, *Zac and the Valley of the Dragons* (Xlibris Press), was released in 1999. His second book, *Mistress of the Dragon* (Publish America), was released in 2001. *The Valley of the Dragons: Dragon's Fire & Wizard's Flame*, first published with Bedside Books in mid-2002, is now republished with Dragon Moon Press as *Dragon's Fire, Wizard's Flame*, released in 2003.

## TONY RUGGIERO

Tony has been publishing fiction since 1998. His science fiction, fantasy and horror stories and novels have appeared in both print and electronic mediums.

His novels include *Team of Darkness* (March 2002, a 2002 reviewer's choice award from Scribes World Reviews), *Get Out of My Mind* (March 2003), *Mind Trap* (June 2003, nominated for the 2003 "Best in Science Fiction" EPPIE and SimeGen Book Reviews), and *Innocence of the Mind* (July 2004). His anthology *Aliens and Satanic Creatures Wanted: Humans Need Not Apply* (August 2003) features some of Tony's favorite short stories including the award-winning story "Lucky Lucifer's Car Emporium," as well as "Electronic Bliss," "Invasion or Subversion" and "Going up?"

Tony retired from the United States Navy in 2001 after twenty-three years of service. He and his family currently reside in Suffolk, Virginia.

While continuing to write, Tony is completing his master's degree in English at Old Dominion University in Norfolk, VA.

Visit his website at  http://www.tonyruggiero.com.

## WEN SPENCER

Wen is the winner of the 2003 John Campbell Award for Best New SF Writer. Her Science Fiction Mysteries, the *Ukiah Oregon* Series, feature a young man with extraordinary senses who was raised by wolves and now works as a private investigator in Pittsburgh. The first Ukiah Oregon novel, *Alien Taste*, won the Compton Crook Award for Best First SF&F Novel. Her new fantasy series, *Tinker*, is a mix of fantasy with a SF edge, romance, and a bit of mystery. It won the 2004 Sapphire Award of Best SF&F Romance. Wen writes what she loves to read and is an avid fan of fantasy, romance, science fiction and (of course) mystery. She lives in the Boston area with her husband, son and two cats.

Visit her website at  http://www.wenspencer.com.

## JEANINE BERRY

Jeanine Berry is the author of the fantasy trilogy *The Secret Sky*, *Dayspring Dawning* and *Dayspring Destiny*. The third novel in this trilogy, *Dayspring Destiny*, won the 2004 Eppie for Best Fantasy Novel. She has contributed to two anthologies, *Twilight Crossings* and *From Within the Mist*.

Her SF and fantasy erotica books include *Destiny Earth*, *Alien Seduction*, *Gabriel's Gift* and *Scent of Magic*.

She is also the co-author of the best-selling SF *Sex Gates* series: *The Sex Gates*, *Masters of the Sex Gates* and *Worlds of the Sex Gates*.

Her web site is:  http://clik.to/Jeanineberry

## ERIK AMUNDSEN

Erik Amundsen started writing fantasy during recess in third grade. He has been a baker, a secretary, a driver and taught students in the US and China and tried (unsuccessfully) to hide from his addiction to words. This is Erik's first publication in twelve years since "The Dragon of the North Sea," which appeared in the youth literary magazine *Merlyn's Pen*. Though writing still keeps him in from recess most days, he spends most of the time he can get out in the forests of New England. He is currently working on the first book of a series, which is threatening to curtail his recess-related activities for quite some time. Erik lives in the northeastern part of Connecticut.

## Evo Terra

Evo brings all of his experiences (of this world and others) to bear in his writings. As a practicing herbal therapist, he has first-hand knowledge of the healing power of plants. And as the co-host of The Dragon Page Radio Talk Show, he's had the opportunity to interview hundreds of fantasy authors, exploring their worlds with them and finding out what makes for the best quality fantasy writing. When he's not traipsing through the Sonoran desert or broadcasting his show, he relaxes with his bass guitar and contemplates the end of civilization as we know it.

Find out more about Evo Terra online at www.asimplerway.com.

## Will McDermott

Depending on who you ask, Will McDermott is best known as the author of the *Magic: The Gathering* novels *Judgment* and *Moons of Mirrodin*, former editor-in-chief of *Duelist* and *TopDeck* magazines, or simply "Dad." Will also writes short stories. He has been published in the *Myths of Magic, Secrets of Magic* and *Monsters of Magic* anthologies for Wizards of the Coast, and in the *Children of the Rune* anthology for Malhavoc Press. Will lives in Hamburg, New York, with his comely wife, three young ruffians and one large, insane dog.

## Kim Headlee

Kim lives on a hundred-acre farm in southwestern Virginia with her husband, children, feral cats, tropical fish, the pasture-tenants' cows and Heaven knows how many deer, raccoons, skunks, pheasants, wild turkeys and other assorted creatures. Headlee is the author of the award-winning, critically acclaimed *Dawnflight* (Pocket Books, 1999). Headlee's newest novel *Liberty* (written under the pseudonym Kimberly Iverson) features a Celtic female gladiator-slave who battles her way to prominence in ancient Rome. *Liberty* is tentatively scheduled to be released by HQN Books, an imprint of Harlequin, in 2006. Further information about these books, as well as Headlee's works in progress, may be viewed on her web site, http://home.usaa.net/ ~ kimheadlee/. She welcomes fans' email at kimheadlee@earthlink.net and, for her Kimberly Iverson projects, kimberlyiverson05@yahoo.com.

## JULIANNE GOODMAN

Julianne has been fascinated with mythos and legend for as long as she can remember. She likes her fantasy dark and her history as accurate as possible. Her historical-fantasy manuscript, *HETAERA*, is RWA's 2004 Golden Heart finalist for Best Novel with Romantic Elements category. Julianne grew up in the Dustbowl of the Midwest—hence her flights of fancy. Since then she's lived in all parts of the country and traveled abroad.

Find out more about Julianne Goodman online at www.juliannegoodman.com.

# About the Editors

### TEE MORRIS

Referring to himself as "the accidental author," this professional actor began his writing career at The Maryland Renaissance Festival with his portrayal of Rafe Rafton, a character featured in his historical epic fantasy, *MOREVI: The Chronicles of Rafe & Askana*. His debut work (penned with Miss Lisa Lee) went on to be a finalist for EPIC's Best Fantasy of 2003. Tee then appeared in Dragon Moon Press' *The Complete Guide to Writing Fantasy*, a finalist for ForeWord Magazine's 2003 Book of the Year award. Tee now steps into his first solo venture with *Billibub Baddings and The Case of The Singing Sword*, a spoof of both the Fantasy and Hard-Boiled Detective novel. With both *Billibub* and *The Fantasy Writer's Companion* completed, Tee returns to Morevi once again with *Legacy of Morevi*, slated for a Summer 2005 release. In between chapters, he writes articles for *Strange Horizons* and reviews movies for The Dragon Page Radio Talk Show.

Find out more about Tee Morris online at www.teemorris.com.

### VALERIE GRISWOLD-FORD

Growing up in a household filled with books, it's only reasonable that Valerie Griswold-Ford had her first novel penned at the tender age of 7. Since then, she's graduated to the real world of writing: now, at age 30, she has five years of journalism under her belt, as well as a chapter in *The Complete Guide to Writing Fantasy*. *The Fantasy Writer's Companion* is her first co-editing position, and her debut novel *Not Your Father's Horseman*, a dark fantasy take on the Four Horsemen of the Apocalypse, is due out from Dragon Moon Press in July 2005. Val lives in Merrimack, NH with her husband and their psychotic Siamese Max.

# About the Artist

## ANNE MOYA

Anne Moya began her career at the age of seventeen with her being commisioned to design a granite sculpture in her home town of Snohomish, Washington. At eighteen, she began Angel Press Studios as a small press comic publisher in 1993. The same year she was awarded the Washington State Artist of the Year as well as her first solo art exhibition. In 1996 she received her AA in Print. After winning various state recognition for her fine art and illustrations, Anne expanded into Graphic Design. Working for 6 years in corporate in-house design, Anne received her BA in Graphic Design in 2002 and entered the freelance field. With her expansive knowledge of print, design and multimedia, Anne continues to return to her roots and persue her passion of fine art and book illustration in her new home of Chicago.

Find out more about Anne Moya and Angel Press Studios online at www.angelpressstudios.com.

# Index

Printed in the United States
119530LV00004B/49-96/P